BEYOND POLITICS:

Essays in Memory of Professor Sanjay Kumar Biswas

BEYOND POLITICS:

Essays in Memory of Professor Sanjay Kumar Biswas

Editor

Dr Ambrose Pinto SJ

KALPAZ

ISBN: 978-93-5128-163-4

Price : ₹ 290

First Published, 2016

Published by

Kalpaz Publications
C-30, Satyawati Nagar,
Delhi – 110052
E-mail: kalpaz@hotmail.com
Ph.: 9212142040

Printed at: G. Print Process, Delhi

Cataloging in Publication Data—DK

Courtesy: D.K. Agencies (P) Ltd. <docinfo@dkagencies.com>

Beyond politics : essays in memory of Professor Sanjay Kumar Biswas / editor, Dr Ambrose Pinto SJ.
pages cm
ISBN 9789351281634

1. India—Politics and government. 2. India—Economic conditions. I. Biswas, S. K. (Sanjay Kumar), 1945- honouree. II. Pinto, Ambrose, editor.

JQ231.B49 2015 DDC 320.954 23

Contents

Preface

Sanjay Biswas was truly a man for all seasons. He arrived at the Indian Institute of Science (IISc) in the mid-1970s. His inclinations were decidedly influenced by an upbringing that exposed him to a liberal view of life and exposure to ideas which were undoubtedly shaped by the romantic view of Marxism, prevalent in the campuses of the 1960s and early 1970s. Ironically enough, he came to Bangalore at the height of the infamous Emergency. I never did get an opportunity to talk to him about his early days at the Institute, when his firmly held liberal views were undoubtedly challenged by an environment where dissenting opinions were rarely heard. Unlike many of us he seemed to be a man of broad and diverse interests; a committed academic engaged deeply in highly technical research on the one hand and one who spent considerable time on social issues on the other. For years I saw him from a distance, a remarkably polite and sophisticated individual with a keen sense of the social responsibility of science and scientists. Many years later I worked very closely with him in addressing issues of academic administration at the Institute. These were chores that academics inevitably have to do as they move up the ladder of seniority at our institutions. This was a period when I got to know Sanjay better and began to recognize the many dimensions of his personality and his interests.

This collection of essays written as a tribute to a friend and colleague who greatly influenced our surroundings, is a reflection of the extraordinarily diverse interests that Sanjay pursued. He was a committed scientist deeply involved in research on tribology, materials and, in later years a champion of developing applications of science and engineering to medicine. He was a teacher who profoundly influenced students by his style and approach to research. He was an activist, with a decidedly Marxist view of the world, undoubtedly influenced by J.D. Bernal whom he greatly admired. Sanjay's essay on 'Marxism and Science', reproduced in this volume, is prescient in many ways. When he died in April 2013, the dramatic transformation of the political scene in India that occurred in 2014, could hardly have been anticipated. Sanjay's, albeit brief but insightful, account of the beginnings of science might well form the starting point for a scholarly debate on the factors that have determined the ebbs and flows of scientific progress over millennia.

In the years before he formally retired at the Institute Sanjay was involved in initiating and spearheading many new programs. As Dean of the Faculty of Engineering he was an enthusiast for the Four Year Undergraduate Program in science. He was particularly excited by the prospect of introducing 'soft courses', which would enable young students to be exposed to the social dimensions and historical aspects of science. In the often charged debates in the faculty, which preceded the introduction of the undergraduate program, Sanjay was a tireless and unfailingly courteous spokesman for the new initiative. He saw an opportunity to seamlessly expose students of basic science to aspects of engineering, an experiment that became possible with the benefit of an additional year of study. Sanjay was a key figure in formulating new research and teaching programs in bioengineering. His extraordinary patience and politeness in discussions was a quality that stood him in good stead in establishing collaborative interactions with other institutions. In the many years that I worked with Sanjay I never heard him say an unkind word about even the most fractious of colleagues. He was positive, almost to an extreme. His optimism could be contagious. When a suggestion, however controversial, was made in a meeting his usual response was 'brilliant'. These qualities allowed him to bring together young members of the faculty (and sometimes older, marginalised colleagues) into collective activities. Sanjay's interests were wide. Tribology, nanomaterials, bioengineering, academic reform and social activism were all part of his daily life. But if he had been compelled to pursue only one of his many interests, I suspect Sanjay would have been a social activist following his conscience. My guess is supported by the essays in this volume which Sanjay would undoubtedly have appreciated greatly.

January 21, 2015
Bangalore

P. Balaram
Former Director of Indian Institue of Science, Bangalore

Introduction

Dr Sanjay Biswas left us all of a sudden on 28th April, 2014 without prior notice leaving a void in the life of civil society in Bangalore and the country. The former Dean of Mechanical Engineering at the Indian Institute of Science (IISc.), still in service at the Institute, his specialisations included bioengineering, tribology, healthcare science and technology. A scientist "par excellance", he had published works with high impact factors. And yet he was a scientist with a difference. His science was linked to the issues and concerns of society. Everything he taught and specialised in was related to life and living. That linkage of the classroom with the outside world had made him a science activist. He was the national president of the All India Progressive Forum and a coordinating member of the Bangalore Citizens' Forum. A driving force behind several ambitious initiatives in the Institute and civil society, Dr Sanjay was a progressive thinker who worked with zeal towards the cause of people and science. Among several voices of opposition to the Pokran test from the scientific community, he was one. To bring awareness on the ill-effects of nuclearisation, he galvanised young people to discuss and debate the issue. He was convener of a meet for scientists and writers protesting against rising religious fundamentalism and remained an active member of Bangalore Citizens' Initiative. As Editor of the Bulletin of Sciences, published by the Indian Institute of Science he had highlighted issues of health and equity, environment and poverty. In all that he did, he was passionate about social justice. He had a special talent to bring people together for common causes. He built alliances across diverse social actors and communities on issues of communalism, nuclearisation, justice and equity. As a professor he led by example. By giving voice to those who struggled for an equal society he set the standards for conscientious citizenship. He was a critic of both communalism and the neo-liberal policies of the Indian state. Through his interaction with students and the civil society he had made people aware of the dangers of a communal and corporate state. As a person committed to the welfare of the workers, he had played a major role in providing the needed academic input to workers organisations to agitate and organise. Sanjay was a dreamer for a world with equity and justice and he could carry many with his ideas that were infectious. He has left his footprints in the hearts of many. With his death we do not want his mission to fade away. To pay a tribute to his memory and to keep his concerns alive we have brought out this volume on some of the central concerns of Dr Sanjay. All the articles are from his friends and associates on some of the emerging concerns.

The book begins with three tributes to Professor Sanjay Kumar Biswas. The first one is from the Professors of the Indian Institute of Science where he had laboured till his last breath. The essay provides a gist of the extent of work done by Sanjay as a scholar and administrator in the Institute. Published first in the "Current Science, Vol. 104, Number 12, 25th June 2013," a publication of the Indian Institute of Science, Bangalore, we have reprinted it here with permission. The second tribute is by Dr Yugal Rayalu from Nagpur winner of the coveted Karamveer Chakra 2012. Committed to empower deprived sections of society, this vocational education professor from Nagpur was given the award in the 'Education to Society' category jointly by United Nations Volunteers (under United Nations Development Programme) India and ICONGO (Indian Confederation of NGOs). He is the Head of the Vocational Department of Dharampet M. P. Deo Memorial Science College. A Human Resource Development Trainer, motivator he had worked with Sanjay on the All India Progressive Forum. The third tribute published earlier in the "Mainstream" is from Dr (Fr.) Ambrose Pinto SJ who worked closely with Dr Sanjay in several civil society initiatives in the city of Bangalore for the last two decades and more. Both founded the

Bangalore Citizens' Initiative and had worked with students on several concerns. Their last venture before the passing away of Dr Sanjay was an animation of a students' manifesto meet for the Karnataka State Elections where students from 20 and more colleges were present.

There is an article of Sanjay we have included in the volume on Science. In this essay Sanjay has argued that there has been a persistent application of fetters to the growth of science in India over the last 5000 years. The fetters have been at the level of superstructure in the earlier times and at the level of infrastructure in the colonial times. In the absence of antagonistic contradictions in the post independent India between a weak capitalist class and feudalism, the social conditions necessary for radical advances in science and productive forces, were not met, while an engineering infrastructure came into being to support the anti-imperialist aspirations of a nationalistic ruling class, recently liberated form colonialism. Dialectically a rising capitalist class did not take ownership of a mediocre science and technology to make radical changes in social relations in its favour. He argues briefly that this meandering status quo is about to change and we may be ushering in a new historic phase where a more focused and powerful bourgeois dominates social relations where certain areas of science advances rapidly amidst very sharp class contradictions between the bourgeois and the working masses of India.

Dr Arun Mitra, the General Secretary of Indian Doctors for Peace and Development, in his essay on Poverty and Health explores the connection between poverty and health. Those who are at lowest rung of poverty are the most deprived in terms of health care. Lack of food is one of the prime causes for health ailments. If the numbers of hungry people have increased one of the important factors is the neglect of agriculture in the phase of liberalisation of the economy. To improve health he opines the necessary steps should be taken for a holistic instead of piecemeal approach with poverty alleviation strategies.

Professor D.P. Sen Gupta is one of the prominent Visiting Professors of the National Institute of Science, Bangalore. He views the nuclear policy of India. While Pokran II was a mistake according to him due the problems in created to the scientific community in India and its failure to deter Pakistan from attacking us, India should explore alternatives to nuclear energy while keeping the nuclear option open.

Dr Thelma Narayan and Dr Ravi Narayan have pioneered community health in India. In their essay they have focused on how civil society and social movements in partnership with academia can and have catalyzed a "Health for All" movement in India and elsewhere. They draw upon their own experiences when they moved beyond academic and research careers in a medical college to become scholar activists working with the voluntary health and development sector, civil society and social movements to promote Health for All. This community health oriented journey which gradually converted a group of health professionals into scholar activists, supporting civil society and movements in solidarity resonates with the key message of the life and times of the late Professor Sanjay Biswas. Sanjay had worked through a constant endeavour to move beyond ivory towered academia and research into the rough and tumble of an unequal social order and the challenges that are faced by all those who work with community and justice issues relevant to the lives of the marginalised and socially excluded. Both authors had the unique opportunity to interact with Sanjay, in the early years of development of SOCHARA, especially with building solidarity and support for the victims of the Bhopal Gas industrial disaster and also in their early efforts to initiate discussion, dialogue and action towards a rational, ethical and India relevant drug policy. The Indian Institute of Science campus was very receptive to both these initiatives in the late 1980's and Sanjay and his department team were a great support. This paper - a small contribution to a memorial publication builds and describes this involvement through two complementary reflections. The first is a brief journey towards a new paradigm when the authors shifted from a medical college into a community resource centre, symbolically moving from a bio-medical model into a social/ community model of health at a work level. The second outlines reflections on the wider implications of such a journey and the development of opportunities and innovative instruments for action that urgently await the solidarity of academia and researchers from the mainstream. Both journeys highlight the need for academia to work as co-creators of a new paradigm of understanding and new framework for action with all those who are grounded in community realities and struggles.

The idea of India as a country in which the state would not discriminate against any person on ground of their religion was something to which Dr Sanjay Biswas was committed to. As such the repeated communal programmes which have rendered fragile the idea of India was something which disturbed him. Dr Sanjay Biswas felt passionately about defending this idea of India and was an active participant is activist efforts to preserve the secular fabric of the nation. This essay seeks to honour this cause that Dr Sanjay Biswas was so passionate about. The article by Aravind Narrain seeks to understand how activists have sought to wrest a measure of justice from a recalcitrant state, in the context of mass communal crimes. In the worst and most difficult circumstances, the only silver lining has been activist efforts to bring a measure of justice for mass crimes or activist efforts to ensure that these kinds of crimes do not recur. This paper will analyse interventions and efforts to ensure justice for mass communal crimes tracing justice efforts in Nellie (1983), Delhi (1984) and Gujarat (2002). Undoubtedly the larger picture is one of a dismal failure by the Indian state to hold accountable those responsible for the murder, rape and destruction of the very way of life of entire communities. However, the story of the activist engagement with the question of mass crimes is not one of unrelieved failure alone. This struggle for justice is never without value as it invariably makes the world a less unjust place.

Professor Mary Mathew from the Indian Institute of Science who had greatly admired Sanjay in her essay on the Psychological Perspective of R&D and Intellectual Property Protection argues the goals of R&D and attitudes towards patents with the intent to make R&D more productive. The overwhelming production of papers in journals and conferences stifle the production of patents. The paper draws from the discipline of psychology since most of R&D effort involves the actions of humans, namely scientists. Using concepts and theories from psychology the paper dwells on goal clarity and positively polarised attitudes towards patents to help Indian R&D become more productive.

The Accusers' Accused, an essay by Dr G. Ramakrishna, former Professor at the National College, Bangalore is a critique on religion that has legitimized caste. The intellectual acrobatics that Shankara, Ramanuja, Madhva and many other Philosophers resorted to was prompted by dogmatic concerns for justifying and consolidating social hierarchy, opines the author. The function of Philosophy is to serve humanity by upholding equality and rationality. It is here the writer finds Debiprasad Chattopadhya head and shoulder above many other scholars of Indian Philosophy.

C. Balakrishnan, President of the Karnataka Progressive Forum explores the impact of neo-liberal economic policies in the city of Bangalore. A green city known as a city of gardens, lakes, flowers and vegetation has been turned into a garbage city with construction of high rise buildings, polluting the environment and causing threats to livelihoods. A city known for peace, harmony and tolerance has been turned into a place for intolerance, divisiveness and restlessness. The developmental model that is imposed on the city from the early nineties has made the city global with congestion, displacement, evictions with increasing corruption and criminalisation with no participation of the people. In the place of the dictated model, an alternative model of development is proposed to make the lives of the people more participative and human.

In a country where majority of the people are involved in agriculture, Dr D. S. Deshpande examines the relationship between poverty and agricultural growth. It is the small, marginal farmers and agricultural labourers who constitute the majority in the sector who are caught in the vicious circle of low investment, low productivity and low income. The urgent need for the state is to intervene with policy changes at the level of land acquisition to protect farm land, at the level of technology, marketing, agricultural research and rebuilding of depleting resources to resurrect the agricultural economy and provide a quality life to people in the sector.

The article by N. Manu Chakravarthy, Professor at NMKRV College, explores the twin issues of justice and equality in the writings of Gandhi and Tagore and highlights why the two concerns are central to nation-building. Two enemies of nation-building, he quotes extensively from the authors and asserts, are narrow ideas of nationalism and principles of capitalism. Gandhi's "Hind Swaraj" and Tagore's "Nationalism" are two texts that could help the country to face the present crisis, he opines.

While paying a rich tribute to Sanjay Biswas for his scientific work and achievement towards establishing an equitable society Narendra Pani explores the role of technology in post-independent India. Explaining the linkages between society, science and technology he highlights the contribution of technology to India's development right from the Nehruvian era to the present. Dr Sanjay Biswas was actively associated with science, science popularisation and working of science policy. Besides, inculcating scientific temper was one of his important fields. The article of Anil Rajimwale in his memory deals mainly with the impact of science on society.

Sri M. Vijaya Kumar is the Vice-President of the "All India Progressive Forum" (AIPF). Dr Sanjay was the founding member of the Forum. The Forum is in the process of building up public platforms for discussions on some of the crucial issues which affect the lives of people in India. Some work has already begun. The essay here essentially covers an explanation of why we need reform in the electoral system and describes the pros and cons of the present electoral system.

Sindhujaa Iyengar while stressing the importance of political parties in our parliamentary democracy makes a critical analysis of the proposed reforms proposed by several official commissions. She makes a plea for an urgent reform of the system.

Justin John, a young man in his late twenties worked as the Director of the Hunger Project and has recently shifted to another civil society organisation CRY. There are several reasons for India to become the hunger capital with more than 30 per cent of people below the poverty line, he says. He pleads for strengthening the Right to food Act; land acquisition polices to favour agriculture without giving in to pressures from international financial organisations to commodity food.

Kiran Kamal Prasad has worked with bonded labour at the grassroots, research, advocacy and lobbying. Slavery exists in the form of bonded labour, he asserts, in spite of denial by state and central governments. He appreciates the role of the judiciary in intervening against the evil by providing directives and guidelines to the states on the issue.

When one goes through all the tributes and articles one discovers that Sanjay was a man with a mission. He was concerned, compassionate and driven by an inner strength. Everything that he did had a dimension of the other. He lived his life being committed to the transformation of the social order. His own comforts and pleasures mattered little for Sanjay. He wanted to make the earth a better place to live especially for the excluded. The volume is sure to ignite the minds and one wishes that the readers would be inspired to continue the mission of Sanjay. This volume would not have been possible without the cooperation of the many friends of Sanjay. One person who needs a special mention is C. Balakrishnan, a member of the National Alliance of People's Movement. He has spent several hours of his time going round and meeting writers to contribute. While I express my gratitude to him, I remain grateful to the many others who have directly or directly contributed to this volume to honour the life of Dr Sanjay Biswas

Dr Ambrose Pinto SJ

Sanjay Kumar Biswas (1945–2013)

*M. S. Bobji, Satish v. Kailas, G. K. Anantha Suresh *,*
Ganapathy Ayappa, Vikram Jayaram,
Sandhya S., Visweswariah,

Sanjay Kumar Biswas, a distinguished tribologist and educator, passed away on 28 April 2013 in Bangalore at the age of 67. With a background of doctoral and postdoctoral work in plasticity, he pioneered many fundamental approaches to studying two moving surfaces that are in contact with each other. This scientific exploration led him to undertake research in many branches of science and engineering ranging from mechanics, materials and chemistry to nanoscience and bioengineering.

Biswas was born on 9 June, 1945 in Kolkata. After graduation in mechanical engineering in 1966 from the Indian Institute of Technology Kharagpur, he moved to the United Kingdom for higher studies. He obtained his Master's degree from University of Strathclyde in 1969 and Ph D from University of Birmingham in 1972. At the suggestion of Professor Satish Dhawan, he joined the Indian.

Institute of Science (IISc), Bangalore in 1976. Since then, he has served IISc in various capacities, including Chair of Mechanical Engineering and Dean of Engineering. The tribology laboratory in IISc had humble beginnings in the hands of Biswas. It is fondly recalled that he was so excited when the purchase department informed him that a new machine, a journal bearing test rig, had arrived on campus that he towed the instrument in a trolley for 2 km from the stores to his laboratory along with his lab members. It was this enthusiasm that helped the field flourish and made his laboratory thrive as a major multidisciplinary focal point in IISc. His legacy in tribology is vibrant even today and his contributions are known around the world.

Tribology is concerned with contact between two surfaces that are in relative motion. Exploring all aspects of tribology led Biswas to several fronts in the field, including contact mechanics, surface roughness, single-point abrasion tests, nano-indentation, nano-tribology and cutting fluids. Since all practical surfaces are rough, it meant looking at how individual asperities – the smallest elements of roughness – interacted with one another. This naturally drew Biswas to the mechanics of materials at nanometer scale and his research moved to nanotribology. Biswas, being a pioneer, exactly knew when to explore a new research topic, develop it, contribute to its understanding in a nontrivial way, and then leave the field open for others to explore. In his endeavours he collaborated with researchers in different disciplines ranging from mechanics, materials and physics to chemistry and biology.

The early work of Biswas and his students on aluminium silicon alloys went on for many years and this work is cited even today. What started as simple curiosity-driven research developed into a major engineering application when modern car-makers turned to aluminium alloys for their engine cylinders. The accumulated knowledge in the wear mechanisms of aluminium alloys provided the groundwork for big automobile companies to design aluminium engines. Similarly, well before technology missions became fashionable, he ventured into the world of ceramics and coatings in collaboration with the industry and academic colleagues from materials engineering. With his ability to integrate other people's expertise with his own background in continuum mechanics and plasticity, these multi-institutional programmes were able to translate laboratory ideas into the real world of engineering tests. The practical experience of applied research that these projects gave the numerous participating students and research staff was truly exceptional in a university environment.

The dynamism and resourcefulness of Biswas is evident from the fact that he managed to procure a scanning electron microscope in 1988 for his laboratory when it was a rare piece of equipment in IISc and India. One of the strong points of his mentoring was making his students develop their own instruments from scratch. This led to many innovations. The pin-on-disc wear-testing machine is one such example. An innovative approach to measure the wear through change in height of the pin rather than its weight led to continuous monitoring of the wear process. This design is popular today and can be found in many engineering colleges across the nation. Other instruments included the high-temperature scratch tester, reciprocating scratch tester, rail wear test rig, erosion test rig and many other machines that formed the basis for tribological studies. He made sure that the instruments were designed to solve problems of direct relevance to the industries that were involved in building as well as marketing some of the instruments. Biswas realised that testing at the macroscopic scale was only part of the story and he embarked on an ambitious foray into nanotribology in an attempt to unravel a molecular understanding of lubrication at contact. In close collaboration with major Indian oil companies, innovative designs were used to develop simple hardness testers for the nano-indentation machine, a surface force apparatus that allowed measuring forces between real engineering surfaces, atomic force microscopy and an *in situ* Raman tribometer to track molecular changes in lubricants. Developing such instruments was a challenge, but Biswas was a man who never gave up and made sure that these instruments were designed, developed and built locally by his students.

One of the notable points in Biswas was the freedom he gave to his students. He made sure that he passed on his enthusiasm and optimism to them. If a student decided to choose a path that was not taken by anyone before, he would not stop the student from doing so; rather he would encourage the student with unhindered backing. It requires quite a bit of courage to have such an open mind. His guidance was built on one simple rule: 'Look deeper into the results and it will get interesting.' This push that he gave students to think deeply into a subject prompted many of his students to pursue research careers. It is worth noting that three of his doctoral students became faculty at IISc.

In addition to being an active researcher, Biswas was also an able administrator who knew how to excite people around him to take new initiatives, and then step aside when things were on the right track, only to move on to another initiative. Within the last five years, he played a pivotal role in increasing the student intake, bringing undergraduate programme into IISc, establishing IISc Press, initiating the bioengineering programme, connecting clinicians and hospitals with IISc, liaising with the Indian Institute of Management Bangalore, and starting biodesign activity at the national level.

Biswas began his bioengineering research in the last few years, focusing on the mechanics of cells. His vast experience and expertise were brought to bear in exploring the mechanical properties of bacterial cell walls using atomic force microscopy, and investigating mechano-transduction of cancer cell adhesion. Just as he was able to connect disparate fields, he was also adept at connecting people from different disciplines. Over the last three years, he brought together faculty from many different departments to create a bioengineering group in IISc. Furthermore, he connected medical doctors with IISc faculty. He had envisioned bringing about a radical change in bioengineering and bio-design in India. After his retirement from IISc in 2010, he occupied a prestigious Department of Biotechnology Chair to work at the Translational Health Sciences and Technology Institute in Gurgaon. He wanted to set up a National Biodesign Alliance to connect major research universities and upcoming colleges with hospitals and industries. The enthusiasm and passion of Biswas were not limited to what he did at IISc. He started and ran for many years a journal entitled *Bulletin of Sciences* to popularise science. He took part in several social activities, including taking a clear anti-nuclear stand and lending support to people who helped the poor and the deprived sections of the society. He also founded the All India Progressive Forum. A truly remarkable trait in Biswas was his eternal optimism. A glass was not just half full for him; it was overflowing.

He was a man of many interests and he lived a full life. He enjoyed music of many genres. He was a connoisseur of food. He loved to travel and trek in various parts of the world. He knew a lot about south Indian temple architecture and rituals and wrote about them in the newspapers. He loved history and literature. Ever friendly and supportive, Biswas and his zest for life brought out the best in people who interacted with him. There was so much more that was to come from him to enrich the lives of the people he worked with, but he left them suddenly on Sunday, 28 April 2013. One is reminded of the immortal lines of Mir Saqib: which can be translated as 'The world was listening to me in rapt attention; It was I who slept off while narrating the story.' These words befit Sanjay Kumar Biswas who was agile in his scientific and other pursuits until the very end. He is sorely missed by his family, friends, students and colleagues, all of whom celebrate a life well lived.

Professor Sanjay Biswas–An Intellectual–A Crusader

Dr Yugal Rayalu

The founder President of All India Progressive Forum, Professor Sanjay Biwas coming from an elite Institution of higher education, "The Indian Institute of Science, Bangalore," was committed to take knowledge and development to the grass roots. One of the major projects that he had taken in the last years of his life was combining rural health with solar power! Today the two go hand in hand in various parts of the country.

It was Professor Biswas who inspired me and my colleagues at Nagpur to go for the 1st National Youth Convention under the banner of All India Progressive Forum (AIPF). Professor Biswas was invited as the Chief Guest of a National Law Seminar held jointly by AIPF and Raison Law School, at Nagpur. While interacting with the young Law students the idea of holding a National Youth Convention came to his mind. It was on his insistence that this convention was held at Nagpur, which was inaugurated by the Vice Chancellor of Nagpur University. Professor Biswas was the Chief Guest of the concluding function of this convention. Today four State of AIPF Committees have planned to have State Youth Conventions on the lines of the National Youth Convention. Thanks to Professor Biswas youth are in the focus at AIPF.

At Hyderabad we all had assembled for the four days National Workshop on "Socialism." Professor Biswas was one of the participants. There was a team of twenty young students from

Jawaharlal Nehru University (JNU). It was the first such exposure for these young scholars. They were hesitant to speak during the sessions where some intellectuals were very active in the deliberations. To benefit the young students some of us mooted the idea of holding a separate session for all the young students. The elders were not ready for the proposal. Professor Biswas intervened with a brilliant idea. "Just add a post dinner session for the young scholars" he said. The idea was accepted with a small change. On the third day a session was added after the last session of the day, from 6.00 pm to 8.00 pm, so that the local participants if they wished could go home while the session continued. Surprisingly all the local delegates including some political leaders, preferred to wait till the end of this special youth session. The twenty young students from JNU and some eight young students from Hyderabad and Chennai participated. The session was a grand success. That was the concern of Professor Biswas for the young people!

Professor Sanjay did a lot to AIPF. One of the best ways of honouring him would be to strengthen the AIPF and take it to every nook and corner of the country. This must become an intellectual platform of the common citizen. Today unfortunately real issues of the people are being brushed under the carpet very cleverly. In the run up to the elections to the 16th Lok Sabha none of the political parties had brought forth the issues that concern the lives of the common citizen of this country. Some leaders talk of religion while others talk of caste and community. They attack each others at a personal level for opportunistic reasons. Highlighting people's issues puts the political parties in a tight spot because once elected to power they have to fulfill the promises made. If the habit of political and intellectual discussion is killed then politics really becomes a game of the scoundrels. We need to save our democracy from becoming a cesspool of mindlessness. The main aim of AIPF is that.

It is true that the sudden death of Professor Biswas gave a jolt to AIPF. We were soon going to organise the All India Conference of AIPF. His departure shocked us all. Some people were quick to prophesise that AIPF would soon wind up. These people were proved wrong. It is true that the AIPF was the brain child of Professor Sanjay Biswas. In a demonstration of a true leadership quality Prof. Biswas created a dynamic collective leadership within AIPF that soon took the organisation to every nook and corner of the country.

Our greatest tribute to this great man would be to make this organisation a confluence of thoughts and opinions that would take the cause of the common citizen of India into the forefront of the democratic functioning of our great Republic. While others are busy fighting to be a part of the leadership of democratic Institutions, let us prepare ourselves to fight for the preservance of democracy. Let AIPF become the meeting point of great discussions! Long live Professor Sanjay Biswas! Long live AIPF.

A Tribute to Dr Sanjay Kumar Biswas (1945 to 2013)

Dr Ambrose Pinto SJ

Sanjay was a Professor at the Indian Institute of Science and I was a teacher at St. Joseph's College. He was a mechanical engineer and I taught political science. While he was a communist, I was a Jesuit, a member of the Catholic Church. He was a Bengali and I am a Mangalorean, born and bred in the state. We met more than two decades ago. We were different and yet not once did we feel that we were not comrades in a common mission. We grew into intimate friends and collaborators in a common mission of making a difference. At least once a week we spoke to each other or met to converse, to plan or to organise. He was a frequent visitor to the campus and the house and we had sat over a cup of coffee or tea conversing and discussing on the interventions we could make to make the young aware and agents of change several times. As soon as I heard that Sanjay was critical in the hospital I requested a former student of mine who had come to meet me to drive me to the Fortis Hospital that evening. Hardly 20 minutes of coming out of the hospital, Dr Sanjay had passed away. I was disturbed no doubt. Sanjay I thought had at least another ten years of fruitful work to do. The immediate response was why was Sanjay so careless about his health that he had to go so early? I had spoken to him just three days ago while he was in England and Sanjay did say he was stressed. Could he have gone to the hospital earlier and given us the privilege of working with him for a different world for a decade more? The warm memories and the concerns on which we had worked together kept haunting me that night and I was there at his house next day to bid him adieu. After spending an hour around his body and joining the procession for the crematorium, it was emotionally impossible to see his body moving into the electric furnace at the Hebbal crematorium. I wished that Sanjay lived. I decided to move out of the place since I did not desire to see that extinction of a life I had deeply come to revere and appreciate. I returned home with a sense of loss as well as gratitude.

Sanjay was a Perfect Gentleman

In the two decades and more of my association, I thought of Sanjay as a perfect gentleman. In spite of his high academic standing he was respectful of others with tremendous sensitivity to the feeling of others. He was considerate to those around him and extremely polite in his actions. Students were highly appreciative of him. He has lectured to students, animated sessions for civil society groups, addressed priests as well as teachers of the college. In everything that he did he was calm and yet able to present whatever he had to present to the audience in a very pleasant and convincing manner. People felt at ease with him. He was never dogmatic and willing to discuss and debate concerns and issues with an open mind. Students admired him and teachers appreciated him. Civil society groups felt he was a part of them. Whatever may have been his preoccupations, when he was at a session he was there fully alive. He treated every question and every person with respect and humility. In the two decades and more of our association, not once have I seen Sanjay annoyed, angry or irritated. For students who hailed from economically weaker sections, he had a soft corner. He met people and students outside the formal group work and cleared their doubts. Those with a mission in life could contact him and he was easily available to them.

Sanjay was a Scholar

As an academician of repute Sanjay had developed sharp focus and a complex, deep and sophisticated understanding of many of the issues in mechanical and bio-engineering fields. His academic world however was not restrictive. He was inquisitive about the world around him and was quick to articulate his views and opinions on concerns affecting society. He had shown a persistent determination to get to the bottom of issues. He was passionate in his explorations and was seen as passionate in whatever he did. He was well connected with fellow scholars and was recognised as one. With large number of publications, he was productive and acknowledged as a leading academician in his field. There are various kinds of scholars. Most of them do not make sense to the people. They have an ivory tower existence. Sanjay was different. His context of research was people and he always posed the question to himself more than anybody else how his work would benefit the large masses of the country. What was impressive about Sanjay was that he was equally competent to speak on major concerns that confront society and help people analyse society from the perspective of the poor. In other words, he was a social scientist as well, not through training but by his own making. Much of his scholarship arose from his deep association with people.

Sanjay was an Activist

In spite of being employed in the Indian Institute of Science, Sanjay was not in favor of the state at all times. When he felt the state was repressive he stood up and had expressed his dissent. He was there in the numerous protests against Gujarat carnage of 2002, the demolition of the mosque in Ayodhya and attacks on churches in Karnataka in 2008. When India decided to exhibit its strength by the Pokhran blast, along with his fellow scientists Sanjay protested and joined the larger protests of civil society against the nuclear policy of India. He was for a nuclear free world. He was our annual guest, resource person and participant for 6th August, anti-nuclear day programmes of civil society for many years and had convinced students why they must carry on their struggles for a nuclear free world. Not only was he an activist, he spent time working within colleges and schools to educate others, maintaining cultural practices and music as an act of resistance, developing national and international networks and forming alliances across movements. He saw the need for change and was driven by passion to share facts to galvanise people and students for change. He had a vision for society and he always held a different world is possible. Activism was natural for him. He held the belief that he can make a difference and he has the power to do something on issues of communalism, nuclearisation, electoral reforms, trade union rights, the neo-liberal economic policies that have adversely affected the people and the rights of the poor. Sanjay worked with us in protests, sat with us in dharnas and educated us in several issues of concern for the country. His last work with us was a students' manifesto for the elections in Karnataka 2013, a document that was brought out by the students of more than 60 colleges. He was there as a resource person to begin the process and he came for some of the meetings encouraging students and affirming them without trying to put his thoughts and yet raising important questions.

More than anything else, I will miss the person of Dr Sanjay and his great humanity. He was a dreamer and a visionary. Not once did he speak about his self and his needs. He was never selfish. He was a man for others who always thought of improving the quality of life of the masses of India. Science made no sense to him apart from being at the service of the people. In the area of health he was determined to provide for the country cheaper instruments to reduce health care costs. As a progressive he dreamt of an all India progressive front that could change the future of India by making the state more concerned, more compassionate and more sensitive to the needs of the peasants, workers, the unorganised sector and the poor. While I pay my tribute to Dr Sanjay and express my gratitude for the inspiration he had been to me personally and to the students of city colleges where we worked together in several campaigns and works I am sure we will be able to carry forward his dreams and visions for a new and different India than the present one. Thanks Sanjay for everything. You were a great human being. You looked at the world and the people as human beings and you saw a hope in everyone you met. At no point of time even in the most depressing situations you had given up hope and you were an optimist and you gave us hope. It is that hope that a new world is possible that would help us to struggle. Though you are not in our midst you inspiration will remain alive with us.

For New Age: Marxism and Science

Professor Sanjay Biswas

Background

The primary source of Marxian thought on 'Science' is the work of Fredrick Engels. Engels in his book 'Anti Duhring' and in his monumental exposition 'Dialectics of Nature' explores the relation which arises in matter in constant motion, bringing about quantitative and qualitative changes. His fundamental discovery much influenced by Hegelian dialects, emerges, as what we call today 'dialectical materialism'. Very well versed in contemporary developments in science and technology Engels arrives at discernible laws of change. Marx profoundly interested in the development of knowledge and understanding in biology and geology evolves the framework of historical materialism where human societies are seen to change within the framework of dialectical laws; as forces of production and production relation come into conflict radical new changes are enforced. Marx contributed the last chapter to 'Anti Duhring' and worked closely with Engels throughout his working life as the latter developed his theory of dialectical materialism. Engels died in 1895 and the world has witnessed a century of debate where the unity of dialectical and historical materialisms have been demonstrated, where each of these categories have been supported and opposed in isolation from each other and where the dialectical and historical materialism have been opposed to each other, often in attempts to denigrate the contributions of Engels. More than hundred years after Marx and Engels wrote their classics, these debates, which have analysed Marxism, acutely, have strengthened Marxism. Marxism today, stands as an irrefutable and established tool for analysis and understanding of the evolution of natural processes in its relation with human society, but most importantly, is an invaluable guide for action to bring about changes in human condition. In the words of Helena Sheehan "arguably, Marxism is still the only mode of thought capable of coming to terms with the complexities of contemporary experience. It is still unsurpassed in its capacity for clarity, coherence, comprehensiveness and credibility. Within its resources are perhaps the only possibilities for penetrating the meaning even of events that its previous adherents never anticipated. The potency of Marxism is not so much in any of existing tenets as in the habit of large - scale and deep rooted thinking, discerning the trajectory of history as it comes, looking for a pattern of interconnections where other see only random chaos, going back further into the past, reaching order within the present, facing with greater composure into the future."

It is within this context we pose a general query in the words of J.D. Bernal; what is the social function of science? This begs further questions; what is that human activity called science? Does science have a social function? What is that complex dialectical relationship with society which legitimises science as an indispensible and integral part of human existence in a pararoma of social change? I am not competent and therefore do not even attempt to answer these questions in any comprehensive way. This essay compiles a set of my observations, about the motivation, practice and outcome of science, especially within the Indian context. The Marxian method allows me to avoid a random walk and focus my observations.

On a day-to-day basis human beings have been active to observe natural phenomena as they occur independent of human intervention as well as the changes which occur because of human intervention. Such observations more often than not have been motivated by a desire to uplift human condition but have principally led to cognitive systemisation of their experience towards generalisations, theories and models. The cognitive outcome has moved them to the next level of more complex observations, experimentation and theory where higher levels of interventions are practiced at a higher level of human condition. This is a very broad sweep of what one may designate as the scientific activity. What we will argue here is that the activity is not linear in time and is deeply social. Its social character on the one hand precipitates human development while on the other hand it may allow dogmatic imposition of separation of the cognitive from the practical which builds social and intellectual fetters which are detrimental to the scheme of human development.

History of Science–The Beginnings

One of the earliest observed trends in the history of science is the pursual of the dogma that one pursues exploration of nature out of sheer enjoyable curiosity, because nature is there. This takes many forms. There is an abstract ideal, in 'form' such as symmetry or an omnipresence endowed with everything perfect. Such an ideal motivates human activity to achieve the ideal by sheer contemplation. Greek geometry, Hindu religious rituals and Turkish miniature paintings are typical trends. The motivation for idealist scientific pursuit may or may not exclude observation and experimentation (as opposed to pure contemplation). We come up at one extreme with the Brahminic statement "Gods detest observations" to the other extreme where rich landlords delved into experimental Chemistry and Physics in England because it was an interesting thing to do. What we have to understand is that such motivation for scientific activity though highly individualistic and subjective are not socially disconnected; they are very much related to stages of social development. The Brahminic idealism is much posited in acute social stratification on caste lines, where manual labour by the lower castes is denigrated. The pursual of the platonic ideal form takes place in a similar social milieu where the thinkers and slaves are rigidly separated. The scientific activities of English scientists happen when leisure and resource are available to a few in a semi - feudal society. The story repeats itself in many ancient and medieval societies such as in ancient Egypt where a leisured class evolves on the surplus from the land to contemplate perfect but useless pyramids. While some of the observations and inferences of such idealistic pursuits especially when it was based in experiments are useful as they are taken up and used by later generations of scientists there is no gainsaying to state that such pursuits could happen only in highly stratified societies and the practitioners more consciously than otherwise strengthened social oppression.

That social separation of mental work from manual work leads to fetters on observation and proof based scientific practice is well read from the history of ancient and medieval society but what is frightening is that such social conditions may lead to the breeding of a dangerous ideology advocated and propagated by idealist philosophers and metaphysical scientists. Bernal argues that such a breed justifies a 'fascist ideology' of brute force under mystically inspired leadership. He talks about "a rising practice in school in the post first world war Europe where reason is dethroned and the man who asks for proof of a fact before he will believe it is dismissed to the bottom of the form and told to write 500 times "I must not ask for proof"......books and sometimes their authors are burnt because they ask for proof or question someone's intuition about the nature of the universe".

In discussing social 'fetters' on scientific activity I shall cite two further examples of complex historical roots which generate as well as which release such fetters. We have briefly discussed the feudal roots of abstract scientific practice in the seventeenth century England. These fetters are shattered and the practice receives a death blow with the discovery of colonies, source of primary raw material for production and a concomitant rise, first of mercantile capitalists and then industrial and financial capitalist classes. These profound changes in production relations broke the fetters as under and took science to a new level where a utilitarian philosophy and practice of science come into force. An additional blow to the old system comes from Darwin where the metaphysical world of science disappears to be replaced by a creator less universe and a science of practical utility at the service of the bourgeois who stood to profit immensely form such a change. My second example gives a brief, but I hope, a contextual history of science in India.

Indian science starts on a glorious note about 3000 BC in the northwest of the country. In a situation of productive agriculture and innovative irrigation, large surplus is generated to yield exquisite civil engineering works, practical geometry and corresponding mathematics. Further enrichment takes place through maritime trade. While the script remains unread our knowledge is speculative, but archeology suggests that it was a prosperous society with mild social stratification without a major invocation of theistic and mystical inspiration. The civilisation, without a knowledge of the use of iron gets wiped out by 1750 BC; what is remarkable is that their knowledge of geometry which arises out of practice than contemplation, gets passed on to the post Harappa Vedic society.

The next phase, is what one may sweepingly term as the Vedic period, is called the dark age of Indian science. Primarily a pastoral society based on an animistic and nature based ideology, it moves to primitive and then to a more class based agricultural society in its later period as the forests are cleared, mineral resources are unearthed and trade routes are established. By about three-four hundred BC a rigid class/caste based society comes into being leading to a highly authoritarian Mauryan regimes. In the first thousand years of this period was a time of settlement, scattered political leadership and low productivity, certain level of botanical classification and educational disciplines come into being, but in general pottery, civil engineering, metallurgy and theoretical sciences reach possibly their lowest level in Indian history. Certain knowledge of geometry and construction survives from the Harappan period and Sulva Sutra records the use of such knowledge in building of temples and altars. What is of a great deal of interest is that it was only the manual labour which was the repository of such knowledge and their relegation to the lowest rungs of the society by the ruling elite ensures that such knowledge has no channels and routes of furtherance and development.

Moving on to a somewhat later development in the early part of the first millennium we come across the Carakas and Susruthas. Using the botanical knowledge accumulated since the days of Parasara they built up a people oriented medical practice in the northern part of India. Within an ideological framework that 'whatever is good for curing a patient is justified' these roaming doctors chronicle two large medical treatises of medicine and surgery, based on local plant based medicine and surgical tools made by village ironsmiths. This first major breakthrough in Indian medicine known as Ayurveda is framed within an atheistic ideology which drives them towards a proto – materialist world view. Popular amongst the people, they come into sharp conflict with the Brahminical ruling class. As far as we know they were brutally suppressed by the 4th–5th century AD and a fraction of the Ayurveda was left to be rediscovered by the 17th–18th century in Tibet. Just like in the case of the Sulvas another great beginning of science was fettered and killed to maintain the status quo in social relation. Astronomy was one more area which suffered. The prevailing Brahminical militancy against 'observation' prevented the development of observational astronomy. At the beginning of the millennium, Aryabhata arrived using mathematics and primitive observation at the rudiments of a heliocentric solar system which challenges the Vedic notion of a geocentric universe. Aryabhata and his followers over the next four to five hundred years suffer because of this conflict till they had to give up this genuinely scientific position. Another instance of social fetters choking a great beginning in a branch of science in India!

The foregoing discussion demonstrates that development of knowledge through the practice of science opens up wide ranging potentials for human development. However, when such developments, in economic and human terms, in a particular stage of history are in consonance with the interest of the ruling class resources are invested to encourage the development. When they are in conflict, fetters are imposed on scientific activity, such fetters may be at the level of infrastructure or the superstructure, concrete historical condition determines the special characters of such a fetter.

History of Science – The Middle Period

We explore below the above social relation of science in a more contemporary setting. One of the questions which are frequently asked is why Indian science, in spite of such glorious beginnings at different historical periods, could at no time sustain such development as a continuum. For a Marxist to make a board statement in answer to that is not difficult, but as Marxists we would like to understand, in the words of Lenin, 'the concrete conditions'. A sharp progress of scientific activity had not taken place in India, since the brilliant beginnings made at the very early times, were thwarted by the ruling class. Over a very long period, almost till the advent of the British, some modest technological innovations in textile, road building, metallurgy and agriculture take place as and when required by the ruling class to maintain its hegemony. Science to develop needs legitimacy by the prior history as much as encouragement from the ruling class. The history of science in India tells us that advancement in science cannot be taken for granted; it is not an abstraction but it is very much related to concrete historical conditions and class relations.

Two things happened with the advent of British colonialism. As raw material needed for manufacture and industrial capitalism in Britain become available in the colonies, certain developmental interest were brought in by the British for appropriate transport, roads, communication and mining. Technological institutions such as Roorkee University and Bengal Engineering College come into existence while survey and classification of natural mineral and vegetable resources of India took place. While it was advantageous in general to train Indian engineers in these areas for maintenance, it was categorically stated that in India any institutional framework for fundamental and applied research was unnecessary and counterproductive. Firstly, there was the rise of Indian capitalists, such as Mr J.N. Tata. With growing familiarity with the metropolis Indian capitalism sought the opportunity, no doubt using the technological knowhow form Europe, to start industries. Secondly, the same familiarity bred aspirations in educational structures to undertake researches in some areas of basic sciences as well. While the industries such as Tata Steel and Bengal Chemical continue through to independence the spurt of very high class scientific research practiced by Boses, Saha, Bhaba, Sarabhai etc, was short lived. The human resources trained by this individual brilliance continued through the independence but the spark remained short lived.

The new ruling class in the 19th century Europe owned the means of production which allowed them to exploit labour which became a market commodity. The process leads necessarily to accumulation of capital. To maintain its hegemony the capitalist class had to perpetually accumulate capital. For sheer survival fierce competition had to take place between individual capitalists, cartels and transnational corporations. Between competitors the one who could reduce more the cost of production without damaging its profit margin survived. This necessitated perpetual technical change, facilitated by increasing automation, greater utilisation of materials with elimination of waste and saving of capital costs owing to more rapid turnover. In general the result is a reduction in working costs for the same production or more usually a greater production for the same working cost. To reduce working costs perpetually apart from innovative factory organisation and, speeding up of the worker or lowering of wages, perpetual technical changes had to take place supported by scientific advance. This science to realise its full potential had to work within a broadly rational society where ideological constraints imposed by mystical religiosity to human activity, in general the hallmark of the superstructure of the previous historical stage, had to be minimised if not fully eliminated. The superstructure needed for this development was important and Marx sets it out very clearly in 'Grundrisse'. The conception of scientific method, he maintained, had to be grounded in an epistemology that stood in contrast to both the British empiricist theory of knowledge and French reductionism and to the idealist theory of knowledge. Against the empiricist view he stressed the necessity of abstraction. Against the idealist view, he stressed the foundational role of the concrete reality. The correct scientific method, he stated, is a process which started with concrete complex concepts and proceeded by way of analysis and synthesis to abstract simple concepts. The end result was the reproduction of concrete situation. The concrete was not so much the starting point as the result of the process, a process involving both observation and conceptualisation. This is the dialectic of the abstract and concrete. Both Marx and Engels in their various studies of the historical evolution of knowledge demonstrated that departures from this methodology, in practice, leads to fetters to scientific activity.

Contemporary Science

Marx and Engels were profoundly aware of the scientific and technical changes in their times, that were making possible the reduction of necessary labour time and transforming the very character of necessary labour. They saw even the most "pure" natural science as inextricably linked to technology and industry, as well as to a whole range of human practices. Every social order posed characteristic question, investigated certain problems, organised the division of labour in its distinctive way and even thought the abstracted in different categories. Every social order gave its own shape to the development of science and technology. Scientific concepts were socially evolved and bore the imprint of technological objectives, class interests and of other forces of that time. Scientific theories were the product, not only of experimentation and thought, but of historical condition. Certain theories could only arise under certain historical condition, but not under others.

The struggle for independence saw the rise of national bourgeois who joined in the struggle against the British to lay the foundation of industry and some institutions of education. In some cases the need for positive linkage between scientific education and research and industry was clearly seen. Raja S.C. Mullick, Mahendra Lal Sarkar and P.C. Ray in Calcutta and J.N. Tata in Bangalore laid the foundation of institutions which would aid the growth of a scientific culture to support industrial growth in the long run. Such instances were few but the idea, that if capitalism has to take roots in a post independent India, 'Science' has to play a role in progressive evolution of productive forces, became a point for discussion in many circles. Given this background, however weak, the post independent nation building discussions, within the 'right' and the 'left' included science in their agenda. 1958 saw Prime Minister Nehru shepherding a historic resolution on 'scientific temper' in the Indian parliament.

Starting from post industrial revolution Britain and the present day 'developed first world', witnessed a relatively uniform and linear growth of science and other necessary infrastructures of education, health and communication at the service of industrial and finance capital; no doubt on the foundation of super profits acquired by imperialism. Capitalists and bourgeois governments invested in science to maintain the engine power of capitalism. A prevailing social rationality was necessary and was established and maintained to ensure that there was no serious crisis in the progress of science. Such background and motivation for the growth of science was almost non- existent in post independent India. India emerged into a general ambience of cultural irrationality, a very weak and patchy infrastructure of health, education and communication and a very poor pre – history (more than 1000 years) of scientific activity, in short as a country steeped in backward feudalism. The productive forces at best developed skewed and distorted. Within intense debates about directions and ideology of development, the more left oriented political leadership gained ground on an anti-imperialist ticket of self reliance. Massive infrastructural industries, educational institutions such as the Indian Institutes of Technology to produce the human resources for such industries and a chain of national and industrial laboratories to generate practical know how at the service of mechanical, metallurgical, chemical and electrical industries, agriculture and medicine came into being. No Darwinian revolution took place on the Indian soil and in spite of tardy induction of science in school curricula irrationality remained a strong social force. Except rationality all the prerequisites for the growth of industrial capitalism were put in place, the only problem was the absence of a capitalist class victorious over feudalism to lay the foundation for a steady growth of productive forces and science, to champion its own class interest.

We will discuss later the absence of any major contradiction between feudalism and early capitalism in the post – independence period and its effects on the character of scientific advance. It is worthwhile to note at this stage that one of the potential harbingers for radical changes in productive forces, the superbly trained technical manpower (viz. from the IITs) to train, whom our planners had invested heavily, emigrated to the USA. In the absence of the necessary social conditions their potential remained unutilised in fulfilling its historic role. The developments of CSIR, ISRO, DAE, DRDO and public sector infrastructure industries provided a bulwark against neocolonialism within a short time frame, but no class which needed science for its survival came into existence. No mechanism which ensures a smooth and steady growth of scientific activity and therefore knowledge in a natural way driven by class contradiction came into being.

The above does not imply that in India there was no development of a capitalist class. Capitalism grew but within a framework, at least till very recently, quite different from the way capitalism developed in Europe and the Americas. In a different historic phase the class draws the surplus value by exploiting the working class but to develop the necessary productive forces there existed at these historic times a reservoir of knowledge and knowhow with international capital which the Indian capital could draw upon by becoming a subsidiary or by purchasing them without having to motivate national scientific activity. It used the human resources produced by the state and private capital to maintain the productive forces but it never needed an "Indian Science" as an engine power for the development of its productive forces. Conversely, science and innovation developed in the strategic sectors of space, defense and atomic energy where there are no overt class contradictions. Science in these sectors has prospered supported directly by a state which projects nationalistic bourgeois aspirations. A further impediment occurs in the Indian scene to the growth of clear cut capitalism – it is the coexistence of a vast economic sector, where the class relations are feudal. Not only does this militate against the development of a rational culture, necessary for the growth of science and productive forces, the Indian capitalism closely allied to the feudal land relation never struggles to establish a clear cut class hegemony which would ensure sharp rise in scientific activity exclusively at the service of industry. Science at the service of agriculture would perhaps take roots in the future supported by rural capitalism but such a connection is presently in its infancy.

The overall assessment of the quality and quantity of advanced scientific activity in India may be (1) there are very few institutions, such as the Indian Institute of Science, where world class scientific activities are practiced. Such institutions survive through massive infusion of government funding and till quite recently were totally isolated from the spheres of production. Their overall social impact is to generate very high quality manpower who in a minute number man national laboratories, some industrial R&D sectors in India and abroad. (2) National laboratories and industrial laboratories generate practical scientific knowledge which is not very innovative but does support the engineering activities of the public sector (3) Mission oriented activities in the strategic sector generate high class engineering innovation and knowledge. There is a high turnover of manpower in this sector and one way mobility to the multinational companies. (4) The great number of Indian Universities, traditionally supported by government funding, languish at the lowest level of innovative scientific activity. Minimal government funding and near total dissociation with productive activities in industry, agriculture and medicine may be the principal causes for this failure.

The most recent period of Indian history may mark a qualitative shift in scientific activities in India. While it is too early to make judgments there appears to be a heightened but patchy growth of scientific activities. There has been a strong growth of private capitalism in the information technology, biotechnology and manufacturing sectors. With freer access of the multinational corporations to the Indian market and infrastructure the Indian private capital stands to compete fiercely with the MNCs. To be competitive both private and public sectors in India are turning more and more towards indigenous scientific and engineering resources. Private investment in relation to traditional government funding in institutions of science and engineering is on the rise.

Generalisation

We come to a point in our discussion where a perennial debate about science and social development raises its head within the framework of historical materialism. Social scientists of the erstwhile Soviet Union, Europe, India and other developing countries debated fiercely in the 1960s and 1970s the question "is capitalism a necessary pre-requisite for socialism?" In India there was no doubt the construction of a large public sector and concomitant industrial R&D

in the infrastructure sector, promotion of higher institutions for training of technology oriented human resources, development of a high technology strategic sector and the growth of national laboratories in the public domain. While such thrusts strengthened national sovereignty, did it provide an expanding domain of socialised production and a corresponding rational superstructure for the ordinary people of India to establish class hegemony towards socialism? In hindsight the answer is clearly a no. Why? All the five year plans and other developments happened where the economy remained a mixed one, feudal relations dominated national politics, mass education up to the level of university was inadequately attended the and the investment in agricultural was peripheral. A reasonably robust but mediocre culture of engineering practice developed in this scenario but the social condition necessary for what Bernal called the "unpredictable radical changes" in ideas in science never happened. It is such changes as the 'steam engine' and 'mass production' which produce the radical changes in productive forces which triggers radical changes in production relations as much as the impending production relation creates the necessary condition for those radical changes in productive forces. In the first 40 years of post independent Indian history the social relations between the capitalist class, feudal landlords and the working masses were such that they could never create the conditions necessary for radical developments in productive forces. Even if such development did occur by chance, the social relations of this historic phase was such that, they would not have changed radically in to a new historic phase. The feudally dominated mixed economy though endowed with an anti-imperialist character could never generate such changes. What the steady but mediocre growth of science, technology, human resources and infrastructure have done in India is to build the base which has been used by an incipient capitalist class for their own growth towards a more radical and focused capitalist class. This has deepened the contradictions between the classes. The 9 per cent growth rate we champion today is a reflection of this. We also witness appropriately, the steady return of a large number of very high class scientific and technological manpower back to India from the West at this specific historical juncture. To go back to the debate, the dream of the 50s and 60s remains unfructified; the socialisation of infrastructure, given the concrete social condition in post independent India has not socialised production and does not leap frog us into socialism. We are in the process of building modern capitalism and sharp classical class contradictions. What role feudalism will play in this is a question which we will know in the near future. I end with a reading of J. D. Bernal's "Social Function of Science".

Bernal on Marxism and Science – The Future

At any given moment we can see the composition of the economic and political forces of the times, their necessary struggle and the new condition which will be the result. Beyond that we can only foresee a process which has not ended and will necessarily take on new and strictly unpredictable forms. It is a method and guide to action and not a creed. The relevance of Marxism to science is that it removes it from its imagined position of complete detachment and shows it as a part, but a critically important part of economic and social development. In this process it separates science from its perennial fetters of metaphysics. From Marxism we obtain the driving force of scientific advance and this consciousness can become embodied in the organisation of science for the benefit to humanity. Science will come to be recognised as the chief factor in fundamental social change. Steady process of technology improvement provides for regular increase in the extent and commodity of life. Science should provide a continuous series of unpredictable radical changes in the techniques themselves. Whether these changes fit in or fail to fit in with human and social needs is the measure of how far science has been adjusted to its social function. For the full value of where science can take us we have to wait till the end of our struggle. Such an end marks the beginning of a new episode in history. Then mankind will come into its material heritage, and, far from needing science less, will make even greater demands on it to solve the greater human and social problem which have to be faced. To meet this challenge science itself will have to change and develop, and in doing so will cease to be a special discipline of a few and become the common heritage of mankind.

Nuclear Future of India

Dr D.P. Sen Gupta

The BJP Government had assumed power for the second time after the first BJP Government had collapsed within 13 days of its assuming power. Even within the 13 days the Government contemplated carrying out a nuclear test at Pokhran. But time was short. Soon after assuming power for the second time the Government went ahead and in 1998, the Pokhran test was carried out. Some of us were horrified. Amongst the 'some' were Professors A. K. N. Reddy and Sanjay Biswas and a few others. It was apparent that BJP was flexing its muscles and trying to prove to the world in general and to Pakistan in particular that India was a "Nuclear Power". The Prime Minister Sri Atal Behari Vajpayee's slogan "Jai Vignan" rented the air. India wanted to prove its scientific capability to us in India and to the world that India is capable of producing a nuclear bomb indigenously. Pakistan obviously was not sitting idle. Three days later, Pakistan exploded the bombs it had allegedly procured from China. Everything was in the open now. Pakistan was waiting for an opportunity to prove to India and to the world that Pakistan wasn't lagging behind India. "So, be careful".

Reddy, Sanjay and I and several others were not convinced that Pokhran II served India's interest and world peace. In an interview to "Outlook" I made my point, stating that nuclear bombs do not promote peace and hardly prove our scientific excellence, repeating something that had been done by the Western countries several decades earlier. I expressed my apprehensions about the sanctions by the western countries, U.S. in particular on India and how our scientific research would suffer. I did state that nuclear power for production of electricity is absolutely necessary for India. I have partially revised my opinion since then for reasons I would come to later in this article. I wrote a number of articles in different newspapers stating my strong reservations about the Pokhran II test and invited tirades and nasty mails. Sanjay and I were branded as anti-national and even considered security threats to the Indian Institute of Science having relinquished faculty positions in England, to serve our country in our modest ways. A meeting was organised in a hall inside a hotel to protest against Pokhran tests. The meeting was half way through when a procession from VHP entered the hotel premises and pounced on the speakers and the members of the audience. But for the timely intervention of the police, summoned by the manager of the hotel, there would have been casualties.

Fifteen years have passed since the test and if we take stock of the losses and benefits of the Pokhran II test, we have very little to show in justification of the test. In fact, doubts have been expressed later as for the validity of the claims made about the scientific success of the explosions. So it wasn't "Jai Vignan". The test did not prove to be a deterrent to conventional war. The Kargil war soon followed. If it was a deterrent, Kargil should not have taken place. Research in Indian Institute of Science suffered badly for many years because of the blanket sanction imposed on importing chemicals and instruments. Other research Institutions in India suffered just as badly. We certainly could have held our head high as a nation that was capable of making nuclear bombs and yet refrained from testing them and producing high quality research in other fields.

Let us come to the question of how much investment of scientific efforts and resources should India make to produce nuclear power. It may not be widely known that the total amount of nuclear energy produced by India is a meagre 3 per cent of the total electricity generation of 800 billion units a year. Wind generation of electricity comes very close to generation of nuclear energy. India lacks uranium and hence we bend backwards to ensure that we have a steady supply of the fuel from other countries. The nuclear disaster in Fukushima has made the world sit up. Even France which has had 75 per cent of its electricity from nuclear power generation is systematically reducing its dependence on nuclear energy. Germany has announced stopping of nuclear energy production by the year 2022.

Apart from the possible threat of a disaster that a nuclear fission reactors hold, our acute shortage of fuel and a sell out to the terms and conditions of a country that agrees to supply the fuel to India, a very long incubation period and huge hidden costs make nuclear power generation unattractive. The costs of solar and wind power generation are rapidly coming down and in view of the extensive solar energy that India receives, our emphasis in electricity production on which India's economic progress will squarely rest, must be now on alternative sources including reducing T&D losses. We should however keep our nuclear option open for future years when fusion energy may turn out to be a technical possibility with endless resources of hydrogen isotopes and disaster free performance.

Poverty and Health

Dr Arun Mitra

Since 1972 poverty has been defined on basis of the money required to buy food worth 2100 calories in urban areas and 2400 calories in rural areas. Poverty is one of the main problems which have attracted attention of Sociologists and Economists. It indicates a condition in which a person fails to maintain a living standard adequate for his physical and mental efficiency. It is a situation people want to escape. It gives rise to a feeling of a discrepancy between what one has and what one should have. As of 2008 statistics, the World Bank has estimated that there were an estimated 1,345 million poor people in developing countries who live on $1.25 a day or less. Out of this 50.9 per cent live in Sub Saharan Africa, 44.4 per cent in South Asia, 16.8 per cent in East Asia & pacific and 8.2 per cent in Latin America and Caribbean. On the other hand 0.04 per cent of people belong to Europe and Central Asia and a similar number are from Middle East and North Africa. Thus extreme poverty remains an alarming problem in the world's developing regions. According to Haq, 23 per cent of the globe's population lives in South Asia, while it accommodates 40 per cent of the globe's poor. The most recent data released by the UN Food and Agriculture Organisation which bases its study on under nutrition has estimated the number of poor to be 925 million in October 2010. The number of hungry people has increased since 1995-97, though the number is down from last year. The increase is due to three factors:

(1) Neglect of agriculture relevant to very poor people by governments and international agencies;

(2) The current worldwide economic crisis and

(3) The significant increase of food prices in the last several years which has been devastating to those with only a few dollars a day to spend.

The figure of 925 million people is 13.6 per cent of the estimated world population of 6.8 billion. Nearly all of the undernourished are in developing countries. Looking at some more statistics:

1. At least 80 per cent of humanity lives on less than $10 a day.
2. More than 80 per cent of the world's population lives in countries where income differentials are widening.
3. The poorest 40 per cent of the world's population accounts for 5 per cent of global income. The richest 20 per cent of the world's population accounts for three-quarters of world income.
4. According to UNICEF, 22,000 children die each day due to poverty. And they die quietly in some of the poorest villages on earth, far removed from the scrutiny and the conscience of the world. Being meek and weak in life makes these dying multitudes even more invisible in death.
5. Infectious diseases continue to blight the lives of the poor across the world. An estimated 40 million people are living with HIV/AIDS, with 3 million deaths in 2004. Every year there are 350–500 million cases of malaria, with 1 million fatalities: Africa accounts for 90 per cent of malarial deaths and African children account for over 80 per cent of malaria victims worldwide.

1.1 billion People in developing countries have inadequate access to water, and 2.6 billion lack basic sanitation. Some 1.8 million child deaths occur each year as a result of diarrhea. There is loss of 443 million school days each year from water-related illness. Harmful economic systems are the principal cause of poverty and hunger. The causes of poverty include an extremely unequal income distribution in the world and within specific countries. Ongoing conflicts add to the problem. Principal underlying cause of poverty and hunger is the ordinary operation of the economic and political systems in the world. Essentially control over resources and income is based on military, political and economic power that typically ends up in the hands of a minority, who live well, while those at the bottom barely survive, if they do. Health status in developing countries is adequately reflected in health indicators. For example in South Asia the mortality rates for infants continue to be as high as 58 to 84. Maternal mortality remains at 350 to 540 and under-five mortality ranges from 83 to 107. Overall life expectancy has barely gone above 60 years and is as low as 43 in some parts!

To move closer to the goal of health for all we must look back at the concept of public health. According to Charles-Edward Amory Winslow, a public health expert. "It is the science and art of preventing disease, prolonging life and promoting physical and mental health and efficiency through organised community effort for the sanitation of the environment, the control of community infection, education of individuals in principles of personal hygiene, the organisation of medical and nursing services for the early diagnosis and preventive treatment of diseases, and the development of the service machinery which will ensure to every individual in the community a standard of living adequate for the maintenance of health" (Park: 2000).

Thus solidarity and equity are the essence of public health and that cannot be a function of technology alone. This spirit was imbibed by the Alma Ata Declaration, which conceptualised health as the core function of development, encompassing the securities of life, livelihood, and basic services including food, health, education, housing, sanitation, drinking water, electricity, and transportation. The Declaration emphasised the interdependence of health and the overall progress of communities based on principles of self-sufficiency and affordability (WHO: 1978). Improving health called for a comprehensive approach whereby primary health care was seen as "the key to achieving an acceptable level of health throughout the world in the foreseeable future as a part of social development and in the spirit of social justice."

Article X of the declaration says that an acceptable level of health for all the people of the world by the year 2000 can be 'attained through a fuller and better use of the world's resources, a considerable part of which is now spent on armaments and military conflicts. A genuine policy of independence, peace, détente and disarmament could and should release additional resources that could well be devoted to peaceful aims and in particular to the acceleration of social and economic development of which primary health care, as an essential part, should be allotted its proper share.'

The critical issue is that, historically, health of the labouring classes has always been the last priority in any sector of the capitalist economy. It becomes an issue only when labour organises and fights for itself (Qadeer 2004). Many nations have enhanced the degree of exploitation of labour by withdrawing their privileges. Several countries have made laws against the interest of the working class who are losing secure employment through closures, retrenchments, and casualisation, causing further deterioration in their living conditions and health.

What we would like to underline here is that there has been shift from the holistic perspective of Winslow and the Alma Ata Declaration to another that treats health as techno-dependent and amenable to commodification. To push this biomedical perspective a theoretical shift is taking place that affects public health at the level of concepts, resources, system management, availability of technical know-how, self-sufficiency, and above all, cohesion and co-operation between those who are responsible for public health as well as those who are its recipients (Qadeer). The shift in concept is evident in the WHO itself when it recently proposed a behavioralist model of intervention that places individual responsibility at centre stage (WHO: 1996). The challenge before it has been redefined to address only population control and some selected communicable diseases at the cost of its earlier broad-based approach.

By the 80s, the policies of the South Asian countries began to be influenced significantly by the Bretton Woods institutions, specially the World Bank. The developing countries had to accept structural adjustment policies (SAP) under the economic development based on market economy in line with the present day corporate driven one way globalisation. The governments in the developing countries changed laws in favour of multinational corporations and the local elite while denying the basic fundamental rights to the working classes. The rights to hold protests and unionise have been curtailed. Subsidies to the poor have been taken off. Job security taken away and employment generation is in the form of contract labour with low wages even in public sector what to talk of the private organisations. The priorities in the agriculture production also shifted from the basic food to the produce that was to be used by the elite in these countries. All this have further resulted into increase in the problem for the lower income groups.

The local pharmaceuticals industries suffered under the new patent regime of the WTO. As a result, prices of newer drug increased. The Government of India closed down its prestigious public sector Indian Drugs and Pharmaceutical Limited (IDPL) which produced bulk drugs and vaccine producing unit Central Research Institute (CRI) at Kasauli (Himachal Pradesh) which used to produce cheap vaccines. Indian Pharmaceutical industry produced cost effective drugs not only for Indian Population but also for several other developing countries in Asia and Africa. Major part of health care now being propagated in the name of health tourism, is being promoted and offered by corporate hospitals and is out of reach even for the middle classes of India what to talk of the vast poor majority. The stress has completely shifted away from the communicable diseases which till date form the major health problem. WHO shifted its own concept of Alma Ata and started collaborating with the pharma MNCs. All this has created new problems for the health of the poor.

Despite the tall claims of high economic growth in India, startling figures were reported by the Arjun Sen Gupta committee appointed by the Government of India in 2008 which concluded that 77 per cent of Indian population lives on less than Rs.20 (Less than half a US Dollar) a day. The Planning Commission of India has lately fixed the Below Poverty Line for those earning Rs 15/- (1/3 US$) a day in rural areas and Rs 20 (less than US$ 1/2) a day in urban areas. This has drawn strong criticism from the public. Acting on a Public Interest Litigation the Supreme Court of India has asked the government to explain as to how it expects people with this low income to get 2400 Calories every day required to sustain a quality life. No wonder the neo-liberal economic order has utterly failed to meet the people's desire of a quality life. Corporate-led, finance-driven globalisation has successfully transferred wealth from labour to capital. This has resulted in inequality and exclusion on a massive scale which, combined with the pressure on water and other environmental resources, is likely to fuel new conflicts.

For economic growth and almost all of the other indicators, the last 20 years [of the current form of globalisation, from 1980–2000] have shown a very clear decline in progress as compared with the previous two decades [1960–1980]. The fall in economic growth rates was most pronounced and across the world.

- Progress in life expectancy was also reduced.
- Progress in reducing infant mortality was also considerably slower during the period of globalisation (1980–1998) than over the previous two decades.
- Progress in education also slowed during the period of globalisation.

It is during this period that the urge to have control on world resources by the developed world increased. This can be seen in the continued arms race with 4.46 Billion US$ expenditure per day. The USA alone spends nearly 42 per cent of this. After the end of cold war and fall of Soviet block the new excuses have been invented to justify their posture like 'to save the world from terrorism, and to establish democracy in other countries'. This is evident from the aggression on Iraq which caused collateral damage and now double standards over events in Arab world. Focus of wars has shifted to Asia and other developing regions. South Asia has fallen into the trap of nuclear arms race and is a centre of continued violence by the non-state actors.

At the end of 2005, the global number of refugees was at its lowest level in almost a quarter of a century. Despite some large-scale repatriation movements, the last three years have witnessed a significant increase in refugee numbers, due primarily to the violence taking place in Iraq and Somalia. By the end of 2008, the total number of refugees under UNHCR's mandate exceeded 10 million. The number of conflict-induced internally displaced persons (IDPs) reached some 26 million worldwide at the end of the year. Providing exact figures on the number of stateless people is extremely difficult. But using the statistics above 1.02 billion people suffer from chronic hunger while 36 million people are displaced [UNHCR 2008].

The whole issue thus poses a big challenge before the right thinking people and organisations around the world. To improve health of the people the spirit of Alma Ata has to be revived. WHO should impress upon the governments around the world to take necessary steps for a holistic instead of a piecemeal approach to health care and devise policies accordingly. Poverty alleviation strategies have to be designed to reduce gaps in the society. It is most essential that a society based on justice and equality be created through international relations based on the principles of mutual respect for the territorial and geographical integrity of the nations and an economic order which gives equal opportunities to people and nations around the world to participate in the development process through the utilisation of natural resources. Modern technology has given us ample opportunity to develop true globalisation rather than corporate driven one way globalisation. Wasteful expenditure on arms race has to be shed and all problems have to be solved through mutual dialogue. It is here that IPPNW can play a big role.

References

- Imrana Qadeer–Challenges for Public Health in Contemporary South Asia 2004
- Haq Mahbub Ul (1999–"Human Development in South Asia 1999: The Crisis of Governance", Oxford, Oxford University Press, pp 13-17)
- Susan George - Globalisation & War, International congress of IPPNW. New Delhi 2008

- Amartya Sen: Poverty, evil and crime
- Michel Chossudovsky, The American Prospect, Jan 1, 2002 V13 i1 pA2(5) - America's War for Global Domination
- Prof Arun Kumar JNU, Delhi–GLOBALISATION AND INDIA'S DEVELOPMENT
- 2011 World Hunger and Poverty Facts and Statistics - World Hunger Education Service - http://www.worldhunger.org/articles/Learn/world%20hunger%20facts%202002.htm
- SIPRI

The Role of Civil Society, Social Movements and Academia in Catalysing "Health For All"

Dr Thelma Narayan & Dr Ravi Narayan

"The people have the right and duty to participate individually and collectively in the planning and implementation of their healthcare"

The Alma Ata Declaration, 1978 (2)

"For too long the medical profession and the medical education sector have been directed by professional control and debate. It is time to recognise the role of the community, the consumer, the patient and the people in the whole debate........What is needed is a strong countervailing movement initiated by health and development activists, consumer and peoples' organisations that will bring health care and medical education and their right orientation high on the political agenda of the country. All those concerned about 'peoples needs' and 'peoples health' will have to take on this emerging challenge as we approach the end of the millennium."

SOCHARA, Vhai, 1998 (26)

"The participation of people and people's organisation is essential to the formulation, implementation and evaluation of all health and social policies and programmes. Strong people's organisations and movements are fundamental to more democratic, transparent and accountable decision making processes."

- The People's Charter for Health - 2000(1)

I. The Journey towards a New Paradigm in Health

We began our journey into understanding the community based challenges and framework of primary health care in the pre Alma Ata years in the department of Community Medicine in a medical college in South India. We worked at the community level using health cooperatives, local health workers and partnership strategies with the government and the community to enhance the goals of primary health care. This led to expanding the range of Primary Health Care activities to preventive and promotive services, appropriate technology, and development activities. We were however constantly faced with the dilemma before most primary health care workers realising early in their action response that the biomedical response was inadequate for a more complex social/community context of the primary health care challenge. The Figure-1 shows how a cough syrup as treatment for a patient with chronic cough is inadequate for the cough which is likely to be linked to underlying issues of poverty, injustice, lack of protective facilities at home and work, poor housing, myths, social exclusion and other factors that are important determinants of the chronic condition.

"Moving beyond the bio-medical frame work A Challenge!"

Figure -1

We were inspired by the work of two professors whose research work symbolised a shift from a biomedical paradigm to a socio-epidemiological paradigm. We are privileged to have known both of them as Philosophers and Guides at various stages of this process.

Professor Bannerji formerly Professor and Head, Centre for Social Medicine, Jawaharlal Nehru University, New Delhi, worked and studied 17 villages in India, in the 1980's, visiting them regularly to understand their experiences and perceptions of health and health services. He concluded and taught that '*Health service development is a social-cultural, process, a political process, a technological and managerial process with an epidemiological and sociological perspective*'. Similarly, Professor Geoffrey Rose, an illustrious epidemiologist at the London School of Hygiene and Tropical Medicine, well known for his work on salt and hypertension wrote a treatise after a very successful career of teaching and practicing epidemiology that "the *primary determinants of disease are mainly economic and social and.........medicine and politics cannot and should not be kept apart*".

One of the authors used the approach of these two professors to study Tuberculosis as a community health problem within the framework of public health policy analysis. In her doctoral study over 200 patients who had been labeled defaulters of the TB treatment programme in rural districts of Mysore in Karnataka, were interviewed to understand the processes leading to the default. Many social, economic, political and cultural factors were identified which distorted the TB programme. From all the evidence a new frame work of the understanding of TB and its causation was hypothesised which covered different levels of analysis and each level of analysis leading to a different level of control strategy (see table -1). The study also made a critique of the recently introduced DOTS programme from a socio-epidemiological point of view identifying its limited biomedical focus and suggesting a community based re-orientation. From direct observed treatment schedule (DOTS) to Community oriented treatment service (COTS) was the suggested paradigm shift, together with a societal understanding pointing to inequalities at various levels to the need for a more effective countervailing power to move towards an equitable distribution of resources.

It is a challenge for epidemiologists today, to move beyond a superficial epidemiology that focuses in an orthodox way on the bio-medical aspects of a health problem and therefore results in techno-managerial program solutions to a deeper assessment and measurement of social, economic, cultural, political and ecological evidence that will enable them to look at deeper determinants of ill health like poverty, gender bias, conflicts, stigma, social exclusion and evolve social and community interventions to respond to this larger framework of understanding. Many health professionals who look at these deeper social determinants and social solutions are often misunderstood as activists, whereas what they really are doing is being socio-epidemiologists who look at determinants of an unhealthy society rather than disease and individual ill health. Professor Denis Burkitt, (well known for the epidemiological description of Burkitts lymphoma in Africa) described this dichotomy in the 1970's by creating two categories of public health professionals – "floor moppers" and "tap turners off" and two categories of public health researchers – "intracellularists" studying the molecular basis of disease and health in their quest for new drugs and vaccines and "balloonists" studying the determinants at community and societal level. ((Figure -2) These are the type of future health professionals needed with special skills and social sensitivity to support the journey in every country towards Health For All and now Universal Health Care .

In 1984, having moved beyond the medical college, along with several colleagues, we evolved the Community Health Cell which later developed the Society for Community Health, Awareness, Research and Action (SOCHARA) as a space for experimentation, reflection, and solidarity with the new social model of health supported by tap turners off and balloonists closely aligned with civil society and emerging social movements. Involvements with the medico friends circle (MFC), the health networks in India and Asia and close involvement as a resource centre with the emerging community health movement in the country followed.

In 2000 AD, our centre was an active participant of a gathering of nearly 2500 primary health care enthusiasts, public health professionals, and health and social activists from 17 states in the country who travelled in 4 people's health trains to Kolkata for the 1st National People's Health Assembly. Our centre had with others facilitated the collaboration of 18 national networks into a loose coalition and supported the evolution of 5 booklets, published in several languages which ultimately became the manifesto of a People's Health Movement. At Kolkata the Jan Swasthya Abhiyan (JSA) was launched as a sort of second freedom struggle symbolically representing the journey towards freedom from ill health and under development. Later, a little over 250 participants travelled to Savar, Bangladesh to join around 1300 people from 75 countries, who gathered for the first Global People's Health Assembly. The assembly was to assess and explore why the Health for All by 2000 AD goal had not been reached. The People's Health Charter which evolved as a situation analysis and an action manifesto presented a new framework for public health professionals and policy activists. It reiterated that "h*ealth is a social, economic and political issue and a fundamental human right" and that "inequality, poverty, exploitation violence and injustice were at the roots of ill health"*. Based on this new understanding it prescribed actions that tackled the economic, political and social challenges of health; countered war, conflict and disaster and environmental health challenges; and promoted a people oriented health care based on the rights paradigm. Since this meeting and as a follow to the People's Health Charter, a global People's Health Movement evolved in which our centre played an important catalyst role including facilitating and hosting a global secretariat from 2003 to 2006. The most significant feature of the evolving PHM was the increasing involvement of academics and researchers and their metamorphoses into health activist professionals. The four key initiatives of the movement have included the deep involvement and engagement of academia and researchers from a large diversity of disciplinary backgrounds. Three alternative world health reports - "*Global Health Watch- I, II and III*" provided the socio-epidemiological evidence to back this new framework of health and health action. Academia, researchers and activist from all over the world have contributed their analysis to these documents and reiterated the challenges of the multidisciplinary approaches that are required to support public health policy processes. Similarly a group of academia and researchers have come together to initiate the International People's Health University (IPHU) to train young professionals and health activists in understanding the links between globalisation, inequity, and health and the health rights paradigm. Another process has been the development of a group of young activist professionals who are trained to attend, and watch the WHO decisions-making process on health policy issues as a group of WHO watchers. All these three supported by academia and researchers complement the larger more grounded Right to Health initiatives in different countries supported by country level circles and a broader coalition of Health For All oriented activists and enthusiasts.

SOCHARA has been deeply involved with this process at several levels and from 2003, has begun the evolution of a community health learning program for young professionals from multidisciplinary backgrounds to understand this paradigm shift in our model of health and to adapt their work to being part of a countervailing power linked to the community.

II. The Journey towards Health as a Social Movement

1. The Global People's Charter for Health (2000), the first of many progressive documents since the beginning of the new millennium, noted that: ***"Health is a social, economic and political issue and above all a fundamental human right. Inequality, poverty, exploitation, violence and injustice are at the roots of ill health and the deaths of poor and marginalised people… Health is primarily determined by the political, economic, social, and physical environment and should, along with equity and sustainable development, be a top priority in local, national, and international policy making".***

It echoed the Alma Ata Declaration of 1978, which had noted that ***"the promotion and protection of the health of the people is***

essential to sustained economic and social development and contributes to a better quality of life and to world peace... the attainment of the highest possible level of health is a most important social goal whose realisation requires the action of many other social and economic sectors in addition to the health sector".

It also echoed the Ottawa Charter for Health Promotion -1986 that had noted—"***Good health is a major resource for social, economic, and personal development and an important dimension of quality of life. Political, economic, social, cultural, environmental, behavioral and biological factors can all favour health or be harmful to it...... Health promotion works through concrete and effective community action in setting priorities, making decisions, planning strategies and implementing them to achieve better health. At the heart of this process is the empowerment of communities- their ownership and control of their own endeavors and destinies***".

All these declarations and charters have a common running thread. They emphasise that social change is a pre-requisite to health; that health is a crucial component of social change; and that involvement and empowerment of communities to strengthen social change and the 'Health for All' goal is a crucial and significant component of the process.

2. The State and Civil Society as a Countervailing Power

The role of government in bringing about change mediated through the political process and political institutions including elected parliaments is well established. Every government establishes certain institutions and procedures for making and enforcing rules, and collective decisions which includes the evolution of policies including health policies. The government is supported in this role by the judiciary which deals with an oversight on the legalities of the decision making process; by the military which provides national security and protection against conflict from external sources; and various other institutions that facilitate accountability and transparency.

The capture of the institutions of state by the elite and the exploitative, oppressive practices in some states has been critiqued.

With an increasing confusion about the role of the state and the increasing emergence of multi state actors – transnationals and the subsequent weakening of state institutions there seems to be increasing need for a countervailing power supported by people and community and especially by those in the community who are marginalised or socially excluded by the current economic, political, social and cultural policies to work towards developing equitable systems. For health the role of the public health system is paramount, and this needs to be strengthened and balanced by a strong civil society. It is the ability to demand/expand/occupy the space for social justice oriented engagement, voice, negotiations, dialogue or even press for evidence based discussion that is becoming the main justification for the salience of the civil society/social movement phenomena. This also explains the wide spectrum of the phenomena–with a range of campaigns and movements that have emerged both at national and global level. SOCHARA had suggested such a health policy initiative by civil society in India in 1998. This report called the Independent Commission on Health in India (ICHI) had a contribution from us which highlighted the need for such an approach as a policy imperative.

COUNTERVAILING MOVEMENT

"For too long the medical profession and the medical education sector have been directed by professional control and debate. It is time to recognize the role of the community, the consumer, the patient and the people in the whole debate.......What is needed is a strong countervailing movement initiated by health and development activists, consumer and people's organisations that will bring health care and medical education and their right orientation high on the political agenda of the country. All those concerned about 'peoples needs' and 'people's health' will have to take on these emerging challenges as we approach the end of the millennium" - ***Source: SOCHARA, VHAI, 1998 (26)***

---

3. The People's Charter as a Multi-Sectoral Document – Towards Health For All (HFA)

The Global People's Health Movement (PHM) which evolved in Savar, Bangladesh in 2000 AD, the People's Charter for Health, and various country and issue circles of the movement that evolved subsequently, probably represent the most well known face of civil society and social movements involved in promoting the right to health and health in all policies towards the HFA goal. The People's Charter for Health – PCH - now translated in over 40 languages is probably the most significant manifesto for health in all policies. The sections of the health charter and the range of policies that are suggested to be promoted are shown in the table below. These key recommendations of the charter represent the most comprehensive, recent outline of the challenges towards Heath for All and health in all policies.

4. Roles of civil society in the efforts towards Health for All

Civil society organisations/ and social movements have played multiple roles in recent decades to stimulate 'health' for all policies. It is impossible to make a complete or comprehensive list of all the roles that have emerged in recent decades. However as illustration of this diversity of roles – ten key roles are described with some relevant examples.

Representing the voice of the people

Some civil society organisations and social movements see themselves as representing the voice of the people especially the poor marginalised or socially excluded, as the main role in health action and health policy evolution at various levels. The most well known example in the current global situation is the People's Health Movement (PHM). The People's Charter for Health evolved as a response to this global gathering and dialogue and in the last decade and many more country level circles of the People's Health Movement have evolved to apply the goals of the charter in national context as well. Participants attend and are involved as informed and concerned citizens.

TABLE: C - PEOPLES HEALTH CHARTER 2000 AD AND SUGGESTIONS FOR HEALTH IN ALL KEY POLICIES	
THRUST AREA	**POLICY CHALLENGES**
HEALTH AS A HUMAN RIGHT	• Formulate and enforce policies and practices that respect Right to Health
TACKLING THE BROADER DETERMINANTS OF HEALTH	• Transformation WTO to prevent violation of social environment, economic and health rights • Cancellations of Third World Debt • Agricultural policies that guarantee food security and equitable access
SOCIAL AND POLITICAL CHALLENGES	• Public Health Rights protection in IPR • Taxation of speculative international policies • Health, equity, gender and environmental impact assessment
ENVIRONMENTAL CHALLENGES	• HIA/EIA for development project • Reduction of green house gases • Occupational and health safety policies and legislation • Laws to control bio-piracy of traditional and indigenous knowledge. • Environment and social audit of development projects.
WAR, VIOLENCE, CONFLICT AND NATURAL DISASTER	• Radical transformation of UN Security Council • End sanctions used as instruments of aggression against health of people • Policies for prevention and response to natural disasters • Policy against militarization of humanitarian relief organization
PEOPLE CENTERED HEALTH SECTOR.	• Oppose privatization and commodification of health care • National drug policies including price control • Patients and consumers right policies • Radical transformation of WHO • Policies for Comprehensive Primary Health Care (CPHC) and Health for All • Policies against privatization of public health services.
Source: People's Charter for Health (1)	

Advocacy and Lobbying

Many civil society organisations and social movements have focused their action on advocacy and lobbying for health system responses and health policy changes. The best example in recent years was the Treatment Action Campaign, in South Africa. This campaign by civil society led to availability of anti retro viral treatment to patients living with HIV-AIDS in the country and also to increase in the access of generic drugs for HIV-AIDS in the country. Depending on the nature of the problem and the availability of democratic space for dialogue and engagement this form of engagement can take different shapes. The role is primarily to encourage the state to change its health policy in response to the needs of the people in general or the specifically affected group.

Watchdog Role

Civil Society Organisations (CSOs) often gear themselves up to play a watchdog role with regard to the health situation, health programs, health policies, by watching, analysing, and reviewing policies and their implementation in the field. A good example is the Global Health Watches of the People's Health Movement which every few years in coordination with fraternal organisations, in different parts of the world and academics, researchers, health professionals, and health and development activist watches, by making situation analysis and policy reviews that result in the different global health watches. The reports usually have four sections focusing on the health care sector; beyond the health care sector; holding to account different, global, multilateral health institutions, and finally resistance and catalysis towards change. This Watchdog role is also now emerging at regional and country level. In India, the People's Rural Health Watch initiated by the People's Health Movement in India (*Jan Swasthya Abhiyan*) reviews the performance of the Rural Public Health System and analyses issues arising out of its implementation.

Research and Policy Analysis

Some civil society initiatives have focused on collecting data and conducting situation analysis and action research studies on a consistent basis focusing on theme such as equity, gender, social exclusion and other themes. Among the best known of these are the Global Equity Guage Alliance -GEGA (36) and EQUINET in Africa. GEGA is a key partner of PHM's Global Health Watch Alliance and GEGA members are spread out in many countries where the focus of equity watch is at national level. EQUINET is the regional network for Equity in East and Southern Africa. In 2012, EQUINET published the Regional Equity Watch and has been gradually moving towards producing country level watches as well. The focus of research and policy analysis in all these efforts is on Social Determinants of Health, redistributed health systems, exploration of gaps in social participation, political support and public leadership in health. In India the most well known research groups in health in civil society is CEHAT – Centre for Enquiry into Health and Allied Themes, which recently has further divided into three focused units under the same trust on issues of Women's Health, Community Action for Health and Medical and Public Health Ethics.

Communication

Civil society and social movements have all developed very good publications and education material for people's education on health, health systems and health policies to enhance their informed involvement. The People's Health Resource Book in India which brought together five little booklets prepared for public education in India as a buildup to the national health assembly and the first People's Health Assembly are well known. Hafldan Mahler the DG Emeritus of WHO and one of the key architects of the Alma Ata declaration described these little booklets as *"the best expressions of primary health care concepts and its politics that I have ever read. They are the bible of the Primary Health Care, a glorious milestone on the tortuous road to Primary Health Care."* The global PHM has also used communication through the website quite effectively through the PHM exchange which keeps a very large number of health policy activists, health professionals and contacts and associates of the movement on everything that is going on at different levels in system development or policy advocacy and engagement.

Participatory Governance

In this role civil society is engaged with health policy making and public health systems through various activities of dialogue and or monitoring and evaluation in a formal mechanism of participatory governance. Two of the best recent examples are the community monitoring engagement of civil society with the National Rural Health Mission in India through the Advisory Group for Community Action at national level and Community Monitoring engagements at state level. In Thailand through the National Health Act, civil society is now formally involved in planning and monitoring through mechanism such as the National Health Assembly which is an annual gathering of civil society to advice the government on health, equity, and policy issues.

Involvement in multi-sectoral Planning

All over the world civil society and or social movement representatives are increasingly being invited to participate in planning, for policy reform, health system development, and evolving responsive health programs and community action. In recent years such civil society involvement has increased in WHO reports and similar exercises. World Health Reports 2008 on Primary Health Care had strong civil society representation. The WHO Commission on Social Determinants had civil society members as commissioners and in the knowledge networks, and also organised dialogue with civil society all through the commission process at various levels. In India the Planning Commission, Steering Groups on Health and also on Traditional and Complementary Alternative Medicine (locally term AYUSH) and all the ten Task forces of the National Rural Health Mission have had strong civil society representation. These have been multi-stakeholder dialogue and planning processes involving also private sector, academia, researchers, and experts from beyond the health sector. In states like Karnataka in India, mulit-sectoral planning exercises initiated by government have shown phenomenal openness to civil society participation by inviting civil society leadership to convene and facilitate the whole exercise with government, resource persons, being part of the exercise but not necessarily leading it. The two best examples are the Karnataka Task Force on Health and Family Welfare -2001 and the recently concluded Mission Group on Public Health of the Karnataka State Knowledge Commission of 2012.

Horizontal and Vertical Networking

Horizontal and vertical networks among civil society organisations and associations to evolve network and coalitions has been increasingly taking place at country, regional and international level to raise awareness and evolve advocacy, campaigning and policy action towards 'Health For All' at all these levels ever since the Alma Ata Declaration 1978. Among the most well known of these networks is an informal circle of health professionals, health and development activists in India – the medico friends circle (mfc), which began pre-Alma Ata in 1974 and has remained an alternative 'thought current' and policy advocacy group all these years with its own bulletin and website and e-group. The Global People's Health Movement arose out of the coalition of 8 international networks that came together to organise the first People's Health Assembly. These were the International People's Health Council; International Organisation of Consumer Unions; Asian Community Health Action Network; Third World Network; Women's Global Network for Reproductive Rights; Health Action- International; Dag Hammarskjold Foundation; and Gonoshasthya Kendra (See section 11 for websites)

Another such process of networking has been the annual World Social Forum and the Regional and National Forum associated with the process initiated in Porto Allegre which has brought together social movements and networks to dialogue around global and national issues. Most of these annual events also have health oriented groups, networks, and movements coming together to discuss share and dialogue around emerging health challenges at various levels. One such key health fora linked to the WSF process took place in Mumbai in 2004 when the WSF process moved for the first time from Brazil to India and the well known Mumbai declaration was one of the definitive outputs of this significant gathering of health activists.

Building Capacity of Civil Society

Civil society organisations have evolved various capacity building strategies to build knowledge skills and attitudes among health and development activists to understand the health situation and challenges and be involved in advocating health in all policies. The International People's Health University of the People's Health Movement which runs courses on Health Equity and Globalisation in all parts of the world in many languages for public health professionals and health and development activists and action initiators is a good example of this. At the national level a good example is the community health fellowships offered by SOCHARA in India which includes the one year community health learning program and the two years community health fellowship program for young professionals from multidisciplinary backgrounds (See Additional Reading for websites)

Campaigns and Movements on Specific Health Problems

Civil society and social movements all over the world and at various levels – local, national, regional, and global have focused on campaigns and policy action around specific health themes and problems be they–HIV AIDS, Street Children, Mental Health, Rational Drug Policy, People with Disability, Elderly, Child labour, Sexual minorities, Women's Health, Child Rights, etc. Three of the most well known campaigns have been the Treatment Action Campaign (TAC) in South Africa; The Campaign Against displacement by dams (*Narmada Bachao Andolan*) in India and the Right to Water Campaign in Bolivia. Among the larger international networks the following – IBFAN (International Breast Feeding Action Network) working towards the International Code of breast milk substitutes; and WGNRR (Women's Global Network on Reproductive Rights) are significant examples.

Innovative Instruments of Engagement

Many innovative instruments are emerging in this new space of dialogue and innovation in civil society to engage with the main stream and state policy. Some have been selected for this paper from many others. These innovative instruments of engagement have begun to enter public policy documents but are still waiting to be introduced into mainstream courses and training programmes.

Social Watch

The idea of monitoring and analysing closely the emerging trends in situation analysis, data, statistics, and performance outputs and impacts by civil society groups outside the formal public health system, at all levels has been gaining ground over the years, providing space and opportunity for trend analysis and comment which is different from the official reports. The Global Health Watch of the People's Health Movement; the Global Equity Gauge Alliance; and the People's Rural Health Watch, in India, described earlier are three good examples. The most innovative website that has been developed based on access to health and development data and indices from UN sources is 'Gapminder' which focuses primarily on Equity and related trends between regions and country. Today it has become a major teaching and training tool as well.

Peoples tribunals/Citizens Juries

Another instrument of engagement which has been developed in many regions by civil society is the idea of people's tribunals and right to health hearings. In this innovation an informal jury of legal officials is setup and representatives of the community or patients/ citizens at large are invited to share their experiences of the health services and programs, in the presence of health and development officials of the Government. This platform provides people to air their concerns and invites government officials to respond to these concerns in generic ways. In India the Right to Health hearings organised by the People's Health Movement at regional and national level in collaboration with the National Human Rights Commission has been a good example of this approach. A people's tribunal on the World Bank Policies in Health and Development has also been organised. In some countries these are also called citizen juries. In recent years the National Rural Health Mission strategy document has internalised this instrument providing space for *Jan Sunwai's* (people's hearings) and *Jan Samwad* (People's dialogue). The Ministry of Environment in India has recently included this instrument in the Health and Environmental impact assessment (HIA and EIA) which is mandatory as part of emerging state and national environmental policy to mitigate the health and development hazards of unplanned development, migration and displacement. As part of this process the local community is also invited to assess the needs and the plans in a participatory process.

Health Assemblies

In the last decade regular, often annual assemblies of health and development activists have been organised at state level, country level, and internationally to bring civil society and social movement representatives together to share experiences, analyse the impact of campaigns and plan strategies locally, nationally, and globally in a spirit of solidarity. The most significant were the global people's health assemblies organised by the people's health movement in Savar Bangladesh, 2000 AD; in Cuenca, Ecuador in 2005 and in Cape Town South Africa in 2012 leading to the People's Charter for Health, the Cuenca declaration and the Cape Town statement.

Campaign Innovations

Campaigns have been the sheet anchor of civil society action on health issues. Starting from the orthodox trade union led protest / solidarity marches –campaigns have innovated other expressions of solidarity including Kala Jatha's, songs, street plays, human chains and candle light vigils. In Latin America a new culture of solidarity through music, street theatre, and other art forms. Groups like Greenpeace have taken this further through symbolic and creative action to get the message to decision makers and policy makers.

Health Manifestos

As part of the political process it is not uncommon for civil society and social movement groups to dialogue with formal political parties before state and national elections. This has been going on for years with different civil society organisations raising issues and facilitating dialogue with different groups. However with increasing recognition that Health in All Policies requires also the All for Health approach and the evidence that Health for All requires action on Social, Economic, Political and Cultural determinants that go far beyond ideologically determined action, there is increasing effort to evolve health manifesto's, policy briefs, and charters that are then distributed to all political parties with a message that Health is too important to be left to one group or the other. This approach which has now begun to be applied by the People's Health Movement in India by the development of a Health Policy news brief in 2004 before the national elections and a people's health manifesto in 2009 before the national election has begun to increase the importance of health on the political agenda of the country. In 2004 the process contributed along with other factors to the reorientation of the emerging National Rural Health Mission towards the policy of communitisation even more emphatically, which was sustained by civil society participation in task forces and advisory groups of NRHM. This trend has now begun to emerge at state and district level before elections at this level. It is too early to demonstrate the impact but perhaps the increasing public dialogue on universal health care in the country is at least one obvious impact of such engagement.

Health Policy Processes

Sustained policy engagement and dialogue is another process instrument which needs to be identified as an increasingly effective tool. The evolution of community monitoring and community action for health in the National Rural Health Mission in India: the development of the draft National Health Act and the concept of National Health Assembly in Thailand and the changes in distorted childhood immunisation policies in state of Tamilnadu in India are three examples of such sustained processes in three very different situations and levels. The World Health Report 2008 on Primary Health Care records this role of civil society and social movements in its section on Mobilizing the Communities by noticing this instrument of engagement in India, Bangladesh, Chile, Western Europe and Mali, demonstrating that this is now an increasing global trend and experience.

Conclusion:

This increasing collaboration between civil society, social

movements, academia, researchers, and others have significantly contributed to the idea of paradigm shift in health and the need for a countervailing power or process from bottom up to encourage the journey for Health For All. This bottom up process has more recently been described as 'Globalisation of heath solidarity from below'

1. The Paradigm shift

Public health systems, health projects and programmes have most often been constructed in a narrow bio-medicalised framework, with a focus on disease rather than health and well being, despite the 1948 WHO definition which tried to shift the focus to all aspects of well being – physical, mental and social. The Alma Ata declaration began a new thrust by shifting the focus to social justice, equity, social development and rights. Civil society and social movements have tried to take this forward with limited success because the biomedical paradigm is so deeply entrenched. This paradigm shift must be appreciated by policy makers, academics and researchers if health in all policies is to become a reality. They must be encouraged to appreciate the six shifts – a shift in focus from individual to community, a shift in dimensions from physical and pathological to broader psychosocial, cultural, economic, political and ecological dimensions, a shift in technology from drugs and vaccines to education and social processes, a shift in the type of service from social marketing and providing models to enabling, empowering and autonomy-building processes and initiatives, a shift in the attitude of people from patients and/or passive beneficiaries to people and communities as active participants, and a shift in research focus from molecular biology, pharmaco-therapeutics and clinical epidemiology to socio-epidemiology, social determinants, health systems and social policy research.

2. 'Globalisation of health solidarity from below':

In recent years key WHO policy documents note the increasing role of civil society and social movements in our efforts towards revitalising primary health care and our efforts towards action on the social determinants of health. Two statements drawn from significant

WHO documents in the last decade–World Health Report (WHR) 2008 and WHO –CSDH 2008 clearly emphasise that at the highest level this new countervailing power is being increasingly recognized as crucial and significant partners in the journey to Health For All.

The first of these taken from the WHR 2008 highlights the importance of mobilising the participation of the people. It notes *"The history of the politics of the PHC reform in the countries that have made major strides largely unwritten. It is clear however where these reform have been successful, the endorsement of the PHC by health sector and by the political word has invariably followed on rising demand and pressure expressed by civil society………..There is an important lesson there; powerful allies for PHC reform are to be found within civil society. They can make difference between a well-intentioned but short–lived attempt and successful and sustained reform; and between a purely technical initiative and one that is endorsed by the political word and enjoys social consensus".*

The second taken from the report of the WHO Commission on Social Determinants of Health, 2008 emphasises new champions for health equity by noting: *"As community members, grass root advocates, service and programme providers, and performance monitors, civil society actors from the global to local level constitute a vital bridge between policies and plans and reality of change and improvement in the lives of all. Helping to organise and promote diverse voices across different community, civil society can be a powerful champion of health equity".*

The way forward is clear. We need to move towards a social and community model of health and we need to enhance the creative energy of civil society and social movements as a social change stimulus from below. The most crucial requirement for that is the increasing openness of our academia, our researchers, and our Intelligentsia to this engagement. The late Sanjay Biswas did this all his life and set an example. Will more walk this path less travelled?

Additional Reading:

a. Society for Community Health, Awareness, Research and Action (www.sochara.org)
b. Community Health Wikipedia- India: www.community health.in
c. People's Health Movement: www.phmovement.org;
d. Global Health Watch: www.ghwatch.org;
e. International People's Health University: www.phmovement.org/iphu;
f. medico friend circle: www.mfcindia.org
g. Global Equity Guage Alliance: www.gega.org.za
h. Gapminder: www.gapminder.org
i. Community of Practice on Accountability and Social Action in Health: www.copasah.net

Mass Crimes and Impunity: The Indian Experience

Arvind Narrain

Mass crimes in India: A story of impunity

A mass crime is necessarily a story when there is an attempt to either annihilate or subordinate an entire segment of the population solely on the ground of the person's religion, race, caste, political opinion or social status. One is referring to a situation of a intentional break down of law and order of such a scale that murder, rape, looting, arson are committed on a large scale against one particular social or political group. This breakdown of law and order, which allows extraordinary systematic and targeted violence to become the order of the day, can only happen when the state intentionally decides to absent itself from its responsibility of ensuring the security of life of all its citizens.

Therefore, the one element which distinguishes a mass crime from a murder or rape is the element of state complicity. By complicity, what one means is that the state does not necessarily directly participate but is involved and allows the crime to happen. The state in fact plays a facilitating role by both direct acts of commission and acts of omission all of which ensure that the mass crimes are committed.

The history of mass crimes in India can broadly be divided into three categories.

- Firstly, the targeting of persons based on their caste as evidenced by numerous cases of caste based massacres in independent India. In terms of mass killings of Dalits, each state has its own particular history of terrible violence. In the history of India among the terrible atrocities inflicted on Dalits the list is a long and depressing one. The list would include Karamchedu and Chundur in Andhra Pradesh, Keelvanmani, Melavalavu, and Kodiyankulam in Tamil Nadu, Khairlanji in Maharashtra, Shahpur and Kambalapalli in Karnataka to Shankarbiga, Narayanpur and Ekwari in Bihar. Many seemingly obscure villages are for a brief moment put under the national spotlight for the brutal treatment of Dalits.

- Secondly is the targeting of persons based on their perceived political opinions. The majority of targeted crimes which come within this framework would be the operations by the Indian state against the Naxalites. In recent times, a clear example is what comes within the legal understanding of a mass crime is the terrible violations carried out by the state sponsored militia the Salwa Judum in Chhattisgarh. The crimes have been of such a scale that thousands of tribals have been forced to take refuge in Andhra Pradesh in a mass internal migration with at one point 45000 tribals living in a pathetic condition in relief camps in Andhra Pradesh, constituting an internally displaced group within the boundaries of India.[1] While arguably the situation is one of an internal armed conflict, there is no doubt that in the course of this conflict terrible crimes amounting to mass crimes have been committed by parties, the state as well as the Maoists.
- Thirdly is the targeting of persons on the basis of their religion. In terms of the number of people affected, clearly this is the largest category. Among the major communal mass crimes in which the Indian state is complicit and for which there has been no accountability are the Nellie massacre in Assam in 1983, 1984 programme against the Sikhs in Delhi and the destruction of the Babri Masjid in 1992. The history of impunity for communal mass crimes was inaugurated with

> the birth of the Indian nation. The independence of India and Pakistan was accompanied by a mass scale slaughter of at least eleven million people perhaps making it the largest mass crime in history.

This article will focus on the third form of mass crime, namely the targeting of persons based on their religion and activist efforts to bring about a measure of accountability. This article will analyze efforts to bring about justice in Nellie (1983), Delhi (1984) and Gujarat (2002)

The Nellie massacre in Assam

The Nellie massacre remains one of the forgotten massacres in Indian history. The 1983 massacre was perpetrated in the context of rising tensions in Assam over the influx of Bangladeshi immigrants. On 18th February, 1983 over 2000 Muslims in Nellie in Assam were, murdered by those who lived in the surrounding villages. This anger against immigration was allowed to be used to perpetrate a programme against Muslim citizens of India, resident in Nellie and the surrounding villages. According to a study by Japanese scholar, Makiko Kimura, the reasons for the massacre differed according to the three groups involved in the massacre. According to the victims, it was their participation in the elections which were boycotted by other communities for which they were punished. According to the perpetrators who belonged to the Tiwas community it was the kidnapping of girls from their community by the Muslims and according to the leaders of the All Assam Student Union (AASU) (the leaders of the anti-foreigner agitation in Assam), it was the appropriation of land by the Muslims of Tiwas who were tribals.[2]

Post the programme as per a study done by the "Centre for Equity Studies", six hundred and sixty eight first information reports or FIRs were registered in relation to the violence in Nellie. Out of these, charge sheets were finally filed in 299 cases, and the remaining 389 cases – or 56 per cent of cases – were summarily closed even before the virtual amnesty that followed from the Assam Accord. After the Assam Accord was signed in 1985, the Government of Assam petitioned to withdraw cases under section 321 of the Criminal Procedure Code, 1973, in all the trial courts that had live cases, citing lack of evidence in all of these. The courts accepted the applications, and agreed to the discharge of all the accused.[3] As a result, the question of legal accountability was buried within two years of the massacre and not a single person has been held accountable for the Nellie massacres of over 2000 Muslims.

Even in terms of remembering by civil society, there are no fact finding reports on the Nellie massacre. The only official memory of the massacre is in the "Tiwari Commission Report" which was submitted in 1984 but has still not been published. [4] Even in terms of compensation for the deaths and loss of livelihood, the survivors got only a paltry sum of Rs 5000. The predominant response by both state and civil society to the Nellie programme has been silence. The silence has been broken in bits, but with no serious implications for the breaking of impunity. Even in terms of activist documentation, the mainstream human rights groups have no reports on Nellie. Among the kinds of violence perpetrated, the question of sexual violence was not even raised. So we have no knowledge of whether and to what extent sexual violence was perpetrated. [5] However the massacre remains far from forgotten in the minds and hearts of those who suffered unbearable loss.

Harsh Mander writes movingly about a visit to Nellie and its environs in 2008 to remember what happened with the survivors of Nellie. Mander narrates the story of one young man which serves as a reminder of why till justice is done, the stubborn memory of unbearable pain will continue to haunt the survivors. In his early thirties, Mohammed Monoruddin began to cry inconsolably as soon as he sat before us. "My brothers, sisters were all killed, hacked into pieces," he recalled. "I was seven years old then. I saw my parents slaughtered in front of me. I saw another woman being killed and her child snatched from her hands and thrown in fire. I wept in terror all day. The CRPF came in the evening and rescued me. Later we came to know that our house was torched. Nothing was left. All our belongings and stores of rice were gone in the fire. My elder brother, who was in Nagaon, brought me up. But I feel so lonely."[6] The Nellie massacre is really a story of an abysmal failure to render any justice to those who had lost so much. The fact that the pogrom does not even register in the consciousness of human rights activism as does Delhi (1984) or Gujarat(2002) points to the stage of the struggle in Nellie i.e. remembering what happened and not allowing it to be forgotten.

Anti Sikh Programme, New Delhi 1984

The 1984 anti-Sikh programme following the death of Indira Gandhi when for three days from 31 October to 3rd November, 1984, Congress goons were allowed to run amok in the streets of the capital. The Joint PUCL-PUDR Report, 'Who are the guilty?' makes clear that it was acts of omission and commission at the very top which resulted in the death of over 2733 Sikhs, rape of Sikh women and the destruction of property belonging to Sikhs. What provided perhaps the most horrifying microcosm of the massacre was the burning alive of over 400 Sikhs in just one block in Trilokpuri. As the Joint PUCL-PUDR Report 'Who are the guilty?' makes clear "when members of our team reached Trilokpuri at about 7 a.m. on November 3 we found the survivors-old men, women and children, some of them with severe burns, huddling together in the open in the main road. Weeping women narrated to the how their men folk were slaughtered and alleged that in some cases the police directed the attacks. Many among the survivors told us that Dr Ashok Kumar the local Congress (I) Councilor had instigated the mob. The entire Sikh community in the area, they said, was left at the mercy of the mob for two full days till arrival of the CRP. As soon as we entered Block 32, we were greeted by a strong stench of burnt bodies which were still rotting inside some of the houses. The entire lane was littered with burnt pieces of furniture, papers, scooters and piles if ash in the shape of human bodies the unmistakable signs of burnt human beings. Dogs were on the prowl. Rats were nibbling at the still recognizable remains of a few bodies.[7]

While the report is horrifying in its description on the kind of brutalities inflicted on the Sikh community, what underlies is the message that the 'guilty' remained at the helm of the state. At the very apex was the then Prime Minister, Rajiv Gandhi who showed complete inaction in the face of a massacre carried out on the streets of the very city in which he lived. To add insult to injury, Rajiv Gandhi in an infamous speech in the Boat Club is reported to have said 'when a big tree falls the ground will shake' in effect legitimising the needless deaths of innocent Sikh men, women and children for the assassination of Indira Gandhi.[8] The Prime Minister also referenced the anger of the people to Indira Gandhi's assassination thereby indirectly legitimising the pogrom.[9] It is also significant that at no point in time did Rajiv Gandhi even reach out to the Sikh community to express his contrition for the massacre of innocent persons. Of course, the massive electoral victory of Rajiv Gandhi was built on stroking Hindu anger against the Sikhs. Post this massive victory, Rajiv Gandhi had no compunctions in inducting all the top men thought to be the executors of the pogrom i.e. H.K.L. Bhagat, Sajjan Kumar, Kamal Nath and Jagdish Tytler into his cabinet.[10]

Post this massacre in the heart of Delhi, the Congress government after a great deal of pressure instituted a Commission of Inquiry headed by Justice Ranganath Mishra. The Mishra Commission did what is acknowledged to be a whitewash of any responsibility for the pogrom. The only window of accountability the Mishra Commission left open was to set up two committees to examine details of compensation as well as accountability. The Jain Banerjee Committee recommended that FIR's be filed based on affidavits filed before the Mishra Commission. It was this small window which was exploited by activists to push for prosecution of the main perpetrators. As H.S. Phooka and Manoj Mitta trenchantly observe, it took an entire decade for the first and only FIR to be lodged against H.K.L. Bhagat in 1996. H.K.L Bhagat was finally arrested in 1996 and taken to the Court complex. As Phooka and Mitta observed, the court room was full with 10,000 people gathered outside it and Bhagat's legal team consisted of a battery of 100 lawyers. Bhagat employed the tactics of intimidation even as he sought to insulate himself by all means possible from the reach of the law. By feigning illness, Bhagat got himself admitted to a hospital instead of the jail. Finally, H.K.L Bhagat succeeded in evading legal accountability as he died and hence did not stand trial for the crimes of 1984.

However, the pursuit of justice was not entirely in vain. As Phooka and Mitta observe, "One tangible consequence of our relentless follow up of the case was the steady decline in the size of Bhagat's contingent in the court. If he came to the court for the first time with a battery of 100 lawyers and a 10000 strong crowd of supporters, the same Bhagat came with just his son, bodyguards, and a solitary lawyer, towards the end of the proceedings... This was a clear measure of the loss of his political clout during the pendency of the case".[11] As Phooka puts it, 'I draw solace from the fact that even if Bhagat escaped conviction in the court of the law, our pursuit of that leader, over two decades in the court of the people, was not entirely in vain.'[12]

The struggle for justice was also kept alive through the appointment of another Commission headed by Justice Nanavati to enquire into the causes of the violence of 1984. The Nanavati Commission after five years delivered a report which can at best be described in the words of H.S. Phooka as 'a mixed bag'. The entire top leadership of the Congress party of 1984 was indicted including H.K.L. Bhagat, Jagdish Tytler, Sajjan Kumar and Dharam Dass Shastri. However, the Commission found no evidence that Rajiv Gandhi or any other high ranking Congress leader at the level of the then Union Government was involved. The value of this indictment remains in the court of public opinion and not necessarily in the court of law. This is because in 2004 those indicted including Sajjan Kumar and Jagdish Tytler got tickets to contest the elections from Delhi. However post the tabling of the Nanavati Commission Report in parliament, the Union Government was forced to ensure that Jagdish Tytler resigned from the cabinet and Sajjan Kumar from the Delhi Government.[13] The tabling of the Nanavati Commission Report and the debate on the action taken also saw an emotional speech by the Prime Minister Manmohan Singh who for the first time in the history of the Congress party apologised for the pogrom. The symbolism of a Sikh Prime Minister apologising for the harm caused to the Sikh community went some way towards assuaging the hurt suffered by the community. "I have no hesitation in apologising not only to the Sikh community but the whole Indian nation because what took place in 1984 is the negation of the concept of nationhood and what enshrined in our Constitution. So, I am not standing on any false prestige. On behalf of our Government, on behalf of the entire people of this country, I bow my head in shame that such thing took place. But, Sir, there are ebbs; there are tides in the affairs of nations. The past is with us. We cannot rewrite the past. But as human beings, we have the will power and we have the ability to write better future for all of us.[14]

The ghosts of 1984 continue to haunt those who were named in the Nanavati Commission report as the indictment made sure that neither Jagdish Tytler nor Sajjan Kumar, were able to contest elections again. Each time the Congress party made efforts to give them tickets there was an uproar which meant that they invariably had to step down. The criminal proceedings have not succeeded in pinning accountability on any of the perpetrators. Though the names of some of the big wigs such as Jagdish Tytler, Sajjan Kumar and H.K.L. Bhagat have cropped up in the hearings of the various Commissions of Inquiry, in the end nobody has been held accountable. The only continuing reminder of the 'injustice' of 1984 lies in the memory of the victims and the civil society fact finding reports which have pin pointed responsibility at the very top of the administration.

Gujarat 2002: Towards another narrative?

Post the burning of a bogey of the Sabarmati Express in Godhra, violence was unleashed against the Muslim community in Gujarat. For five days from Feb 28 to March 4, 2002, there was systematic and targeted violence against the Muslim community. There were over 2000 Muslims killed, Muslim women were raped, property belonging to Muslims was destroyed and 235 dargahs/mosques were destroyed. There was an attempt at destroying the very basis of physical, biological, cultural and psychological life of the Muslim community in Gujarat. The state was complicit in this attempt. Post 2002 over 4000 FIR's have been filed with a majority of them having been closed for so called lack of evidence. However, for the first time in Indian history, the events of Gujarat 2002 were not allowed to be forgotten. A courageous band of activists followed a few cases closely with a view to ensuring that there would be justice for those who lost so much in the carnage. Some of the significant successes of activist interventions in the post Gujarat related cases include convictions for mass crimes perhaps for the first time in Indian history. There have been convictions by trial courts in cases of mass crimes in a number of cases. Till now 96 persons have been convicted for their role in the mass crime - 32 in Naroda Patiya, 11 in Bilkis Bano, 31 in Sardarpura, 18 in Ode and 4 in Best Bakery. In the convictions till now perhaps the most significant is the conviction of the 32 persons in Naroda Patiya. The decision in Naroda Patiya will be discussed in greater detail as it provides a worm's eye view of what it takes to ensure that there is conviction for mass crimes as well the limitations of the existing legal framework.

***State of Gujarat* v. *Naresh Agarsinh Chara and others*[15] (The Naroda Patiya Case)**

On 28th February following the Godhra train incident, in the locality of Naroda Patiya, a violent mob systematically went about the task of murdering and maiming Muslims, raping Muslim women and destroying Muslim places of worship and houses. The orgy of violence which went on the full day was accomplished using deadly weapons and was to the accompaniment of slogans such as *'slaughter, Cut, not a single Miya should be able to survive, Jay Shri Ram'* etc. The destruction concluded with the burning (dead or alive) of members of the Muslim community.

In the case which was finally before Justice Jyotsna Yagnik, what was on trial was the series of incidents over the course of the day which resulted in the death of over 98 Muslims, serious injuries inflicted on over 124 Muslims and the rape committed on Muslim women. What also was on trial was the criminal responsibility of Mayaben Kodnani and others for the conspiracy to commit the said offences. During the course of trial 327 witnesses were examined and 2392 documents were produced. The charge sheet listed offences from conspiracy, murder, gang rape, causing grievous hurt to forming of an unlawful assembly. The entire process of accessing justice right from filing FIR's to ensuring a fair trial was an uphill struggle. In fact it was only the intervention of the Supreme Court which resulted in a relatively fair investigation. Because of all these difficulties the struggle of the victims of Naroda Patiya continued for ten long years. It was only in August of 2012 that a 1969 page judgment was delivered by Justice Jyotsna Yagnik in the Naroda Patiya case convicting 32 people for the above mentioned offences.

The Naroda Patiya Judgment: The Judges reasoning

Overcoming procedural hurdles

The substratum of the reasoning of the judge is a keen awareness that this is an extraordinary case. The case has been sent back for fresh investigation by none other than the Supreme Court and the facts of the case have to do with an extraordinary break down of law and order. Considering this scenario the judge was inclined to look at procedural issues which can often stymie the struggle for justice differently. *Firstly,* with respect to the fact that investigation itself was faulty, the judge asserted the principle that *'defective investigation, that too a deliberate defective investigation or deliberately kept loopholes are no ground for acquittal.'* The Judge constructed a mental picture of the days when the massacre happened and was able to emphasise emotionally with the situation on February 28, 2002. The judge observed that, *'the picture was so gloomy and sad that the complaints of the Muslims were not taken...It seems that the entire negligence, lighter attitude, carelessness in the investigation, insensitive attitude towards victims and their agonies etc. all was surely aimed at to see to it that at the end of the entire investigation if not all statements, then at least of majority witnesses should be saying that, "they do not know any member of the mob".'*

Secondly, the crime was difficult to prove as there was no "corpus delicti", no body was recovered. Integral to the crimes committed at Naroda Patiya was the throwing of persons, both dead and alive into the flames. As one eye witness observed, *'four women of the society came there who were giving kerosene to the men of the mob and those women were telling' that 'kill these people and then burn them.'* Taking this problem, which is often integral to the nature of mass crimes into account, J. Yagnik by drawing on case law finds that, *'recovery of dead body is not necessary and it is held that conviction for murder does not necessarily depend upon Corpus Delicti being found.'*

Thirdly, Justice Yagnik was also not inclined to give the benefit of the doubt to the accused because none of the deadly weapons used during the carnage were recovered by the police. As J. Yagnik succinctly puts it, *"the evidence shows that most of the accused were armed with deadly weapons and are guilty of rioting being armed with deadly weapons". 'The weapon is not actually recovered from them, but it is immaterial in the circumstances.'*

Speaking truth to power: Eye witness accounts as the basis of conviction.

The evidence which forms the heart of the judgment and is the basis of the convictions is really the eye witness accounts. The eye witnesses in this case have all suffered grievous loss with some of them seeing their family members killed. The demeanor of eye witnesses who have suffered so much of trauma is observed by the Court. The Court notes that *'during the deposition many of the witnesses were finding it very difficult to control rolling down their tears on their cheeks. They were eager to show their burnt limbs, their injured limbs and explain their losses to the Court. Many of the parent witnesses were unable to describe about the death of their children in the riot, they became so emotional that very often needed to be consoled and offered a glass of water to complete their deposition.'* In the absence of almost all other forms of evidence, forensic, recovery of weapons, it is eye witness testimony and the reliance placed upon it by the judge, which forms the basis of the Naroda Patiya convictions.[16] This judgment at its heart is really about the courageous testimonies of witnesses who persisted in their quest for justice in spite of overwhelming odds. The witnesses went ahead and testified to the almost unbearable loss they had suffered in spite of continuing intimidation. A particular example of this form of courageous truth telling is the testimony of PW 158 which is extracted below:

> Here several people were cut and killed like entire family of Kudratbibi, Jadi khala, her two daughters-in-law, family of the PW, family of Kausharbanu, the family of maternal aunt of Kausharbanu, brother-in-law Salam of Gauri Appa etc. At this time, his wife Zarina, daughter Fauzia, cousin Abdul Aziz, Haroon, Yunus, wife of Yunus jumped the wall, they were cordoned by the people, his wife was dragged by four men, she was attacked, her left hand was cut off by sword, her right hand was attacked by sword, her head was injured by sword, she was given hockey blow in her leg, her clothes were being pulled and torn off, not a single cloth remained on her body, she was made naked.....
>
> Even at the water tank, there was screaming of 'kill- cut', all the men of the mob have attacked different persons with the weapons in their hands, four women of the society came there who were giving kerosene to the men of the mob and those women were telling that 'kill these people and then burn them', he knew the four women since they were purchasing bakery products which he used to sell. Even he was also battered by acid bottles on his right hand, flesh came out from his right hand, he was also injured, he had also sustained injury on his hand, hip and head, the clamours of only 'save, save and save' were heard, the mob has killed his mother Abedabibi, sister Saidabanu, daughter of sister Saida - Gulnaaz, Jadi Khala, Kudratbibi, their family members by pouring kerosene and burning them.......
>
> They learnt about survivals of their relatives and met each other...... The witness felt that their house, their world were all ruined, he added that "even today I get knee jerks and I am shaken, upon remembering, I feel I am very upset and will undergo brain hemorrhage on remembering the occurrence of that day." His wife told him about the occurrence with her, they were so helpless that they had to shut their mouths, they were giving statement but, were not knowing as to what they were saying and what

they were missing, the PW could not identify the four who dragged his wife.....

The testimony speaks to a collective dimension of violence involving an orgy of murder and rape. The chilling aspect of the testimony emerges from the number of defenseless people who the witness testifies to having been killed. The violence is sexualized with the clothes of women being pulled off and them being made naked. The deeply personal and humiliating nature of sexual nature of the violence is hinted at with the witness saying that his '*wife told him about the occurrence with her, they were so helpless that they had to shut their mouths*'. The consequences of this almost overwhelming violence is literally world shattering as the witness notes that on remembering, '*I feel I am very upset and will undergo brain hemorrhage on remembering the occurrence of that day*'. It is on understanding the various dimensions of the violence as well as the impact on the victims that the incredible courage of the victims shines through again and again.

The honesty of extra-judicial confession: Why did Naroda Patiya happen?

The sting operation conducted by Ashish Ketan of the Tehelka resulted in videographed interviews with three accused in the Naroda Patiya case.[17] All three interviews were treated as extra judicial confessions under Section 24 of the Indian Evidence Act. The extra judicial confessions were the other piece of evidence implicating both those making the confession as well as the other accused in the crimes committed at Naroda Patiya. The extra judicial confessions which were cited by the judgment also need to be quoted in part as they throw light on numerous aspects of the crime.

The gist of the confession of Babu Bajrangi was that:

- I shall not stop working for Hinduism until I die. I have personal notions about Hinduism. I have no fear even if I am hanged. Now, there won't live any Muslims in India. The moment I saw corpses lying in Godhra, that very night I had decided and challenged that, 'there would be four times more slaughter in PATIYA than that of GODHRA.'..I have two enemies, the Muslims and the Christians...

- We slaughtered Muslims; Patiya is half kilometer away from my house. I and the local public were there to do the massacre at Patiya. If one would go to Godhra, one would be provoked and would determine to kill all the Muslims then and there. We retaliated at Patiya. In Patiya, we had secured the highest death toll.

The gist of the confession of Suresh was that:

- If fruits (saying for girls) were lying, the hungry would eat it. In any case, she (the Muslim girl) was to be burnt; hence somebody might have eaten the fruit.
- 2 to 4 rapes or may be more, might have been committed. Who would not eat fruit? In whatever number Muslims are killed, it is still less. I would not leave them. I have too much of rancor (malice) against them (Muslims). Even I had also raped one girl, who was daughter of a scrap man (one who is in business of scrap) – named Nasimo. She was fat. I raped her on roof and then thrown her from there. I smashed her, cut her to pieces like 'achar' (pickle)."

What the extra-judicial confessions do is describe in great detail what exactly the accused did that day. More importantly, they give us a direct insight into the mind of the accused. If there were doubts as to whether rape did happen on that day, it is set at rest by Suresh's casual description of the act of rape and murder of a Muslim woman. What both confessions give is the chilling evidence of the deep motive underlying the killings. It is the hatred of the Muslim community which is at root of the orgy of violence. The confessions give us a hint that the crime is not one which can be contained within ordinary criminal law as the intent is not only to murder or rape as the IPC describes it but rather the intention to eliminate the hated race, the Muslims. The crime which is executed by the mob is nothing less than what is referred to as the 'crime of crimes' i.e. genocide.

Conspiracy to commit murder, rioting, unlawful assembly, inflict grievous hurt

In a large mob it would be close to impossible to prove the individual culpability of each of the members for every one of the offences committed. What serves to connect the various actions of the mob to one another legally is the law on conspiracy. Under the law on conspiracy what needs to be proved is that the various members of the mob had a prior agreement to do a series of illegal acts. If there is such a prior agreement then the various members of the mob are responsible for all the actions undertaken by any and every actions undertaken by anyone who is a part of the mob. The judge finds that there was indeed an agreement among the members of the mob. The finding is that *'the accused were tremendously over charged with the idea to take revenge with the Muslim Community as a whole and they were totally out and had clear objects in their minds of doing away with maximum Muslims and to destroy, damage and demolish their religious place and property'.*

Rape in the context of mass violence: A crime without traces?

The problem J. Yagnik faces when it comes to the offence of rape is that there is very little evidence left of the offence itself. The chilling extra judicial confession of Suresh when he brags about having raped a woman called Nasimo and then cut her into piece provides an insight into the methods of the killers. The methodology was clearly rape followed by murder to be followed by burning; hence there is very little evidence of the original crime which survived. The only place where the evidence of the crime survived was in the memory of the perpetrators as well as the memory of the victim survivors. The undoing of impunity for rape was really the fact that Suresh felt impelled to boast about 'raping Nasimo'.[18] It is this extra judicial confession which J. Yagnik uses to convict Suresh of the crime of rape.

Further the history of mass crimes of the nature of that perpetrated at Naroda Patiya are closely tied in with sexual crimes. In fact mass crimes and sexual violence go hand in hand and we owe a debt of gratitude to J. Yagnik for making that connection clear through the appreciation of evidence. However nobody else is convicted of rape as J. Yagnik does not see the conspiracy hatched on 28 February, 2002 to include the commission of the crime of rape. This is mystifying, particularly as she very clearly delineates the acts of rape committed in the course of the murderous assault and quite clearly rape emerges as an integral part of the conspiracy both from the eye witness testimonies as well as from the extra judicial confessions.

However, J. Yagnik is very clear on one point, i.e. that the crime of rape was committed. The eye witness testimonies combined with the extra-judicial confession are sufficient to arrive at the conclusion. Further, J. Yagnik understands why victims might want to testify about a crime in which the perpetrator is unknown. Zarina testifies to being *'attacked by four men and that she was gang raped there. She testifies that four men had attacked on her with the help of sword, string of her petticoat was cut off and that a severe sword blow was given on her hand by the attackers. Having nakeded her, she was gang raped.'* However Zarina was unable to identify the attackers. J. Yagnik concludes that:

> When PW-205 is not implicating any of the accused, it is clear that she does not have any other intention in her mind for narration of this incident, except ventilation of tremendous violation of her human right and constitutional right before the Court. The loud cries of such victim of crime if not heard by the system, it is mockery of justice. Here, it sounds quite fitting to record the deep concern of the Court about violation of human rights and constitutional rights of the victim who was subjected to gang rape.

In giving a dignified hearing to Zarina's tale of horror and woe, Justice Yagnik understands something very deep about justice. It is very important that the victims be heard and be believed. The pain of those who have suffered unbearable loss needs to be acknowledged. This acknowledgement of pain and loss can itself begin the process of healing. J. Yagnik goes on to order compensation for Zarina. The compensation is ordered in full recognition that *'no compensation in fact, is weighty enough to wipe out the permanent scar, effect and impact on the mind of the victim of the crime of gang-rape'*. Rather the compensation is a recognition that, *'the Court is concerned with the commission of crime primarily since that is to take care of subsistence of rule of law. The international concern for the impacts of sexual offences against women guide this Court that this victim needs to be compensated.'*

The Naroda Patiya judgment: Bringing a sense of closure?

In the Naroda Patiya incident 96 persons were murdered, 125 injured and gang rape was committed on unknown number of women. The brutality of the crimes committed emerged from the intentional killing, maiming, raping and then burning of members of the Muslim community. If the 'iron rod' emerged as symbol of brutality in the Delhi rape judgment, the phrase repeated by J. Yagnik, 'grilled meat' to refer to the ruthless burning of Muslims both dead and alive symbolizes the horror of Naroda Patiya. The other image which dominates the horror and in fact emerged as the emblematic horror story of the Gujarat pogrom was the ripping apart of the stomach of the pregnant Kausar Bano by Babu Bajrangi.

The remarkable judgment by J. Jyotsna Yagnik was able to acknowledge the horror suffered by the residents of Naroda Patiya. Justice Yagnik understood that the reason, even after ten years the victims in spite of all odds were still pursing the claim to justice related to a deep rooted need to right the balance. The wrong which was done had to be righted, before one could even attempt the process of closure.

J. Yagnik demonstrates sensitivity in understanding the context of communal violence and she puts it *'The Court is not sitting in Ivory Tower.'* It is this appreciation of the context of a communal mass crime that ensures that defective and complicit investigation is not allowed to checkmate the quest for justice. Even when there is no possibility for conviction, J. Yagnik understands that victims need to be heard. The process of empathetic hearing itself[19] combined with the judgment has brought about some measure of closure to a horrific chapter in Indian history. What is apparent is also that the evidence before J. Yagnik far outstrips the narrow limits of the crimes defined in the IPC. The offences committed on that day were not only acts of murder and rape committed against individuals persons. In its deepest sense they were crimes committed with the avowed intent to eliminate in whole or in part the Muslim community in Naroda Patiya. As such the crime was really what is referred to as the 'crime of crimes', i.e. genocide, a crime against a collectivity which is not recognised by Indian law.

Conclusion

The search for justice for victims of mass communal crimes remains very much a work in progress. There has been some significant progress due to Herculean efforts by activists and others committed to the idea of India, but much remains to be done to ensure that such crimes do not recur. It is unfortunate that Gujarat (2002) was followed by Kandmahal (2008) as well as Muzafarnagar (2013), thereby letting us know that the work of human rights activism has to continue.

References

1. See http://cpjc.wordpress.com/reports-by-fact-finding-teams-on-salwa-judum/ For Reports by various human rights organisations on the situation in the Dantewada region.
2. Makiko Kimura, The Nellie Massacre of 1983, Sage, New Delhi, 2013.
3. Pritharani Jha, Surabhi Chopra et al., Accountability for Mass Violence, Centre for Equity Studies, 2012.
4. http://www.tehelka.com/an-untold-shame-2/ accessed on 7.11.13 Also see Makiko Kimura, The Nellie Massacre of 1983, Sage, New Delhi, 2013.
5. *Ibid.* p.135
6. Harsh Mander, Nellie: India's forgotten massacre, http://www.hindu.com/mag/2008/12/14/stories/2008121450100300.htm accessed on 22.11.13.
7. http://www.pucl.org/Topics/Religion-communalism/2003/who-are-guilty.htm accessed on 7.11.13

8. Responsibility flows downwards from the then Home Minister PV Narasimha Rao (later to preside as the Prime Minister over the demolition of the Babri Masjid) to the police officers who either choose to do nothing or actively aided the criminal elements. http://www.tehelka.com/when-a-big-tree-falls-the-earth-shakes/ accessed on 7.11.13 Also see Manoj Mitta and H. S. Phooka, When a tree shook Delhi: The 1984 carnage and its aftermath, Roli Books, New Delhi, 2007.
9. *Ibid.*
10. *Ibid.*
11. Id. p.186.
12. Id. Page, 187
13. Id. Page, 204.
14. http://pmindia.nic.in/RS%20speech.pdf accessed on
15. Sessions Case Numbers - 235/09, 236/09, 241/09,242/09, 243/09, 245/09, 246/09 & 270/09 - Common Judgment.
16. The recent acquittal of all the accused in the Laxmanpur Bathe massacre was based upon the High Court discrediting the eye witness testimony. What is singularly absent from the Laxmanpur Bathe judgment is an acknowledgment that a mass crime is an extraordinary situation which demands a measure of sensitivity from the judge and an awareness that in a situation of mass crime, there will be procedural lapses which however should not be allowed to pervert the course of justice. Further the credibility of eye witnesses need to be assessed with respect to their demeanour and the fact that they are victims as well, a point the Court misses totally. See State of Bihar v. Girija Singh and others, Death Reference No.5 of 2010.
17. The sting in the story, http://archive.tehelka.com/story_main53.asp?filename=Ne080912Coverstory.asp accessed on 16.10.13.
18. What is it in the psychology of the perpetrator that urges him to undo his own safety by bragging about his unspeakable crimes? Hannah Arendt explores this question in the context of Adolf Eichmann who post the holocaust, found refuge under a false name in Argentina. But during his exile, 'his only compensation consisted in talking endlessly with members of the large Nazi colony, to whom he readily admitted his identity' It was finally one such interview with a Dutch journalist which resulted in the Israelis getting to know about his whereabouts and what followed was his abduction, trial and hanging. See Hannah Arendt, Eichmann in Jerusalem, Penguin Books, London, 1994. p.238.

19. Ashish Ketan in his account of giving testimony in the Gujarat riot related cases documents the contrasting ways in which witnesses were heard: 'I got a full sense of the odds stacked against the victims in their quest for justice when I was summoned to depose as a critical witness in the Gulberg Society massacre case. The judge before whom I appeared was BU Joshi. A victim, Sairabehn, who had lost her only son in the Gulberg massacre, was humiliated by Joshi in the open court. When Rupabehn Modi—whose son went missing in the riots and on whose life the film Parzania was made—while recounting the events of the day broke down in court, Joshi didn't even allow her to take a break or have a glass of water. The contrast to J Joshi could not be more striking': 'I was called to testify in the Naroda Patiya case in December 2011. The trial was conducted by Judge Jyotsnabehn Yagnik. Not only was she completely impartial and fair in her conduct, she ensured that the defence did not humiliate me to entertain their clients seated in court, during the cross-examination. "Witnesses are the eyes and ears of my court. They come at my invitation and are the guests of this court. You may ask him whatever is relevant to your case but I will not allow you to insult him or make wild remarks about his character," Judge Yagnik told the defence lawyer.' - Ashish Ketan, The sting in the tale, http://archive.tehelka.com/story_main53.asp?filename=Ne080912Coverstory.asp accessed on 17.10.13

The Psychological Perspective of R&D and Intellectual Property Protection

Mary Mathew, Professor Indian Institute of Science

Introduction:

Almost anything has a psychological nature to it. This includes Research and Development (R&D) Management, or Intellectual Property (IP) Management practice. The psychological nature stems from the fact that human beings are at centre stage. Even in situations like climate change, humans indirectly play a role, affecting outcomes. In situations where humans are directly involved and financial investments are very high, the role of humans is worth constant discussion. In this qualitative paper, the psychological nature of humans is dealt with in terms of goals of R&D and attitudes towards intellectual property practice, namely patents. It is assumed that goal clarity about R&D, and positive attitudes towards patents will propel a scientist to be more productive. The paper intends to throw light on how R&D can become more productive. When R&D is productive it produces intellectual property in the form of publications (conference or journal papers) and patents.

In this paper, the link between R&D and patent generation is stressed. A little over decade ago a diagnostic study on 52 Indian R&D scientists showed that there were many reasons why patent outcomes are low (Mathew, 1997). Despite improvements, patent production remains low in India. India has an imbalance between publications and patents. The 2010 scientific publication record in

India was about 65,487 papers and the corresponding patent filing by Indians was about 8312 (DST, R&D statistics, 2013). This implies that the goal of R&D is only partially understood. It is understood as a method to obtain more publications. Goal clarity can induce productive R&D that produces the right balance of papers and patents.

Goals of R&D

Analysis of R&D investments is an ongoing activity. World trends show a conscious increase year on year with R&D budgets. The 2014 Battelle R&D Magazine provides the global share of R&D expenditure in different countries (see Table 1).

Table 1: Showing the percentage share of total spending in Global R&D

Country	*Year 2012*	*Year 2013*	*Year 2014*	*per cent of GDP for year 2014*
USA	34.5	34.0	33.9	2.8
Europe	23.1	22.4	21.7	2.7*
India	2.7	2.7	2.7	0.9
China	15.3	16.5	17.5	2.0

(Source: Battelle, 2014)*

This is an approximation, the highest being Finland with 3.5 per cent, the range within Europe is anywhere between 2.0 per cent to 3.5 per cent.

From Table 1 we see that India has a share of 2.7 per cent with no increase expected in 2014 (forecasted), unlike its ambitious partner China who has increased its R&D spending for the year 2014. Battelle forecasts show that China is expected to surpass US R&D spending by year 2020. The gross expenditure on R&D (GERD) is $465 billion for USA and $44 billion for India. This amount of $44 billion is a substantial investment in Indian R&D for year 2014.

To understand R&D productivity better, goals of R&D are discussed. Process experts may insist on not focusing on the goal, whereas, goal theorists will insist on focusing on the goal.

Nevertheless, an investment of $44 billion justifies the need to understand human variations in goal clarity perception. Humans always have varied goals, for instance, to create wealth, acquire power and prestige, to solve human suffering and to serve the poor. How a human chooses goals and works towards them can be characterised as his or her psychological nature. The goal can be to 'do nothing' or 'entertain one-self'. This might appear goalless to some. However, it is indeed a goal to those without goals. Goals of R&D do not end in the method but in the outcome, implying that the goals of R&D lead to important outcomes of publications and patents. The goals of R&D do not stop there either; these publications and patents must further reach society and the needy user via markets. Usability of R&D outcomes at the end of the road is the ultimate aim of R&D when investments are at $44 billion. Usability can be understood in the context of publications and patents. A paper publication, conference or journal, is read by scientists of academia and industry. If the paper is found useful, the paper is cited. Citations imply that others found use of the paper, but whether it reached society via the markets or not is difficult to pin down. There is no need for a user to report back to the author of the paper that the paper was used. This assumes that the content in the paper has know-how relevant to some user's process, product or service. This may not be the case always though, and only few papers may lend themselves to be readily used for a process, product or service. Since feedback to the author is limited unless the author or Technology Transfer Office is directly contacted by the user, the relevance of the paper to society is never understood by the author. It is only assumed by the author. If the paper must be relevant to the needs of society then it is most often the industry that must pick up the paper and further use it. This implies that academia does write papers for use by industry, if industry finds it worthwhile to adopt or adapt. But industry's motivation to report back to the author is minimal since there is no legal need to report back to the author if the paper was used. Since this feedback loop is not automated by law, one does draw a blank in due course, since other than citations, the paper does not generate feedback about its use in society and markets.

This is not the case with patents. Compared to paper publications, patents are closer to industry, users and markets in the value chain. Patents will vary greatly in their distance to market. Despite their protection system, they are accessible to all. They are available for viewing in public databases and can be seen by industry or any other academic or government user at various points of time. More important, the inventor of the patent must be contacted for anyone to use the patent by law. If they do not, then there is a chance that they would have infringed the patent. Infringement has dire consequences. Since this action stems from the patent act, which is the law of the land, it is legal and enforceable. This law will deter anyone using someone else's patent without the permission of the inventor. Given the legal situation of a patent, the inventor of a patent has negotiation power with a potential user/customer of the patent. It is evident to those who work on bringing a patent to society and markets that much has to be done to the patent to get it there. This will involve further investments and R&D work. Such activity needs the cooperation of the inventor and the customer of the patent, for example an industrialist. Today, the trend is to patent only if the patent is commercially worthy enough and useful to society. In fact the definition of the patent is about newness, non-obviousness and usefulness. Deciding whether to publish ones R&D results via a paper or patent or both is a decision that is crucial if one has to reach one's R&D outcomes to society via the markets. The author of a paper need not bother about it reaching society via markets; however, the inventor with a patent may have this goal as a responsibility due to the law. How to step up patent generation in a country as an outcome of R&D is worth pondering about. This does not mean mere generation of patent numbers, but the generation of patents useful for markets and society.

When R&D only leads to the outcome of publications (and not patents) that do not reach the market then something is amiss. Figure 1 shows three scenarios for a country's overall outcome in R&D. The first (i) is when only publications are the outcome of R&D. The creation of knowledge happens but whether this reaches the market is uncertain and unclear. The third (iii) is a rare case when only patents are generated in the country and no publications. The second (ii) is the balanced case where publications and patents are generated and patents are marketed to reach users, fully completing the intended goal of R&D. Thus, the goals of R&D can be described when the second scenario is operational in a country. These goals will have to manifest themselves in all areas of science and engineering.

Figure 1: Shows possible R&D outcomes at the

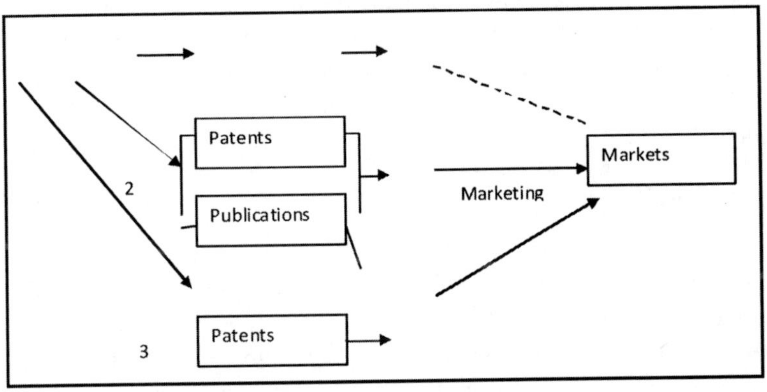

level of a country

It would be simple if humans were merely goal oriented. In the case of patents, for example the goal will be to produce innovative patents (reaching patents to the market) and the method to reach that goal will be via R&D. However, humans are complicated.

If the goal is to reach markets (as markets reach society keeping economics in mind), then humans work to fulfill the needs of a customer using appropriate methods of sales and get paid for it, but unfortunately, this does not mean they do R&D for the same. One might ask why? This is because R&D requires investments where outcomes are unpredictable. R&D is not predictable as is selling a laser printer to a customer in retail business. After a sales meeting the sales person can assess whether or not the sale will go through and if he or she will get paid. This is certainly not the case for R&D and markets. Thus, if the goal is to reach markets, only the ones that have mastered the art of managing uncertainty will use the method of R&D, others will use methods with higher probabilities of certainty, like outsourcing a client's business, banking, selling shares and retailing products. The method of R&D requires deep involvement with science and engineering. There are many needs of users that do not require newer areas of science and engineering. Such needs use public domain and older versions of science and engineering to meet user requirements. This is what business without R&D does. Business using R&D is the harder route to take. It is those that seek to improve things incrementally or radically for a user, that involve themselves in newer areas of science and engineering. Things get more complex when goals are in conflict, but humans assume that goals are the same.

Goal Clarity for R&D

The most complex situations in life arise when humans think they have shared goals, but are confused, and do not understand that they do not have shared goals. A good example is that of two sales persons one from a company in the private sector and the other from the government sector. A sales person of the private sector is certainly more successful than a salesperson of the government sector. They both seem to have shared goals, namely customers and markets, as both are from companies. But, this is really not true. The government sector company has different goals compared to the private sector company although both masquerade as revenue begetting companies in the market. It is not difficult to say who will lose at the stock market. It is almost true that one must allow business for markets to be with the private sector and never with the government since the goal of the government is welfare as opposed to reaching markets. Welfare and profits are conflicting goals and can also have parallel trajectories. Only a few government companies have learnt to balance welfare and profits, BHEL is one such example. When the goals of the company in which the sales person works varies from welfare to profits, it results in two differently performing sales persons.

In the case of R&D, a government company engaged in R&D is different from a private company engaged in R&D. The R&D scientist of the government company is unfortunately immersed in goals of welfare unlike the private company. This is the reason why the situation is celebrated when R&D investments of private sector companies are found to be greater than R&D investments of government companies. R&D investments from the private sector have greater probability to reach to markets than get lost in the sea of knowledge that is published as papers. Currently, in India there is a minor increase in private sector R&D spending. In India during the year 1990-1991, the government R&D spending share was 75.7 per cent (65.8 per cent in 2009-2010), whilst for private sector it was 24.3 per cent (34.2 per cent in 2009-2010), (DST R&D Statistics, 2013).

It is indeed desirable that private sector companies take on R&D in a bigger way. However, the private sector company's top management may not be skilled in the art of managing uncertainty and may be more keen to have speedy profits nested in short term goals. In this case, top managements of private companies by-pass R&D and carry on with sales and outsourcing operations as these are easier to achieve and lead quickly to their desired goal, namely profits. This leads to a situation where profits from activities that are non-R&D based increase in a country and these profits are reflected in the country's GDP as an increase in the rate of services. Given such a situation in India, neither the government sector scientist, nor the non-existent private sector scientist, will produce innovative patents, i.e., patents reaching society via the markets. It does take a lot of patience and competence to deal with R&D as a method for reaching markets. Skills to demystify the uncertainty of R&D are currently missing. When the goal is clearly stated to be R&D for markets, the scientist will stay on track and proceed towards R&D outcomes that are useful to the market. This may require a mix of science, engineering and business education in the human capital attempting such R&D.

Need of the Hour: A new Breed of Scientists

Making scientists who currently work in science silos conscious of user needs and markets involves a modification in scientific skill sets. If changes in scientific skill sets are not possible then the scientist can work with teams of those from the business and management schools. Those in business and management schools are forced to learn the terms society, user, customer, revenue and markets as part of their training. This mix of science, engineering and business scientists can bring out patents that are innovative, meaning patents that have a market and address user needs. Such a group of scientists will have to be multi-disciplinary, and be able to go across disciplines of science, engineering and business, understand prior art deeply, and study user profiles to be able to bring innovative patent outcomes in R&D. Some refer to these as 'T' professionals. Where the length of the T is the core domain the person understands and the head of the T are other broad areas that help the scientist bring out complex solutions for user needs. Clarity of goals of R&D at the individual, organisation and national level may be the starting point of good economic development, beginning with a modification of scientist skill sets.

Goals of Intellectual Property Protection Historically

It is worth understanding the historical goals of intellectual property protection. As a formal practice, it is over 700 years old. It was a practice initiated by monarchs of Europe to protect know-how developed by people of their region. The idea was to help inventors trade their know-how with other business personnel keen to use the know-how in their trade or business. The formal royal protection ensured that the original inventor was made known to everyone in the region. This transaction of the inventor's know-how to another, who might use it, could even carry a fee. The goal of the monarch was to help people confidently sell their know-how. The goal of the people was to gain customers. The goal of the customers who buy this know-how was to use the know-how to better run their businesses and earn their profits. Whilst the monarch had a welfare goal, possibly also to win popularity, that same goal helped inventors and business communities attract customers to themselves. Fortunately, whilst the goals differed for the monarch and his or her people of the region the varied goals worked in a complementary fashion to make everyone in the situation happy. The monarch took care of governance and the people made inventions for business.

In more recent times, namely the last two hundred years, such a protection was formalised by governments of countries (not monarchs) who were keen to harmonise trade practices across country boundaries. The goals almost remained the same even when monarchs disappeared and governments took over intellectual property practice but for one grave change in the goals of inventors. The governments had welfare goals to protect their inventors, rather similar to that of monarchs. Scientists on the other hand began to get distant from the goals of markets, and many intermediate goals appear to have filled this gap. Most scientists did it for the prestige of patent numbers and citations on their websites without a care for the user and markets. This is because most scientists are not 'T' professionals propelled to reach society via markets.

Attitude Theory for Patents

Assuming that the goal is well known to all for R&D i.e. R&D for society via markets, then one expects scientists to be propelled forward in this direction. However, this does not seem to happen despite apparent goal clarity. One approach to understand why humans behave the way they do is the insight provided by attitude theory. To a large extent attitude theory assumes that one's beliefs and psychological feelings towards something will have a bearing on how one will act towards it (overtly seen actions). So, in the case of patents, the beliefs and feelings scientists have towards intellectual property practice will have a bearing on how they act with regards to it. Patents are meant to protect the inventor and dissuade others from using them without the inventor's permission. Whilst this goal is clear to many, there is a certain attitude about intellectual property that is negatively polarized. Attitude theory suggested by many authors over the decades provides useful clarity. An interesting study by Lee and Wong, 2005, on 1390 scientists found that their attitudes do influence patenting intensity.

Attitude Theory

Attitude theory evolved since 1930 to say that beliefs do make humans behave. An attitude is always towards something for example an object, philosophy or practice, in this case towards intellectual property practice and patents. According to Allport (1935) "an attitude is a mental and neural state of readiness, organised through experience, exerting a directive or dynamic influence upon the individual's response to all objects and situations with which it is related". Later in 1960 Katz said that, "an attitude is the predisposition of the individual to evaluate a particular object in a favorable or unfavorable manner" (p. 168). With time Eagly & Chaiken, 1993 felt that an attitude, like all theoretical concepts in psychology, is a latent, hypothetical construct that is not directly observable. And further Ajzen 2005 added that as a consequence an attitude has to be inferred on the basis of tangible responses to an attitude stimulus. In this paper the stimulus will mean patents. While beliefs (the unseen covert cognitive part of humans, essentially thoughts), and actions (the seen overt actions of humans, essentially verbal, written or bodily actions), are both forms of behavior, some theorists tend to distinguish between beliefs and behaviors, where actions are meant to be behavior and beliefs are not. In the following sections it is assumed that, the psychological nature of beliefs and actions about an attitude stimulus, namely patents, will constitute behavior of scientists. It was in 1960 that a very popular and useful classification of attitudes inspired by Plato's writing was found. Rosenberg and Hovland 1960 classified attitudes into three components of cognitive belief systems, affective tendency and action tendency. Although criticized by some and shown by them to be near invalid, the theory is interesting when applied to patents. The three components of their theory are described further and are described in Figure 1.

The first component, namely cognitive beliefs are views and thoughts that a scientist has about the attitude being discussed for example, the attitude towards a patent. Thus, the cognitive belief about a patent refers to the belief systems scientists and other stakeholders have about it. Beliefs may require empirical analysis to support, strengthen and be stamped into minds of individuals. With experience, beliefs will get reinforced. Such empirical analysis will prove whether the belief to be had should be positive or negative. The positive and negative polarity of beliefs can be referred to as their valence. On the other hand, the depth of knowledge a scientist acquires to form their beliefs can be referred to as multiplicity. Given that the cognitive belief systems of an individual are the beginning of positive or negative action, it is the formation of these beliefs that is imperative. Formation of such beliefs requires a depth of understanding through various inputs: reading, discussions, speeches, listening, observing, writing, debating, empirical analysis and so on. Formation of such beliefs follows developmental stages as in maturation and growth. The childlike scientists will then be individuals whose beliefs on patents are yet to form, and they might show much dissonance and oscillation. Dissonance implies lack of clarity. Teenage scientists have beliefs that are more mature since they have better exposure to relevant information related to patents. The young adult scientist then further expands their knowledge and information base through advanced exposure, dialogue, reading, writing and debate about patents. Finally, the mature adult scientists are the ones whose beliefs are grounded and these individuals will show least dissonance and oscillation about patents. They will use their concepts on patents functionally. They will have consonance. Their valence can vary from positive or negative, depending on the beliefs they have acquired about patents.

The second component which is the affective tendency is not about beliefs but feelings and emotions one has about patents. These bio-chemical reactions are triggered based on their beliefs (within) and such emotions and feelings help the scientist validate their beliefs further. Feelings that get triggered from external sources (other than personal beliefs) may also have an impact on beliefs of the scientist. The feedback from these stimuli to the self, act as bits of data that further help in belief formation. It is assumed that beliefs will relate to correlated feelings/emotions. Thus, if the belief is that patents do not fuel innovation then one has a negative feeling towards patents.

The last component referred to as action tendency, where in the "act" is made visible and is seen to self or others, and is the actionable one. Some prefer to call this action "behavior" while others refer to beliefs, feelings and actions as behaviors and segregate the action as an outcome of beliefs and feelings. Irrespective, an action is expected to correlate to the beliefs and feelings for the patent. If a person's beliefs are that patents do not fuel innovation, then one dislikes and has negative feelings towards patents and ones action ensures no action i.e. one does not file a patent. The goal in this example was to fuel innovation. The valence and multiplexity of actions must further be understood.

Since valence suggests that the scientist with attitudes towards patents for example has a favourable or unfavourable orientation (polarisation) towards it, these must be interpreted in terms of actions. Polarized actions that are positive or negative are seen in valence of actions. Varying characterisation given the degree of valence is seen in actions. As the attitude gets more embedded in the individual the polarisations either positive or negative will increase. Multiplexity as mentioned before refers to the number of elements constituting

Figure 1: Attitude theory used to describe attitude towards patents

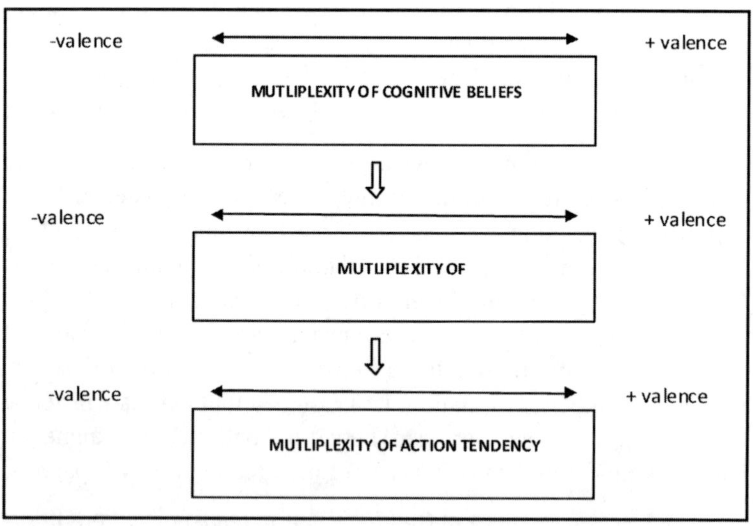

Source of Figure: Author

the potential actions the scientist displays about patents. It can also be described in terms of depth of actions, where shallow actions are the opposite. Plurality by depth comes from education and experience (plurality of beliefs). The deeper the attitude gets embedded in the scientist the greater will be the time spent on familiarizing oneself about patents.

Table 2: Showing polarised attitudes towards patents

Belief negative	Middling	Belief positive
Patents are not good for R&D. Patents deter innovation. Patents are monopolistic. We need not bother about patents, paper publiccations are fine. India has no money to file patents. Companies do not respect inventors. Rewards do not consider patents, promotions happen with publiccations. Patents kill creativity.	I am not sure I know anything on patents. I do not know if the company should file a patent or not.	Patents protect R&D outcomes. My research is patentable. I know when not to file a patent. I can comercialize my patents. Patent revenues will be shared with me. Patent portfolios are essential for innovation and product development. Patents should be budgeted like R&D. Patents provide competitive advantage. Inventors are creative and must patent their works.
Feeling negative		Feeling positive
I hate patents	I am unclear about patents I neither like nor dislike patents	I am proactive about patents, I am happy to patent, it does give me a good feeling
Action negative		Action positive
I will never file a patent. I will ensure that my team also never files a patent. I will tell my top management to avoid patents. I will work with anti-patent groups. I will only publish papers. I will not work with scientists who patent. I cannot help it if my research does not reach markets. I will not read patents.	I will think about filing patents. Not sure what to do about filing or who to contact. It is easier just to write a paper than file a patent. I will attend patent workshops if I have the time.	I will monitor my research work for patentable ideas; I will cooperate with the Technology Transfer Office to file patents. I will talk to customers to sell or license my patents. I will reach my patents to users in markets. I will encourage patent training and patent search databases. I will participate on discussions on the patent act. I will encourage young people to patent.

Given the theory of attitudes, it appears that humans vary on their attitude formation road map. Some are slow to reach the milestone of attitude maturity, while others reach this faster. Some individuals move towards a fully mature attitude system where patents are concerned, and others barely reach the first milestone of knowing what a patent does. Some have partial negative or positive valence whilst some have reached highly positive or negative polarised valence. Some exhibit actions that are correlated to their beliefs and feelings, with much multiplexity, doing many actions for or against patents, whilst others are laid back and engage in no action. For a few the three components are correlated implying they are in consonance, whilst for many there is dissonance; they are confused about patents.

Table 2 describes the various beliefs and feelings of scientists when polarised either negatively or positively where attitudes towards patents are concerned. The middle column is one in which the individual is confused and does not act consistently. The individual who is middling takes some beliefs from either polarised sides and mixes them up eventually sounding illogical. Polarised attitudes are logical. In a scenario where patents are not forthcoming although R&D investments are high it is clear that most scientists are middling or polarized negative regarding patents.

Conclusions

Those scientists that have a positive attitude towards patents will have their beliefs, feelings and actions in consonance, propelling them to act in proactive ways where R&D and patents are concerned. Beliefs of scientists with a positive mature attitude towards patents are easily recognizable when they express themselves. Such a scientist will have vast knowledge on what is meant by a patent. Their beliefs will be positively skewed towards patents. In the process of developing ones belief system, one will find that, there is multiplexity in the information base of what is a patent. The multiplexity comes from the various perspectives one needs to have about a patent. Some of these perspectives of thought are R&D management, patent law, writing a patent document, prior art analysis, management/strategy for patents, and the more recently emerging, patent analytics. Positive beliefs about the legal side involve beliefs about the definition of a patent, the harmonisation movements across countries, their understanding and clarity on the Patent Act, the legal practice namely prosecution, opposition and litigation, and the variations in legal definitions given the nature of technology. Positive legal belief systems can also describe the beliefs about patent examiner's capability, patent examination efficiency, and patent databases for prior art search. The beliefs related to the management and strategy side of patents is better explained from corporate or university systems. These beliefs involve beliefs in practices such as organisation designs (normally structures like committees, processes and decision rules, such that of to file or not to file), more sociological aspects like culture for patenting, belief in dashboards that assess for patent productivity, human resource management (rewards and recognition) of inventors, R&D management, and patent analytics (landscaping technology areas, collaborator and competitor analysis, white space analysis). Beliefs on the financial and strategy side will describe whether the company plans and budgets patent filing and litigation, needs to maintain a patent, supports the technology transfer office, its capability at marketing patents or portfolios, and patent assessment and pricing. Such positively polarised beliefs will have corresponding feelings. All the beliefs mentioned in the previous paragraph will create positive feelings in the individual; such that favourable feelings towards patents are formed. These emotions further fuel action towards patents.

Actions of one with a positive attitude towards patents are many. The scientist supports the legal side of patents by cooperating with the patent attorney, and examiners. The scientist provides all supporting documents to the patent application without feeling that he or she has no time for such paper work. The scientist cooperates to understand the outputs of a prior art search. He or she is willing to alter their pre-conceived stereotypes about the R&D area and modify these views based on the prior art results. They are willing to cooperate with committees that assess the patent for decisions on whether to file or not. They help technology transfer offices in identifying customers and participate in decisions related to how much to price the patent. They may even participate in strategic decisions on whether to license the patent or put it into a start up. Cooperation with the beliefs of a patent is the typical action that will be seen from scientists with a positive attitude towards patents.

Attitudes help a scientist perform in a focused manner and make them competent. If the attitude is positive then they work towards the goals of R&D. On the other hand if their attitude towards patents is negative they work against patenting and try to stop it from happening, implying R&D will not be productive. Congruence in goals and attitudes of humans thus, determine what they become. When the goal is productive R&D, then strong attitudes about intellectual property protection are to be socialised. Individuals whose goal clarity is poor and attitudes are that of childlike scientists will be confused doing actions that are sometimes progressive and often regressive. These form the most unproductive human capital in R&D. The clever ones are those that pretend to be strong R&D scientists, full of R&D funds and investments, with much man power, publications, and possibly reasonably high citations too. However, their R&D outcomes may not be patented and neither would their publications have reached the market. Their citations will be by academic scientists and not by industrial scientists or collaborators. The clever ones will be ones that file patents also, but for the sake of filing. None of these patents too would have reached the market. Their performance is misleading. They appear productive and to have shared goals with leaders, namely, seemingly active R&D. While they did their job in the public eye, in their private eye, they know for sure they managed their mask well and that their intellectual property was not intended to reach any market or society. If it does serendipitously, they will bask in that unexpected glory. The ignorant scientists are the ones who continue to publish not knowing they were to patent too. These need training and exposure.

The psychological perspective of understanding R&D goals and attitudes towards intellectual property protection, namely patents, to some extent provides insights into what is happening with R&D in countries like India. Whilst it may be healthy to have polarisations,

R&D will benefit greatly if the polarisation is positive. Instilling the right belief systems is essential if intellectual property must be an outcome. This belief does not come from mere technical training in science or engineering, but also training in business and technology management. When R&D reaches the market, it helps boost economic development in the country in the long run. If R&D has to reach the markets to trickle down to society, then positive attitudes towards patents will help scientists in general.

Bibliography

1. Ajzen, I. (2005), Attitudes, personality and behaviour (2nd ed.). Maidenhead, UK: Open University Press, (2005).
2. Allport, G. W. (1935). A handbook of social psychology (C. Murchison, Ed.). Worcester, MA: Clark University Press.
3. Arai, H., Intellectual Property Policies for the 21st Century, the Japanese experience in Wealth creation, Policy Advisory Commission, WIPO, December, 1999.
4. Eagly, A. H., & Chaiken, S. (1993). The psychology of attitudes. Fort Worth, TX: Harcourt Brace Jovanovich.
5. Katz, D. (1960). The functional study of attitudes. Public opinion quarterly, 24, pp163-204.
6. Lee, L & Wong, P.K. Individual attitudes, organisational reward system and patenting performance of R&D scientists and engineers, MPRA Paper No. 595, posted 27, October 2006.
7. Mathew, M., Benchmarking Patenting Procedures: A Conceptual Model of the Procedure and Experiences of R&D Scientists, paper presented at the Portland International Conference on Management Engineering Technology, PICMET, Portland, Oregon, USA, 1997.
8. Research and Development Statistics at a Glance, 2011-2012, DST, Ministry of Science and Technology. September, 2013.
9. Rosenberg, M. J., & Hovland, C. I. (1960). Cognitive, affective, and behavioural components of attitudes. In C. I. Hovland & M. J. Rosenberg (Eds.), Attitude organisation and change: An analysis of consistency among attitude components (p 1-14). New Haven, CT: Yale University Press. Open University Press.
10. 2014 Global R&D Funding Forecast, Battelle, December, 2013.

The Accusers' Accused

Dr G. Ramakrishna

A significant enunciation, with copious evidences, by Debiprasad Chattopadhyaya was that the Lokayatas were not always looked down upon by the elitist sections of society in ancient India. Denunciation of the Lokayatas based on their alleged hedonistic approach to life is philosophically and historically quite medieval in thinking. It is one of the heresies spread by the author of Sarvadarshana Samgraha, a text on philosophy in Sanskrit belonging to the 14th century. Drupada of the Mahabharata had no qualms against them, while Kautilya included the Lokayata among the lore that a ruler should be familiar with. Among the Brahmins said to have called on the Buddha once was a Lokayata philosopher as well. The inescapable truth is that the Lokayatas got denigrated profusely because of their unflinching opposition to the system which protected vested interests. This system had no scruples about superstitious beliefs providing a safety valve against possible protests by the masses. Let alone the masses, even an ordinary representative of theirs had to be put down violently lest he provoke others into his line of thinking. Why else would that solitary individual raising his voice against the illegitimacy of Yudhisthira getting anointed as king in Hastinapura be beheaded? Beheaded he was according to the version we have in the Mahabharata. His only grouse after all was that this same Yudhisthira had played havoc with the lives of multitudes of people during the war in Kurukshetra in the name of restoring Dharma. What kind of restoration of Dharma is that where you have to kill a million instead of converting a few of them into righteous persons or persuading them to follow the path of righteousness in general. It is to the eternal credit of the Lokayatas that it was a person professing Lokayata philosophy who had the boldness and decency to cry foul when such a colossal destruction had been perpetrated. The poor Charvaka who had thus remonstrated was unceremoniously lynched by the Brahmin mob, for which act of 'social gracefulness' all the Brahmins in the mob were duly compensated by the king with regards and gifts. The whole episode serves as a fine metaphor for what has apparently gone on relentlessly in our society for quite a long time. As loyal traditionalists, large numbers of the contemporary defenders of the so called Dharma perpetuate the crime in a more complex form today. And that does not apply solely to our own India either, because other parts of the globe are not free from such horrendous deeds against the lowly in society.

The Charavaka consciousness exemplified by the episode just recalled is not by any means an isolated occurrence. In fact, at the core of the Bhagavad Gita lies an interrogation of exactly the same kind, but much more elaborate and disturbing. The extraordinary feat of the Gita consists in marginalising this supremely important sociological question of violence and destruction as an imperative for restoring and consolidating Dharma. The first chapter of the Gita, which incidentally also happens to be the best chapter of that philosophico-religious text, articulates the concerns of the Charvaka of Mahabharata fame when the remorseful Arjuna is overtaken by mortification at the very thought of killing his own kinsmen for the sake of obtaining the throne. It is quite another matter that the super preceptor Krishna preaches that there is nothing like death for the warriors on the battlefield as their souls are eternal and that Arjuna need only be an instrument for killing the 'unkillable' because they have already been killed! A mesmerizing play of words to equal this philosophical fancy is hard to come by in the range of world philosophy. Arjuna's questions are not questions of an anti-hero who wants to find an alibi for fleeing from the battlefield.

On the contrary, there must have been members in the society of the days of the author of the Gita raising such awkward but pressing questions regarding what was transpiring in society. It was viewed as being unjust, not to speak of being irrational as well. The principal foundational principles of those times, subjected to criticism by a section of society, are sought to be justified and defended by the Gita, thereby performing a philosophical task of 'justifying the ways of God to humans'. The most touching question of Arjuna centers round the understanding that one cannot live in peace after killing one's own people (BG. 1.31 and 37). He would rather go without the kingdom for himself than have the three worlds themselves after killing such an enormous number of people of his own milieu. He would not mind getting himself killed instead (BG 1.41). One need not view the entire discussion in the Bhagavad-Gita in the light of the actual battlefield in Kurukshetra. After all, the author of the Gita has chosen that particular form for highlighting his philosophico-religious ideas in the context of his own times. The disintegration of society that would inevitably result from war is abhorred by Arjuna. Of course, disintegration is here conceived of in terms of caste barriers being broken and women being led astray (BG 1.41). It is somewhat intriguing that Arjuna who is so much worried about what might happen if women went astray does not seem to be equally concerned about what might happen if men went astray. But that is beside the point. The orthodox opinion that stratification of society along caste lines is divine dispensation is repeated parrot-like by Arjuna when he expresses consternation about 'permanent values', getting dislocated by war which creates intermixture of castes, as a consequence of which the prescribed death rites would also be a casualty (BG 1.42). The fortress of rituals must not be allowed to be de-sanctified, come what may. But that was precisely the target of the Lokayatas, for which reason they were shunned and demonised. The demonisation went so far as to deny basic ethical norms being sacrosanct for the Lokayatas. So much so, it was averred that these pestilences personified by the Charvakas would go so far as to make merry recklessly, throwing to the winds any sense of social obligation. They might not steal, but definitely borrow from others unmindfully for having a swell time for themselves. It is a paradox that the very people who raised crucial questions about social ethics were portrayed as a socially irresponsible crowd. The Gita promised hope under distressing circumstances by assuring that God would descend on earth to straighten things out whenever they became unbearable (4.7). But no serious philosopher in the Indian tradition ever thought it fit to introspect as to why Almighty God never tried to instill hope by persuading the unrighteous to be otherwise instead of taking the extreme step of bumping them off at one stroke. Secondly, how come that God incarnate is unable to install a just society once and for all so that he does not have to undergo the ordeal of incarnating himself now and again? Idealist schools of thought were annoyed continually, as they are even now, for no other reason than that such questions were raised by the Lokayatas.

This is not to suggest that the Gita presents a view of the Lokayata School. But the point is that the Indian philosophical tradition and its impact cannot be viewed as if it were a monolithic structure. We have karma, adrishta (the unseen), bondage and liberation on the one hand, and the thought of the common folk untainted by such doctrines on the other. One of them imposes a burden on the individual by making him helpless and subordinate and the other prompts the person to action. It is this latter tradition which interrogates the rationale of the beliefs and practices of the other tradition. The principal postulate of the interrogators is that man has the potential to intervene creatively to change the order of things in society if only he interacts with his milieu and understands the principles governing it. Naturally, the two traditions have been polaric opposites, one accepting the reality of the world and the other negating it. Even among those who do not reject the reality of the world, there are some like Ramanuja and Madhva who preach surrender to the supreme deity as the single authentic means for attaining what they call emancipation. Social emancipation is definitely not there on the agenda of these philosophers whose company is quite formidable.

It is a commonplace truth that primitive societies try to come to grips with reality rather than negate it stoutly, or else posit the reality of the world with the rider that there is something more real than reality which ought to be the real aim in the quest of man. Fear and mystery are the two outstanding experiences that we find recorded in primitive societies as evidenced by their belief-systems and ritualistic practices. Fire, rain, thunder, darkness, wild beasts and the like stare primitive men in the face. The means to survival in the confrontation is the ancient magical act. Through this, he gradually moves on to the recognition of some law ingrained in movements within nature that he perceives all around himself. The spelndour of the morning, the starry sky of the night, the warmth of the sun, the occasional floods, wild fires, seasonal fluctuations and similar other phenomena mesmerise him as he gropes in darkness to figure out the law, if any, governing these phenomena. Even a cursory glance at the Rig-Veda brings out this element quite vividly. How then can he deny reality of it all like some future day sophisticated philosophers of the idealist school of thought? The latter, after all, belonged to a period when there were more material advancements along with the knowledge to thus advance.

What Lokayata philosophy does is to retain both the awe and the reality of things around man as experienced by all primitive societies. It is needless to say that the full ramifications of a philosophical school of thought are nowhere to be seen in primitive societies and their rituals. Nevertheless, it is necessary to cognize proto-materialism in its form, scope and evolution. We shall then be able to disentangle ourselves from the inane characterisation of Indian philosophy as a whole as something exclusively idealistic and spiritualistic. It is for historians to discern when and under what circumstances the spiritual discourse struck roots in Indian philosophy. The signal contribution of Debiprasad Chattopadhyaya consists in unraveling this mystery, if mystery it is reckoned to be. It is an infamy, therefore, to consider an anti-idealistic philosopher as a philosophical untouchable in the Indian tradition. Here, for example, is a specimen of the tirade against the Lokayata: "....With the single exception of the Lokayata which insists that all moral conventions and ethical theories have been invented by clever weaklings, no other philosopher would seriously support the view that the preservation of one's earthly existence at all costs is the summum bonum of our life." This is penned by a reputed author in one of the early issues of the prestigious 'Philosophical Quarterly' and it is quite easy to pick out any number of such declarations by our allegedly pious philosophers of yesterday and today. (But let us first be clear that the Lokayata does not speak of weaklings cleverly inventing moral conventions and ethical theories; what they do attribute to the 'clever weaklings' is the diabolical rituals to bamboozle the layman.) The purport of statements like the one just quoted is as much to eulogise the idealist schools as to deride the Lokayata School. If the litmus test is social ethics, how do idealistic philosophers fare in our tradition? Unfortunately, there is nothing spectacular in their mien if the justification advanced by them in favour of social stratification is any indication. Whatever the veracity of the accusations laid at the door of the Lokayatas, one thing is for sure, and that is that they never sullied themselves by advancing preposterous and phony theories to explain the alleged divine ordinance concerning the vertical social hierarchy perpetuated for centuries in our country. On the contrary, they relentlessly laid bare the philosophical emptiness of the idealist schools of thought which professed loftily but practised meanly.

It does not redound to the credit of philosophy to make acceptance of Vedic authority as the sole criterion for categorising philosophical schools as either theistic or atheistic. And yet this is constantly harped upon as the ultimate court of justice to decide what is acceptable and what is not in the realm of philosophy. What is worse, many an Indian philosopher bows down in reverence to the dictates of even ordinary mundane law-givers (hopefully, they are not law-makers, too) as if they were profound philosophers, which they were not. It is strange that our philosophers did not for a moment doubt that truth could be the child of authority and not of time, contemplation, observation, analysis and logic. The Lokayata philosophers sought to move towards that methodology even if they did not conceptualise it in so many words. Of some curiosity is the question of the Jain school. Where does philosophy end and religion gain ground? This question is as much relevant in the context of the Shaiva and Vaishnava traditions as in the case of Jainism. Contemporary Buddhism is no exception either. With all the elaborate rituals of worship, the Jain School could as well have been designated a thoroughly theistic religion, had it not been for the ridiculous criterion of Vedic authority being the yardstick for the classification. The only difference between the Jain school and the so called Vedic schools is that the Tirthankaras take the position of the Veda in Jainism. Both authorities could well be considered as being subject to the limitations of time and perception. It would have been more reasonable philosophically had the views of Jain philosophy concerning the origin of the universe, theory of knowledge and conditions for Arhantship been considered instead. The identity or otherwise of views regarding Pudgala and Padartha respectively in Jain and Nyaya schools of philosophy, for example, could better serve as distinguishing marks. Even so, what exactly does it mean to accept Vedic authority in philosophy? Does the Veda enunciate any specific idea regarding, say, the five elements as constituents of the real world for schools of philosophy to accept it as a postulate and then proceed further in philosophical disquisition? Likewise what about other propositions that fall within the scope of philosophy? It is obvious, therefore, that issues alien to philosophy have been tagged on as limitations for a free philosophical discussion. It is one thing to refer to an idea adumbrated in some Upanishad or the other and accept it and corroborate it, and quite another to be bound by it. Is there one stream of philosophy in the Rigveda, for example? Are the hymns addressed to Agni, Indra, Savitr, Varuna and Ushas fundamental to philosophical speculations? What does one make of the gambler's hymn of the Rigveda as source material for philosophy? Or, of the frog-hymn where the budding disciple recites the Veda like a frog just back from hibernation? How can one convert a piece of good poetry into authoritative philosophy? Further, even granting that there is some very significant philosophical doctrine in the just mentioned hymns, is it consistent with speculations in the Upanishads? And why should it be, indeed? Is there no scope for divergent views in the world of philosophy on questions for which we do not possess final answers?

It certainly is not a sound method to telescope the history of thought over a few centuries into one supposedly infallible doctrine, for the simple reason that it would make efforts over centuries to understand Reality irrelevant, as one obviously is already in possession of authentic 'final answers' to all questions concerning man and the world. The problem of philosophy has been resolved and hence there is no further need for exercising the intellect any more regarding the perennial questions of philosophy. In other words, one makes philosophy redundant by making some apparently divine text as the final authority on questions for which we do not have any single final answer even now! And that is what has been done in respect of the entire range of Upanishadic literature produced over a period of a few centuries at geographical areas largely distant from each other. It is grossly unfair to aver that after a few centuries of philosophical exercises over vastly separated areas, our ancestors arrived at just one philosophical view as the Brahma Sutra-s understood it. Indian philosophy is much more than this one text. Variety in thinking and viewing is what anyone immediately recognises in the Upanishads. It must have been quite boring for anyone to produce so many texts for conveying one uniform idea! This kind of misplaced adulation for the Upanishads reduces the abundantly rich texts into a poorly composed copy-book. Let us put it a little more bluntly thus: The veracity or otherwise of a Physicist's formulation can hardly be judged by the totally extraneous factor as to whether he or she reads his or her Bible regularly or not. A third alternative is not to read it at all at any time and still be a knowledgeable Physicist. The glorious strides that Indian philosophers so valiantly made in their attempt to understand Reality have been pygmied by the brownie and the pixie called Vedic authority for the corroboration of philosophical ideas. It is not only strange but also shameful that our traditional scholars, old and new, have never once given thought to this somewhat elementary detail concerning the history of Indian Philosophy.

For once, the Lokayata School liberated philosophy from this uncalled for encumbrance by looking at the world straight without the 'Vedic glasses' and by calling the bluff of those who foisted elaborate rituals on philosophy. Even if one does not agree with an oriental scholar who described the Brahmana texts that succeeded the Samhita texts as 'theological twaddle', it must unhesitatingly be accepted that there is not much philosophical analysis therein for a philosopher to fall back upon. Debiprasad Chattopadhyaya almost single-handedly, or as 'a one man brigade' as he was once described, put Indian Philosophy on its legitimate course by establishing in no uncertain terms that there are two concrete traditions in Indian Philosophy, like in world philosophy. The relationship between the elements of nature and human consciousness discussed so passionately in some schools of Indian philosophy received its due at the hands of Debiprasad more than in anybody else's hands, although it must be conceded that many others before him had called attention to it. M. Hiriyanna is one of them. The other thing that Debiprasad did was to ostracise the self-proclaimed dictatorial authorities, namely, the law-givers (or Dharmashastrakaras), from the domain of a critical and historical study of Indian Philosophy. Considering that even historians of science at the Academy of Science have no more than the rigmarole that is popular with others, it is significant that a path breaking role has been played by Debiprasad Chattopadhyaya by his focus on what is central to Lokayata as a philosophy. The cliché about the Lokayata being hedonistic or 'Charvaka' being a 'sweet-tongued' fellow no longer seems to have any place in philosophy.

Madhava's stanza in the Sarva Darshana Samgraha which is what has started the game needs to be understood copiously. The stanza runs thus: **Yavajjivet sukham jivet rinam kritva ghritam pibet; Bhasmibhutasya dehasys punaragamanam kutah.** The literal meaning of the stanza is well-known: Live happily as long as you live; enjoy by being a debtor if need be. Once turned to ashes after death, where is there any return at all? Firstly, the first part of the stanza is not much different from the oft-repeated incantation: Jivema Sharadah Shatam (May we live for a hundred years). Modama Sharadah Shatam (May we partake of joy for a hundred years) is among the aspirations voiced. This is sanctified, but "Yavajjivet sukham jivet" is condemned as blasphemy, which is rather odd. Secondly, do we take all such stanzas literally always? If not, why castigate this one for its 'rinam kritva ghritam pibet" part? A devotional poem attributed to Shankaracharya says among other things that it does not help to know your grammar and roots of Sanskrit verbs (Na hi na hi rakshati dukrun karane). Do we take it literally and stop learning grammar in order to attain emancipation? The point is that literary devices are abundantly employed by philosophers for driving home their message; they may grow rhetorical also at times. No student of Literature need be taught that rhetorical expressions are not to be taken too literally. "Rinam kritva ghritam pibet" is one such fine expression and it does not intend to portray a Charvaka as a hedonist, much less a morally irresponsible being. There are umpteen literary devices employed by Shankara in his commentary on the Brahma Sutras.

Students of Purva Mimamsa know what they refer to as 'arthavada' by which is meant the laying of emphasis on a particular prescription in an indirect suggestive way. The usual example given is that the serpents performed a sacrifice. When you say "sarpah satram asata" you are not making a factual statement about the serpents having performed a sacrifice; what you mean to convey is that man has the obligation to perform a sacrifice. When the serpents themselves have performed a sacrifice, how much more becoming is it for man to do so! Arthavada may be a technical term in the Purva Mimamsa, but it is akin to any literary device having a similar purport. It is only for denigrating the Lokayata School that a simple commonplace literary device has been twisted and is being relentlessly continued even now. What the 'arthavada' of the passage under reference conveys is simply this: Ingrain in yourself the way to remain happy in life; don't you be a slave to the barren belief and ritual that have been held before you as the path to happiness; instead, you had better develop the discretion to be happy at all times and at all costs.

Ordaining thus is not a terrible deviation from what is commended in the Ishavasya Upanishad which says that you should live for a hundred years with activities, meaning desirable actions. It is quite superfluous to suggest like Shankara does that action here means various rituals (karmani agnihotradini). Supposing that the 'arthavada' connotation is not acceptable for some prejudicial reason, the further question arises whether a Charvaka will be allowed by his fellow social beings to keep incurring debts to be happy when they also are expected to be doing exactly the same thing as fellow Charvakas. Today the World Bank prescribes conditionalities which our sovereign government accepts, but a Charvaka society will have none to accept the conditionalities when each member of the group here is prescribing conditionalities, the sole condition being 'give me the loan on condition that you don't get it back'. It is not graceful to call the dog mad and shoot it and that applies as much to the world of philosophy as it does to other departments of life. The priestly class has the prerogative to tell its votaries that it is safe to perform the Jyotishtoma sacrifice for attaining heaven (Jyotishtomena swargakamo yajeta), but the Charvaka philosopher has no such elixir-like formula to tell anyone that it is safe to give loans to a Charvaka. There are two snags there: firstly, he does not have votaries like the priestly class has and secondly, the Charvaka does not have a heaven to entice his votaries with! We have yet to hear of a Charvaka Bank which is totally unmindful of its non-performing assets, a euphemism for unreturned loans, like some of our nationalised banks seem to be.

Debiprasad Chattopadhyaya drew the attention of the students of Indian Philosophy to Shantarakshita's "Tattavasamgraha" commented upon by Kamalasheela. This work mentions a certain Purandara as the author of a text on Lokayata philosophy but the text is extinct. What we understand from Shantarakshita is that the philosophical doctrines of Purandara are considerably different from the one attributed to the Lokayata School by the 'Sarva Darshana Samgraha'. It is another matter, of course, that Shantarakshita does not accept Purandara's doctrines. But he does not dismiss the school as inconsequential after making some sniding remarks about its doctrines like some latter day 'philosophers' do. The current crop of critics of the Lokayata School with no analytical approach whatsoever needs to be included among such philosophers. The reason for Shantarakshita in so doing may be that he is, like Purandara, one who does not recognise the authority of the Veda for validating philosophical positions. Madhava, on the other hand, is incensed with the gumption of the Lokayata philosopher in making light of Vedic authority and even lampooning it lavishly. In tune, therefore, with the masters of Vedic rituals who had no love lost for the Lokayatas, Madhava repeats parrot-like what had been traditionally said about the Lokayata School by orthodox schools. That is no sound method for a philosopher, to say the least. It is the examination and evaluation of the epistemology and ontology of a school of philosophy that should be the deciding factor for a philosopher when he is in disagreement with a school of philosophy. That is what Shankara does, for example, when he refutes the position of the Samkhya School which to him is the finalist in philosophical debate. Defeating Samkhya means defeating Lokayata as well, according to him. In other words, Lokayata, like Samkhya, is a school of materialist philosophy and Shankara is prepared for a confrontation with them simultaneously. Had the works of Purandara, Bhaguri and the likes of them come down to us, the ridiculous argument against Lokayata philosophy advanced by Madhava and his ilk might not have been there.

The prime question then is why the texts of the Lokayata philosophers disappeared in the course of history. It is not tendentious or simplistic to suggest that a crucial reason for it was the social philosophy which the Lokayata School underlined. It was against this that idealist philosophers had to fight in order to defend what their philosophy sought to defend. The innate connection between materialism and the people involved in human endeavours is borne out by the history of civilisation throughout the world. A world – denying philosophy may be sweet for an intellectually astute philosopher, but a person who has to live with the sweat of his brow does not have much love for it. What is 'ultimately real' may be a fine academic question, but ploughing and sowing are not mere academic matters. Plato was neither the first nor the last to demean the labourer while making merry with the products of the labour of others. The Lokayata School of philosophy has happily remained at the receiving end in this unequal bout.

Not to be left far behind some philosophers and texts like the Vishnu Purana castigated the Lokayatas in strong terms which are more indicative of anger and apprehension than any philosophical justification. It might also be said that some philosophers took the cue from the Puranas while attacking the Lokayata system. It is interesting to note that the Vishnu Purana has nothing against Lokayata philosophy; its whole ire is occasioned by the fact that the Lokayata does not accept Vedic authority and has no special regard for sacrificial rituals. That the Lokayatas have a severe banter for death rituals is an indication of the demoniac element in the Lokayata system according to this Purana. The text further bemoans that the Lokayatas are under a delusion because of which they allegedly declare that 'the world has no basis or support' external to itself, that the world is primordially evil, and so on. It is because of this that the lokayatas are inimical to the Brahmins in the view of the Vishnu Purana. It is obvious whose interests within the caste hierarchy the Purana seeks to defend and also why orthodoxy has always found the lokayata as a bush of thorns in the otherwise pleasant garden of vertical social hierarchy. Those who wonder whether the Lokayata system of philosophy has anything at all to do with ethics may like to consider if consciousness of social equality is not a fundamental ingredient of ethics in the specific Indian context. The Lokayatas were not satisfied with mere consciousness against a social stigma; they were crusaders against it as well, which says a lot about their ethical values. As crusaders, of course, they did not perpetrate any crime like their counterparts of medieval Europe did, and yet the Vishnu Purana liberally consigns all the Lokayatas to the burning hell out of sheer indignation, but the society at large might not have enthusiastically shared its misplaced spirit for 'punishing' the Lokayatas. Vachaspati Mishra follows the Purana edict as a great loyalist, casting to the winds his true calling as a philosopher. He is more royal than the king when he proclaims that the Lokayatas are 'more brutish than brutes' thereby again proving that his first interest is not philosophy but defence of the social pyramid of his times. Why would so many 'authorities' rave against the lokayatas if their system had not been part of the popular legend of those days?

If it is not some Purana like the Vishnu Purana that guides some Indian philosophers in the evaluation of philosophy, then it is some law-giver who directs them how to distribute their favours. In either case, it is an extraneous thing that makes them evaluate philosophical schools. The whole thing reminds one of the medieval age in Europe when the Church in Rome either frowned upon Science or favoured it depending upon how it might or might not affect papal authority. The only difference is that perhaps India did not resort to the foul act of burning heretics at the stake like Europe did. Possibly the Indian philosophers believed in a more humane way of killing! As far as killing the idea is concerned there is a fine similarity of purpose. A typical instance of the Indian philosophers signing on the dotted lines drawn by the law-givers can be seen in the commentaries on what is called the "Apashudradhikarana" of the Brahma Sutras. The Taittiriya Samhita (2.2.10.2) had earlier averred that the "words of Manu are like a medical potion" (Yadvai kincha manuravadat tadbheshajam). Not many Indian philosophers have raised the question as to why or how the words of a law-giver could be the final verdict on a question of philosophy when it is well-known that such law-givers are by no means pre-eminent philosophers in their own right. Another way of saying this is that philosophy must dutifully subserve the purpose of the existing unequal social order. Shankara has said that a particular statement of Manu (namely, 12.91) implies the refutation of the views of the Samkhya doctrine of Kapila. The exact words are here: Manuna...sarvatmatvadarshanam prashamsataa kaapilam matam nindyata iti gamyate, meaning that while edifying the soul as the substratum of everything Manu has refuted the view of Kapila regarding the elements. Should one not have the integrity to pronounce outright that it is not edifying for a philosopher to lay philosophy prostrating at the feet of a law-giver whose sole purpose is to keep the stultifying social order static? P.V. Kane has hit the nail on the head by saying, perhaps ironically, that "according to Shankara, the author of the Vedanta Sutras has Manusmriti for one of his sources." It passes one's understanding how Manu could be of great help in understanding the true nature of 'what is' (sat), which is the principal preoccupation of the philosopher Shankara. This question may sound quite scandalous to our adherents and irrational admirers of Shankara, 'the Himalayan philosopher' as they like to describe him. But the Himalayan philosopher is not disinterested in the conservation of the social hierarchy of his times. Both the philosophical and the sociological stances of Shankara are evident from his commentary on the Brahma Sutras. The world as experienced by us in our day to day life may be ephemeral according to Shankara, but the vertical social hierarchy in it is not so; it must be defended to the last hilt.

As an illustration for this, we may go to the 'Apashudra-adhikarana' of the Brahma Sutras. That it is the opinion of the Upanishadic passage concerned and not necessarily that of Shankara as well does not hold water. The point at issue in this section (adhikarana) is that the philosophical view highlighted in the Upanishad is not available to the 'low born' (shudra). If that is what the contention of the Upanishadic passage, namely, the Chandogya Upanishad 4.2.3, also is, then that too becomes an example for calumny, leaving the slandering Shankara unexonerated. The paradox of it all is that the philosophical view under reference is a sine qua non for liberation, but that view is, however, not available for a Shudra, which means that a Shudra is condemned to eternal bondage. It is quite another matter that the Shudra in spite of such ignominious strictures continues to struggle for liberation with the help of some other philosophy as evidenced by history. If there is any hope for the so called low born, it is solely in the form of service to the 'high-born', as Manu has said and as Shankara has endorsed!

In the first place, why does the 'low-born' not have the right to gain the philosophical view so much tattooed? The answer is simple: "Because he has no right to study the Veda." And why so? 'Because he is uninitiated' as per law and he is also uninitiable as per the law of the 'high-born' rulers. The 'low-born' is duly warned that any transgression of this ordinance could be suicidal as molten lead might be poured into his ears if he dares to so much as hear the recitation of the Veda, let alone recite it himself. It is hard to believe that a philosopher could be as irrational as this, but Shankara quotes these words of the Gautama Dharma Sutra (2.3.4) with unbashful approval and why should the 'low-born' not hear the recitation of the Veda? - "because he is similar to the cremation grounds." Pray, what logic is this? Suppose one goes and recites the Veda right on the cremation grounds, then what? Oh, no. It is sheer blasphemy. "There is a clear injunction that his tongue must be cut if he recites the Veda and that his body must be rendered as under if he comprehends the Veda," says Shankara, the mighty philosopher. But, are we reading a philosophical text or some nasty edict of a tyrannical Roman emperor? May we submit that the great champions of Shankara's philosophy who want us to accept Shankara lock, stock and barrel should answer that question to themselves first? It is not without some substance that some present day followers of Shankara liken him to Plato. There are many similarities between the two; both consider the world to be somewhat unreal and both uphold slavery, albeit in slightly different forms.

Without going into the details of the context in which all this discourse on the curse heaped on the Shudra figures in Shankara's commentary on the relevant portions of the Chandogya Upanishad (4.2.3), it may be mentioned that Raikva, endowed with sublime knowledge although living in harsh straits, condescends to teach the Truth to Jaanashruti, a wealthy non-shudra, when he offers to gift a damsel if need be to receive the famed knowledge in possession of the former. While doing so, he addresses the non-shudra as a shudra, which is what prompts all the commentators on the Brahjma Sutras to launch a tirade against the shudras and pay rich obeisances to the law-givers in the name of interpreting a philosophical point. The multi-million rupee question for the commentators unhappily is whether philosophical knowledge could be imparted to someone like Jaanashruti who had just been addressed as if he were a Shudra. After taking the literal meaning of the word 'shudra' to begin with, the commentators hold forth eloquently about the prescriptions of the law-givers approvingly and then argue that the literal meaning is not of any consequence in the given context. What else does the word 'shudra' mean then in the given context? The etymology of the word from the root 'shuk' suggests that 'shudra' is one who is perpetually in a pathetic condition, but that Jaanashruti is momentarily a 'shudra' because of his remorseful condition. Whatever the usefulness or otherwise of the excursion into etymology, one thing remains clear and that is that there was no sense of pathos evoked in Shankara for the 'low-born' and yet he was a lofty philosopher.

Ramanuja, Madhva and other greats in the world of Indian Philosophy might have differed among themselves on any number of issues concerning philosophy, but they were all one in equating the 'low-born' with the cemetery. They vied with each other, if anything, in surrendering to the dictates of the law-givers without ever venturing to dictate the law-givers about humanist philosophy, social equality and universal appeal of knowledge. Likewise, they are all strongly united in their opposition to the Lokayata school of thought. There is, for example, a myth bandied about in respect of Ramanuja that he was for embracing everyone into his fold in a truly liberal fashion. But here is a sample of his 'liberalism' (in loose translation) which should be an eye-opener: The low-born are not entitled to perform any sacrifice. It is not something which one can perform by virtue of the material wealth that one possesses. Everyone should follow the course of action prescribed for the different varnas (that is, broadly, castes)....The low-born ought to understand the Brahman by taking recourse to the epics and legends only (Commentary on the Brahma Sutra-s, 1.3.36). Not to be left behind, Raghavendratirtha, the much venerated miracle-man of the Madhva tradition in his "Tattvamanjari" (144) has said all that Shankara has said about the Shudras. He, however, goes a step further to point out that Jaanashruti of the Chandogya Upanishad was not a Shudra, for he possessed a chariot which he could not have done had he been a Shudra! Nothing, therefore, could prevent Raikva from imparting sublime knowledge to him.

The intellectual acrobatics that Shankara, Ramanuja, Madhva and many other Indian philosophers willingly resorted to was occasioned not by any demand of philosophy but by the dogmatic concern for justifying and consolidating social hierarchy which is not an ennobling function of philosophy. If anything, philosophy has the unenviable task of serving humanity by upholding equality, rationality and happiness. To suggest that in the 'ultimate sense' happiness so called is only unhappiness is to be clever by half because even the Bhagavad Gita speaks of the worldly imperatives when it acknowledges 'lokasamgraha' (norms of the actual world) as a value. The Lokayata School of philosophy had no need for such crafty arguments and rationalisation. The Lokayatika, that is, a follower of the Lokayata School, had reason on his side when he boldly accused his accuser of non-philosophical considerations while discussing philosophy. The deft strokes of Debiprasad Chattopadhyaya have restored the right of the Lokayata School to stand head and shoulder above many another Indian school of philosophy while also buttressing the philosophical schools of Samkhya, Vaisheshika and Nyaya. Little wonder, therefore, that shaken savant unsuccessfully moved a resolution once at an All India Philosophical Congress stating that the 'pernicious influence of Debiprasad Chattopadhyaya must be cried a halt to' in order to save Indian Philosophy. Unfortunately for him, history is not on his side. There is no 'pernicious influence' to fear from Debiprasad. All that he meant to do was to drive some sanity into the heads of students of Indian Philosophy. Nobody claims that he succeeded a hundred per cent in this endeavour. But as Bhavabhuti assured us a long time ago, the world is vast and time endless. Kaalohyayam niravadhih vipulaa cha prithvi. History does not run out of time and the time of Lokayata will dawn one day.

Need for an Alternative Vision of Development for Bangalore

C. Balakrishnan, President, Karnataka Progressive Forum

Situational Analysis

Bangalore was once a clean, beautiful, garden city with salubrious climate. It was a city of the peaceful, peace-loving and with a leisurely pace of life. It was a place where gentleness, tolerance, accommodation, honesty, hospitality, warmth and sharing were the accepted modes of behaviour. There were values of simplicity and ordinary life of spirituality here. But now the city has transformed into an ugly, busy, garbage city, devoid of greenery. It has lost its humane qualities of life and become a place of market fundamentalism, corruption, cut-throat competition with an attitude of individualism. It has become a soulless city where the pursuit of material comforts has become the goal of life. Bangalore has the dubious distinction of being the fastest growing city in the whole of Asia. The population of Bangalore has increased from 40 lakhs in the year 1991 to 90 lakhs at present. The same is expected to grow to 100 lakhs by the year 2015. This abnormal growth of population has come about because of the path of development pursued by the government since independence.

Recent growth of the city

The city is facing a multi-dimensional crisis. Beneficiary of the mixed economic model of development, the city had a large number of institutions of higher learning and excellence, defense establishments and Public Sector Enterprises (PSEs) of the Central Government. This sound foundation paved the way for the creation of a scientific, technological and managerial intelligentsia in the place. The trade unions in the PSEs were able to obtain higher wages, housing, healthcare, transportation and social security for the workers. Now Bangalore is considered as one of the seven or eight intellectual capitals of the world. Five lakh jobs out of the twenty lakh well-paid jobs created in the IT sector all over the country are in Bangalore alone due to the availability of skilled manpower, belonging to the highly affluent and elite sections of society. Bangalore is also a significant beneficiary of the globalising process as several lakhs of jobs through business process outsourcing (BPO) from USA and other Western countries have been created. However, this positive development hides several negative trends.

Urban Bias in Development

The Bangalore-centric development pattern in Karnataka in the last few decades has been at the cost of the other towns and especially of the rural areas. Decline in public investments in rural/agricultural sector has ruined the rural economy and pauperised the rural people resulting in their large scale suicides. The neglect of the rural and the agrarian crisis in the state has led to the poor migrating to Bangalore in search of work, wages and livelihood. The influx of migrants has put great strain on the city's infrastructure. In addition, construction boom has attracted about five lakh workers from the other parts of the country. There is a severe crisis in transport, infrastructure, housing, drinking water, power, health care, law and order etc. Attempts are made to solve the infrastructure crisis through massive borrowings from the Centre and various financial institutions, local and international, like World Bank, Asian Development Bank, HUDCO, KUIDFC etc., to construct huge flyovers, metro rails, parking lots, shopping malls and multi-storied housing complexes. The loans available in astronomical sums will come in the form of consultancy, technology, project management and construction contracts to MNCs. Apart from generating huge profits for the foreign institutions and their local collaborators, the loans will place heavy burdens of repayment. Governments have miserably failed to get these loans on our own terms. The loans come with conditionalities requiring privatisation of essential public services, payment of users' fees and reduction of subsidies which make these services inaccessible and unaffordable even more than before for poor communities. The loan burdens are undemocratic, more so because these investments are also made without involvement of the local bodies and local people and are not subject to public scrutiny, review and accountability. Participatory democracy is the need of the hour. It is welcome sign that the Federations of Residential Welfare Association (RWA) are demanding recognition and a voice in the operation of funds. The present system is the hot bed of wholesale corruption.

Skewed Development

A section of the migrants to the city have belonged to the highly skilled sectors. The city has another section of migrants-unskilled, poorer classes working in construction, road-laying, domestic labour, vending and hawking. The city's development of infrastructure has however been geared to meet the demands only of the affluent migrants. The permission given for 100 per cent FDI in the construction industry has escalated land prices and made them beyond the reach of even the middle class. Only a small percentage of the available land is inhabited by the lower and middle classes and people living in slums, whereas a large percentage is occupied by the upper classes.

This kind of huge infrastructure development in terms of highways and flyovers promotes a lifestyle based on private, individual transport and is at the cost of other more desirable social infrastructure. Thus while flyovers and highway are being given plenty of resources, the same degree of resources are not being set apart for making public transport more efficient, for constructing workers' colonies or for strengthening public provisioning for education and health which benefit the poor.

Displacement and loss of livelihoods

Productive resources and wealth are in the hands of ever fewer companies and persons. This is most apparent in the liberalisation of land reform and urban land ceiling laws which allow the government to acquire land in unlimited quantity in the expanding borders of Bangalore at throw away sums, under the 'Law of Eminent Domain' for huge projects such as the Devanahalli International Airport, BMIC (Bangalore-Mysore Infrastructure Corridor) project, IT Corridor, etc., without a public consultation process. We are yet to see the impact of New Land Acquisition Act replacing old Land Acquisition Act of 1894. This results in the displacement of small and marginal farmers in the peri-urban areas and transfer of their land into more powerful and affluent hands, such as the sunrise sectors of IT and BT, builders and non-agriculturists. Most of these investments are made without involvement of the local bodies. Under the impact of neo-liberal policies, jobs have been abolished in the PSEs and government, through voluntary retirement schemes and replacement by contractual and casual labour. The once thriving small-scale industry has been destroyed through destruction of its jobs through opening of markets. The net result is that the jobs lost for the poorer sections far outweigh the jobs gained by the elite sections, leading to jobless growth. While skilled workers in IT and BT sectors get astronomical sums as salaries, those engaged in unskilled, casual and contractual jobs are being deprived even minimum wages. The problem of space for carrying on the livelihoods of the poor and migrants, such as vending and hawking, is also severe as more and more public space is acquired for parking of cars while vendors and hawkers are made illegal and pushed out of existence. Pressure to evict slum-dwellers living on expensive, inner-city land and pushing them to outlying areas, distancing them from their places of livelihood is tragic.

Corruption & Criminalisation of Politics

There is growing corruption, criminalisation of politics and virtual collapse of governance making it incapable of efficient delivery of public services to citizens. The present representative democracy has become dysfunctional with arbitrary power patronage and self-seekers taking the place of people-centered politics and policies. Money-power and muscle-power decide elections. Representative democracy packaged in caste-based vote bank has reached its dead end. Electoral reforms and reforms in the functioning of political parties in spite of a clamour for it are not taking place. The ability of the middle class to pay their way through bribes for their necessities has made them indifferent towards public issues and elections. This has paved the way for criminals and anti-social elements filling the political space and getting entrenched in the power structure by making false promises and exploiting the slum dwellers and lower middle class who are their only vote banks. Ownership of resources, land and productive assets are in the hands of land mafia, corrupt politicians, contractors and bureaucracy. Thousands of acres of government land worth hundreds of crores of rupees are cornered by them. These forces have lured and cheated SC/STs to part with the land and other assets allotted to them by the government. Politicians are only the frontal face of the contractors. Contractors have taken over all major political parties. Despite valiant efforts on the part of the Lok Ayukta to expose corruption, it has been ensured that the institution of the Lok Ayukta does not have adequate powers to bring the guilty to book. Orderly growth of industry and economic and social development of the city will be further jeopardised unless politics is cleansed.

Lack of People's Participation

A top-down approach continues to prevail despite the 74th Constitutional Amendment calling for urban local self governance with people's participation. Many of the mandatory requirements of the 74th Amendment, such as the setting up of a Metropolitan Planning Committee for Bangalore including elected representatives, has not taken place. Instead, para-state agencies, such as BMRDA, BDA, BWSSB, etc., with no accountability to the local elected body, continue to perform the planning functions for Bangalore. Also, several functions related to the basic needs of citizens, such as food security, employment, labour rights, primary education, primary health, and social welfare continue to be in the hands of the line departments of the state government rather than the urban local body. The ward committees, foreseen in the 74th Constitutional Amendment and meant to perform decentralised functions and bring in proximity and accountability of the local body to the citizens, are non-functional. Though the Right to Information Act exists, transparency of the government regarding development works to citizens is yet to become a routine matter. On the other hand, the government has been promoting the setting up of parallel structures, such as the Bangalore Agenda Task Force, in the name of people's participation, which is a body representing only the corporate sector, setting an agenda to serve only its interests. The other stakeholders in the city, especially the poor women workers' groups, various social movements and grassroots groups find no place on these bodies. However, several middle class residents' associations and citizens' movements and NGOs working on civic issues have been playing a positive role in the recent period in empowering citizens to make local governments more accountable.

Environmental Degradation

The transformation that Bangalore has undergone has made a direct assault on its environment, affecting its natural resources, weather, climate, flora and fauna. The city is now warmer by four to five degrees; it has lost about six species of birds; its greenery, especially the roadside trees and the "green belt", is continually under assault; its lakes have all but disappeared or are choked with pollution. Its air is noxious from the fumes of lakhs of vehicles. The noise pollution has reached an unbearable level. Life is stressful due to endless traffic snarls and resultant road-rage. All this has given rise to several pollution-related diseases. Bangalore is facing severe water crisis. While its own local resources of water, from Thippagondanahalli and other sources are drying up, Cauvery water is being brought at an enormous cost to Bangalore, denying it to hundreds of villages on either bank of the river. Within the city too, its distribution is grossly unjust with several slums being deprived of water or having to pay exorbitant sums for it while others use it wastefully for non-drinking purposes. Though Bangalore's roads are flooded each time it rains, its groundwater is being depleted at a very high rate due to lack of recharge.

Cultural Alienation

A more insidious fall-out of the development paradigm pursued is the promotion of acquisitive hedonism, selfishness and individualism, citizens' apathy in social, cultural and political engagement, the building of exclusive enclaves of the rich and cultural homogenisation of the western kind leading to alienation and loss of traditional and historical cultural identity of the city. Despite the material abundance, spiritual emptiness, decline in human values, break-up of families, neglect of old people, stress and depression are also visible, with suicides increasing among middle class urban youth. Growing violence against women is one of the manifestations of this consumerism driven by the media and marketers. The craze for easy money has led to increasing social and economic crimes, murders, dacoities, kidnaps and rapes.

Overall Vision:

There is need for a new alternate vision and search for a development model for Bangalore based on humanism and living in harmony with nature. That vision has to be inclusive where :

- the political, social and developmental factors, especially the urban bias, causing migration to the city along with loss of livelihood and displacement in rural areas are addressed.
- development is participative, pro-poor, pro-women and in harmony with nature; a lifestyle that respects Bangalore's environment, its natural resources and its rich flora and fauna is promoted; Bangalore's growth is limited to a sustainable level defined by its ecological carrying capacity;
- the rule of law, sovereignty of the people, a system of governance that ensures devolution of power, people's right to self –rule and control over resources, prevails; support is given to the local economy, a healthy degree of self-respect and national spirit is cultivated and national honour is upheld;

- human rights including the right to development of all are protected without discriminations based on class, caste, gender, language, religion;
- the values of shared concern, social justice, and humanity determine the life of the community; moral and spiritual values are resurrected to halt growing dehumanisation; synthesis is evolved between science and spirituality, modernity and tradition, functionality and aesthetics;
- diverse personal beliefs and cultural practices that do not violate the human rights of others are promoted and protected; the duty to protect the human rights of others is as valued and practiced, individually and collectively, as the enjoyment of one's own human rights; the various linguistic, religious and other elements giving it its composite culture are protected and nurtured and its diverse people live together in harmony respecting their differences and celebrating their commonalities;
- the necessary institutions are created which facilitate citizens' right to information, and transparency and accountability from the state;

Specific Goals

To make Bangalore a humane city where:

- Its growth is restricted by development of surrounding small and medium towns and cities; migration from rural areas is curbed through massive public investment in agriculture and rural development; inalienable right of the people to basic needs including food, clothing, shelter, health, education, social security and productive work are met as a first call on the city's resources;
- there is full guarantee of employment for at least 200 days of the year to all who seek work; workers are ensured humane and dignified conditions of work with respect to all core labour standards, including provision of social security; those unable to work, the destitute and the homeless, are

provided social assistance to lead a life of dignity; migrants are recognised as sovereign people with sovereign identities and are provided guarantee of protection, dignity and access to basic services;

- compulsory accessible, affordable (free to the downtrodden) and quality elementary education is provided to all children between 6 and 14 years; affordable primary healthcare that is accessible to all; provision of basic amenities such as child care, water, sewage and sanitation to all take precedence over less urgent needs;
- decentralised structures to ensure that citizens have control over and participate in the planning process, outcome and evaluation of development and governance of their areas; each municipal ward functions as a self-reliant community having full powers to take decisions over its affairs and has control over local resources; all loans, aid, trade and investment agreements and instruments are subjected to uniform standards for negotiations and public scrutiny by elected representatives and people to ensure transparency and accountability;
- effective social control and a corporate social responsibility standard is formulated to govern all investments; social infrastructure for health and education and essential services such as water, power and transport will, as far as possible, remain in the public domain; optimum and equitable utilisation of resources for the benefit of the people, providing them adequate space to influence and participate in decisions on resource use and management, is provided; local economy of labor-intensive, small and medium enterprises through people's markets are promoted;
- the rights of women and children, religious, language, sexual and other minorities, the physically and mentally challenged, are given special protection; the family as bedrock of civilisation is strengthened, and old infirm are treated with love and compassion; work ethics, truth, love,

compassion and spirituality are cultivated and the unity and sanctity of life is recognised;

- wealth is tinged with charity, politics with ethics, learning with humility, power with compassion; the composite cultural identity of Bangalore is preserved and spiritual pursuits actively promoted.

Mission For Bangalore Citizens:

- Provide a broad inclusive platform for exchange of views for all organisations, groups and individuals who have a genuine interest in the equitable and sustainable development of the city & prepare a People's Charter/manifesto/agenda through a process of broad based consultation among all sections;
- Become a forum for the study, research, and documentation of the development of the city and its people and disseminate its findings; provide a forum for information, dissemination, awareness creation, debate, informed choice and consensus building with regard to the plans, policies, budgets and investments with regard to the development of the city;
- Ensure that policies of liberalisation, privatisation and globalisation are not pursued at the cost of basic entitlements of the marginalised to their lives and livelihood; mobilise people's power, individually and collectively, to carry out campaigns in favour of alternative policies agreed upon; Carry out advocacy with those in position of power and ability to influence decision making to create political will and commitment to realise a more sustainable development of the city;
- Lobby for strengthening, through amendment, the 74th Constitutional Amendment on urban decentralisation and power to the people in its true spirit; press for the formation of the Metropolitan Planning Committee for Bangalore as mandated under the 74th amendment; press for the transfer of necessary funds functions and functionaries of BBMP to

enable to become a genuine institution of local self government; demand creation of institutions/platforms for tri-monthly interaction between the government (elected representatives, officials and service providers) and the general public, at the city, range and ward level (ward sabhas); through these interactive platforms press for the implementation of the People's Charter manifestos/agenda in a phased and time-bound manner at all levels; to create for bottom-up visioning, planning and participatory budgeting by the people in every ward;

- Conduct training programme for empowering citizens to undertake the functions of planning, implementing, monitoring and auditing work in their respective wards; undertake studies and create awareness and concern about the problems of the differently abled and their integration with the mainstream; undertake studies to identify slums build data-base on the working and living conditions of the slum dwellers, their access to amenities and services, their employment level, status of health, housing education, the special problems of women, girl children, extent of poverty malnutrition etc;
- Undertake awareness creation in slums on their rights and entitlements, various government schemes, use of right to information etc; enable slum dwellers to gain a critical awareness of their reality, undertake capacity building, promote organisation of self help groups, and facilitate problem-solving by slum dwellers themselves; conduct public hearings on the functioning of PDS, government schools and hospitals, implementation of various government schemes, slum development work etc. in collaboration with organisations of slum dwellers.

Immediate and Urgent Task:

Contrary to earlier commitments the Chief Minister Siddaramiah has stated that the city should go to vertical growth only to clear real estate sector's mammoth projects that are awaiting clearance. But environmentalists and city planners are flabbergasted as the city has already reached saturation point. In the interest of all citizens of Bangalore should rise to the occasion and defeat the new move of the government to save Bangalore from further ruin and chaos.

Scientific Temper in the age of STR

Anil Rajimwale

It was the industrial age which basically inaugurated the era of modern sciences and of scientific temper. It is little realised that revolution based on machine changed not only our way of life but also our world outlook. Similarly, present-day STR (Scientific and Technological Revolution) based on electronics is again bringing about a qualitative change. Events preceding, in particular following, the industrial revolution, led to the emergence of new disciplines based upon discoveries in various fields of knowledge, such as mechanics, physics, chemistry, biology, sciences related with the study of heat, energy, 'work' of the machines, behaviour of gases, liquid and solids, and so on. Not only this; the outlook in the social fields also began to change, such as in economics, production, social sciences, history, etc. Thus, an age or era of scientific method began to emerge rapidly. The sciences provided solid scientific facts and proofs about the processes constituting the nature, society and human thought. It was also the era of cultural, artistic and literary renaissance. Gutenberg's invention of the printing press created the material basis for the dissemination of scientific information and knowledge. Art and culture flourished and spread throughout Europe and World.

It was an age of enlightenment and liberation: enlightenment about the new, and the new was coming up all the time, refreshing human intelligence and character, and liberation from the shackles of age-old ideas that had slowed down human development. Science and scientific ideas had to fight their way forward through age-old jungle of outdated ideas, darkness and superstitions. It was an age of titanic struggles between the old and the new, between mysticism and science. Scientists even paid with their lives for their discoveries and new ideas, were persecuted even for saying that the earth revolved round the sun!

Scientific method, instruments of knowledge and concepts gradually established themselves in the course of this struggle, and science became unassailable due to the experimental veracity of scientific truths. Industrial revolution and the consequent industrial age put reason firmly in the driver's seat of human thought. Thought had so far been unsure and confused, based on speculation. Not that there was no science, reason and realism in history. But that had a weak material ground, surrounded by a sea of speculation and superstition. The modern times established reason, scientific logic and scientific questioning on a firm terrain. Philosophy and world outlook took on new forms filled with new content. Philosophical materialism for the first time came into full bloom, backed by science. Even idealism acquired dialectical method. The way we looked at the world changed. Science removed the age-old veils of mystery over natural processes, so also over the social processes.

Knowledge about society became revolutionised. For the first time, it became clear that the human beings created their own tools for production, which became means and forces of production in the course of social development. Around the nature and use of tools was created society. Society, in fact, was created by the use of means of production, around which were created relations among people or relations of production, which in popular language is called society. We began for the first time to interpret society and history in objective and material terms. Sciences and scientific method revealed that society developed due to its own objective laws. It was found that nothing in the world, society and nature was stationary, everything was in motion, and therefore our ideas too constantly changed. The ideas were revealed as the reflection of the material world on our brains, and the social ideas as the reflection of the socio-economic structures, relations and activities. The world started to fall in proper places.

It was also revealed that the human beings made their own history, not in an arbitrary manner, not wishfully and willfully, and not in a subjective utopian way. They made history by following certain laws of motion of nature and society. What science revealed most was the fact that since everything was in motion, therefore, human society also constantly evolved. Certain types of tools led to the creation of certain societies in step by step manner through a change in human relations. These relations were the direct result of the kind of tools that were being used. This simple but fundamental fact and law was revealed only after the industrial revolution. State, nation, community, class, sections, democracy, thought and culture and civilisation were the product of certain interaction of nature and social relations.

Science in Post-independence India

Among the major issues after achieving freedom was the path of development to be adopted, political, economic and social. Science held a key place in the presentation as well as the solution of the questions before independent India. While a whole era of development passed in Europe and some other places, the colonial rule deprived India and other enslaved countries of the means of development and of development itself. It is a strange logic of imperialism and colonialism that while their countries performed feats of industrial and socio-economic growth and development, the same was denied to the countries where they ruled. Capitalism/imperialism do not allow the backward countries to develop industrially. India after independence faced the problems related with resistance from the western countries to its endeavour to develop along industrial and scientific lines. India faced a huge task of industrial and economic growth and development. Coupled with this problem was that of overcoming age-old resistance and survivals in form of obscurantism, traditionalism and a fall-back upon village economy. Centuries of colonial rule had disrupted India's economy including the traditional rural economy, and had released the forces of casteism and inward-looking localism. Development of science and technology was closely related with the path of industrialisation of the country.

Out of these dilemmas and problems, combined with the given international balance of forces, arose what has come to be known as the "Nehruvian framework'. One may or may not agree with Nehru on everything, but it goes to his credit that he firmly charted out a path of development for India, which was largely independent, self-reliant and at the same time cooperative with other countries. One of the main pillars of the Nehruvian path of development was the creation of scientific institutions and a huge pool of scientific personnel. After independence, India became one of the largest reservoirs of scientific institutions and personnel in the world. IITs, scientific laboratories and institutes like the CSIR, DRDO, ISRO, atomic energy establishments and such others were created. During Nehru's time 45 high level central laboratories in various fields were founded. They formed the backbone of scientific research in India. These developments were encouraged and helped by the development of a huge public sector in our country. The importance of public sector units is often under-estimated in India: HMT, BHEL, IDPL, SAIL, ONGC, Railways, Communications, Oil and Natural Gas and so on. The public sector and the scientific institutions have a close relationship, feeding each other. They laid down the basis of self-reliance in science, technology and economy. The recent launch of the 'Mangalyan' is a pointer in this direction.

Development of Productive Forces and Role of Science

It goes to the credit of the path followed in independent India that we see tremendous growth of the productive forces in our country. India really became one of the leading countries in the world in this field. It is due to these institutions that the country has been able to come out of the age-old backwardness and step into a new modern world, of course with its own problems. It is a leading country among the developing ones, and one of the fastest economies, contributing greatly to the BRICS grouping. This has been possible due to the great scientific and industrial base that has been created after independence, of course with the accompanying problems. It is contributing to the development of science all over the world in many fields. Science has become an important productive force in our country. That is why we are able to meet the electronics revolution much more successfully than many other countries. It will be erroneous to deny these achievements of India in the name of its drawbacks. Without them India would today be a subservient country, which it is not. It compares well with many advanced and other economies in some of the important fields.

Scientific Temper and Consciousness

With the development of economy and science, the question of scientific temper has come to the fore. Science demands scientific temper. It is assumed that with the development of sciences and modern methods, scientific temper will develop automatically. But it does not happen that way. Scientific development does create favourable scientific atmosphere, which spreads scientific ideas. At the same time, obscurantists distort scientific facts to their purpose. It has to be kept in mind that in the meantime, the world had gone through a whole series of fundamental scientific and technological innovations/developments, taking the society to progressively higher levels. Science, directly and through technology, had become part of our life, our necessity. But the two world wars also showed that it could be put to destructive usage. Besides, capitalism, and in particular its monopolist and imperialist sections, used science and its innovations more often against the interests of the people. The British rule in India underlined this point. So, the question was that with the development of industry, agriculture and economy in general, and with the use of new methods, how could science and technology be put to public use, in the interest of society. And here emerged the importance of science policy. It is a relatively new field of socio-economic and political field. It has grown out of the necessity of the newly liberated countries to create their own base and to get into the mainstream of industrial development and growth. The basic task before the developing countries was and is how to join the industrial age, direct from the various stages they were in.

This is a stupendous task, and calls for innovative and visionary policies. The post-second world war period first talked of peaceful usage of scientific know-how, which was very much required in case of, for example, atomic and nuclear field. It was a great dilemma. The question of disarmament and peaceful coexistence were direct result of attempts to solve these problems. Among others, they were attempts to channelise scientific development into peaceful and fruitful directions. Science policy has been one of the centre-points of discussions in post-independence India. The country no doubt has achieved much in the field of science and technology, and it would be a nihilist mistake to overlook the achievements, and cynicism to deny the great achievements. We have in our country people sincerely devoted to science and technology who really want to do a lot and with this view want need and demand certain facilities, which they generally find in the western countries or they feel are available there. This sincerity of the middle class scientific professionals cannot be doubted, and they must be put to the best use. We have produced some of the world's best scientists, who have left their mark on the scientific map of the world.

Therefore, creating favourable working conditions for the scientists and academics is among the keys to our development. Indianess and nationalism expresses through the work in this field which needs to be appreciated. This strengthens the Indian nation. At the same time, a lot remains to be done in this field. The question is directly related with education system and the policy framework of education. It is a fact that millions of people are deprived of elementary necessities and facilities in education, health, science, even in elementary means for simple living. Starvation, hunger, lack of clean water, jobs, and such other questions constantly hit our efforts and impact the life of common people. In other words, the question is how to put science and economy at the service of the people? It is a sad fact that our society is thus polarised into two opposites. And in that case we cannot make full use of the potentials of the society and economy. This involves the question of the path of development of our country.

Question of Scientific Temper and Outlook

It is in this context that the question of scientific temper assumes greater importance as we proceed forward. It is a complicated problem and needs to be tackled. India is burdened with age-old beliefs, most of them superstitious, obscurantist and outdated. The pursuit of science cannot be in isolation and in parallel with outdated ideas. In the course of its development science comes in conflict with the old ideas and notions. Mysticism and agnosticism do not go with scientific attitudes; in fact, they act as the drags on its development. Both of the latter trends try to slow down and prevent evolution of science, which is search for truth.

The growth of mass and electronic media is a contradictory process. It has given rise to the dissemination of both scientific and as well as non- and anti-scientific ideas. It is a clear example of use and misuse of new scientifically advanced means of mass communications. Therefore, the forces supporting science need to create their own space in the media and spread scientific viewpoint and facts through it. In other words, media is an important arena of battle of ideas, which can in no way be under-estimated.

Nehru was an atheist, and that was a great asset for the country. He could take decisions and interpret them and frame policies without too many shackles. But most of the others are not atheists. In a sense, it is not a necessary precondition for a scientist to be an atheist. Darwin was a religious person, a believer. Yet he followed the logic of science. And he did not hesitate to put his conclusions before the scientific community, though he and many other scientists had often to resort tactical retreat in the face of the 'public' outcry.

The point is science follows certain logic and argumentation, which flows from the scientific work being done. If one follows that, the work becomes scientific. One need not become irreligious immediately, though at some point many conclusions may fly in the face of religion and religious beliefs. Establishing scientific facts itself negates religious beliefs and religion.

The whole thing is a complicated question. To spread science, one has to repeatedly highlight the cause and effect relations and the scientific findings in and outside the laboratory. After all, sun rises in the east and sets in the west, and this is due to certain natural motions of the bodies. This simple scientific fact has become part of our life. The questions related with the 'whys' and 'hows' have to be inculcated into the mental makeup of the people. The processes have to be explained in detail. Doing that automatically leads one away from mysticism and towards scientific augmentation.

In other words, somewhere science has to be converted into clear-cut theory and the masses have to be educated in it. And here lies the weakness of those who advocate scientific temper. They are not doing enough to inculcate such a temper and consciousness. It is a struggle that has to be carried on at all levels, without of course, hurting the religious sentiments. Yet, it is a crucial struggle of ideas, notions and philosophy.

Scientific temper involves participation of the human being in the natural and artificial processes. The humans are and should be in the centre of activity. This is what needs to be inculcated. Millions of booklets and thousands of lectures are constantly needed for this campaign. It is strange to find the TV channels, even those claiming to be of 'science' propagating mystic, even ghost-stories. This has become a common feature. While it cannot be banned, it can and has to be countered. And here lies the problem and the complacency of those professing science and technology. If science and technology is the reality, then what 'we do' with our own hands and with tools and equipments is the reality, and not some mystic force.

'Mangalyan' and the host of satellites and rockets and missiles are nothing but the results of human endeavour, and not of some mystic force. In other words, such developments involve philosophical and logical struggles. And it is here that the scientists and those supporting science fall short of mark. It has to be driven home that it is the human beings, the government, the organisations and the policies that matter most. Without them the society and the country cannot go ahead. Mangalyan should be the occasion, for example, to propagate scientific outlook, and not just praise the event. It is a great development that astronomical discussions and gatherings have lately increased in connection with many celestial events.

Science versus Obscurantism

It is in the context of the developments in science and technology that the question of obscurantism and superstition becomes increasingly highlighted. At some point in the course of scientific and economic development, the problem of outdated and obscurantist outlook comes in the way of society's progress as a hurdle to its further march. Obscurantism and superstition are an anomaly in the modern times. It reflects a disjoint between our work in science and our social outlook, between the results of scientific work and the attitude to the events outside the field of science and technology.

What we need today is an assimilation of scientific facts, methods and discoveries in all the fields. We need a theoretical, ideological and scientific assault and criticism of all that is outdated, mystic and superstitious. Too much leeway has been provided to reactionary obscure ideas, which cloud our thought process. It is being done in order to further the reactionary socio-economic and political interests.

Here it would be in order to mention that even in the economically and industrially most advanced country, which also is almost the most advanced in science and technology, that is the US, a campaign has been run by the most reactionary and obscurantist circles to ban the discoveries of Charles Darwin. The event is a reflection of the frustration of a section of backward looking forces connected with the corporate and imperialist circles, who take recourse to pre-industrial, feudal and mystic superstitious ideas to justify their opposition to anything progressive.

Something similar is happening in our country too, though not exactly this way. But there is a sudden explosion in the electronic media and outside it of mysticism and obscurantism. This is the only way that the progress of science and technology can be opposed or slowed down. Otherwise all the 'secrets' of nature and reality will be revealed!

What is lacking in our country is the alertness of the scientific community and their responsibility to carry on a sustained campaign and to explain the real nature of things and processes, natural and social, to the people. There are no large-scale movements, efforts and campaigns, no 'social' reform type of efforts and so on. It does not mean that no efforts are being made. There are no doubt substantial efforts. But they are not enough, and they run in fits and starts.

The reactionary forces have reached with their obscurantism to the nooks and corners of the country. All sorts of organisations, socio-political campaigns are being run, literature being distributed, medieval and ancient practices being revived, history being distorted, and common ignorant people being appealed at the most ignorant and basest levels. They are physically going practically to every house in the villages. But let us not think that it is only the rural ignorant masses that are being appealed. The new rising consumerist middle class, most of which is educated, is also being seriously embroiled in this maelstrom of obscurantism.

Why is it happening and why they are succeeding? It is mainly because the historical bloc or front of those holding sane, rational and scientific outlook that was formed in the immediate post-independence India has broken down. At that time they had taken up the task of building India on a giant scale together. That effort was strongly helped on by a scientific approach. It was reflected in the syllabi at various stages of education: from lowest to the highest levels. Schools, colleges and universities and the institutions were being fast inculcated with new thinking, full of hopes, aspirations and optimism. Even though it was a small movement in scope and even when the country was largely agrarian-feudal, thought was filled with positive approach and real hope based on science and new outlook. And here we come to a very crucial question or problem.

Age of STR and Scientific Attitude

We have termed this paper at the beginning as 'scientific temper in the age of STR'. This is very important. We are not only talking of science of the industrial age or only of the recent past. That is very important, and we should carry the scientific tradition and scientific outlook built upon that whole age forward. At the same time, we are today going through the most rapid new technological revolution known as the STR. It calls for changes in many of the existing concepts. We must realise that science itself is a developing field. It changes constantly, with old concepts giving way to the new ones, formulations and hypotheses and concepts becoming obsolete, to be replaced by new ones. And this is a crucial point. The point is that those professing science and scientific temper must themselves become renewed conceptually, and assimilate the new in science itself as also in technology. Without it, the scientific temper is weakened if not lost.

When the computers arrived in India a few decades ago, there were many in the progressive movement who actually opposed them! The grounds given were many, but they ended up actually opposing introduction of new technologies and sciences and thus progress itself. This is happening even now. And this is a disaster. It deprives us of the very tool with which we fight the obscurantist forces! Computers and electronics have inaugurated a new age of scientific and technological revolution, higher, broader and deeper than the industrial revolution. At the same time, the revolution is the most rapid in human history, causing most changes in the shortest time scale, as never before in history. Electronics has penetrated every nook and corner of our life. This fact needs to be used to fight conservative, reactionary and obscurantist forces/outlook.

Therefore, it is obvious that we have to study and assimilate the STR and the ICR, both theoretically and practically. This involves fresh study of the new discoveries being presently made. New facts are coming to the fore not only daily but hourly. In other words, our existing stock of scientific facts is becoming inadequate and insufficient. This has to be understood by those who claim to propagate scientific temper/outlook. The process involves a deep study of new means and methods in science and technology, and at the same time of the new theories and practices. Many theories are becoming obsolete and need to be given up. Science is already rejecting several outdated concepts. The problem arises when those doing social work and at the same time abiding by scientific method or outlook refuse themselves to give up old/obsolete outlook, concepts and theories.

This is already happening and is doing immense harm to the movement of spreading scientific temper.

In other words, you cannot spread scientific outlook and objective method basing solely upon the pre-electronics science and technology, on what is known as the industrial methods alone. We have to move forward towards post-industrial methods, assimilate relativity and quantum science and quantum philosophy and so on. We have to be one with the new social sections that are emerging with the spread of STR, the sections working with new tools, equipments and electronic means.

A lot of mystical nonsense is being spread under the cover of electronics, quantum and relativity, regarding discoveries in the space science and about the new galaxies and so on. The field has virtually been left open for this new kind of mysticism, agnosticism and obscurantism. A new kind of obscurantism is being spread, having wide appeal, based on new scientific discoveries. This has been made possible because those with scientific outlook are proving to be slow to react to the new and latest discoveries. If you are indifferent, and even oppose the new, under whatever pretext, then you are giving way to new kind of obscurantism. Mysticism is built not only on the science that is past, but also on the basis of the new science. To base one solely on the old sciences is also a kind of obscurantism and mysticism. The new sciences are being used (misused) to justify mysticism and throw-back to the ancient thought as a justification.

The scientific social activists should be in the forefront to master and advocate new science, support new technologies in a healthy and robust manner, and become representatives of everything that is new, emerging, scientific and progressive in social and scientific and technological development. They should stop treating the new technology/technologies as something belonging to the MNCs/ corporates alone. They should treat it as people's technology (and science). The other forces like the MNCs and the obscurantist forces actually misuse these developments.

Therefore, scientific temper today also means assimilation and propaganda and educating the masses in the latest scientific development. It also involves sharp debates on scientific world outlook, philosophy and scientific temper. Every person needs to be approached to make him/her aware of the primacy of scientific discoveries and laws, and of the need to develop and use new technologies. This will help people overcome mystic philosophy and any kind of mysticism. The discoveries in the outer space and galaxies as also the events like the space station and Mangalyan etc. will help people to come out of mysticism and to take recourse to the concrete facts for the good of the society and the individual.

A large-scale and widespread theoretical, ideological and people-oriented practical offensive based upon science and technology is the need of the hour. The objective conditions favour scientific outlook, but if no or little initiative is taken to propagate the new discoveries and to show how they can be used for people's good, then these developments cannot be converted into a social force. Many exposures of various 'gurus', so called 'saints' and 'sadhus' are already taking place. This has helped to expose the obscurantist forces to an extent. But it needs to be turned into an all-pervasive social movement. All the people favouring scientific temper need to come together to speed up spread of new scientific outlook.

Poverty and Agricultural Growth: The Uneasy Partners

Dr R. S. Deshpande

The agrarian structure of the Indian economy emerged out of the refractory land tenure system that had a long and deep rooted feudal history (Dantwala, 1996; Deshpande, 2003). Three specific indicators of the agrarian structure continued to dominate the debate all along. First, the density of small and marginal farmers and the shrinking size of holding and the reasons behind the transformation. This placed weak farmers away from the market, unviable for adoption of new technology and therefore stuck to the tenterhooks of the State programmes. The State promised and worked for the mere survival of the weak farmers exactly on the threshold of poverty. The pace of marginalisation was quite fast during the last two decades and that placed a large number of peasants in resource poor situation to push them below poverty line. Second, there has always been high density of agricultural workers (marginal farmers and agricultural labourers) with little bargaining power at their control. The transfer of labour from agriculture to non-agricultural sectors (Lewisian process) is quite slow and wherever such transfers are taking place the welfare of the migrating labour has been in peril. The immiserisation of the migrant labourers across the length and breadth of the country is quite visible. Third, the increased pressure on the household economy (due to increased share of cash needs in the presence of new technology) and the imperfections of markets together caused a large share of farmers to give away farming and join the ranks and files of labourers

(Bhalla, 2006). All these constitute a pre-condition of the distress in the sector.

Immediately after independence land reforms were taken up and these had a myriad story. These institutional reforms did not have any unexpected outcomes and if the prevailing agrarian structure is analysed, it comes out that all of these were half baked policy initiatives. Thereafter, the agrarian issues were dealt more symptomatically and the policy interventions were frequently accompanied by severe negative externalities. Food insecurity was addressed with the rice-wheat technology (that was not the food of the poor) that provided food grains, but in the process inflicted neglect on coarse cereals and consequently the farmers growing these crops also suffered. Development of irrigation was taken up through surface and groundwater sources and the externalities were soon realised. Market led commercialisation process was introduced and that threatened to bypass the most vulnerable among the farmers. In all these initiatives the agricultural labourers remained mute partners, always to suffer the distress but rarely could partake in the gains. The current phase of agrarian crisis has also raised many such questions and specifically some of them directly affecting the vulnerable in the sector. As a routine drill a new policy package has been worked out and this focuses on credit, technology and input delivery system. This package emerged mainly from an ill-founded assumption of a 'technological fatigue' (Narayanamoorthy, 2007; Deshpande, 2005). Basically, it does not flow from the ground and stays in the top-down framework as usual.

Among the questions to be answered and issues to be discussed here we begin from the responsibility of the State to the functioning of the market. The Constitution of India in its Directive Principles under article 38(2) provides *"The State shall in particular, strive to minimize the inequalities in income and endeavour to eliminate inequalities in status, facilities and opportunities, not only amongst individuals but also amongst groups of people residing in different areas or engaged in different vocations."* Farmers as a group today feel let down by the policies of the State that puts them relatively in severe disadvantageous position compared to their peers in other sectors. This is made abundantly clear by many analysts in the recent past (Ghosh, Jayati, 1997; Bhalla, 2006; Chand and Jha 2001). In other words, even if the State is not directly discriminating against the farmer as a group, but the policies are sufficiently provocative in increasing the welfare gap between the farmers, agricultural labourers on one hand and the remaining workers on the other.

Genesis of the Crisis

India's agricultural sector cannot be compared with that of many countries especially those significantly participating in the international trade. Among the major constraints faced by the sector prominent is the low average size of holdings as a base for production and high density of uneconomic holdings. About 99 million small and marginal farmers inhabit the sector with only a small proportion of farmers generate some marketable surplus. During the last five decades the rural population has grown about 2.49 times but the number of agricultural labourers has grown more than that (almost by 3.91 times). That increased their density in rural sector. The market conditions in factor as well as product markets are far from satisfactory; and finally India never had a sustained presence in the international trade to participate pro-actively in the process of globalisation. Besides these, the gains from trade hardly percolate to the agricultural labour. These overt constraints provoked the uses of terminology like 'level playing field' while analysing comparative performance of India vis-à-vis its trading partners. It is quite clear that the production as well as domestic and international trade environment in India is not comparable to many of its competitors (Nayyar and Sen, 1994). Therefore, the significant question crops up whether agriculture and agricultural labourer will always be at the receiving end? How this should be avoided, is a major policy issue to wrestle with.

Over the last five decades, Indian agricultural sector performed under various constraints. The performance during late sixties, mid seventies and early eighties helped to overcome the problem of food insecurity. The performance of the last two years of eighties was remarkable and that was not exceeded in the following decade (See Figure 1). GDP from agriculture grew at an annual rate of 3.4 per cent during 1980s, but it registered only 1.8 per cent growth between 1997-98 and 2000-02. As can be seen from figure 1, the decade of nineties has recorded positive growth in GDP in most of the years except two years, but the post 1997 situation is bad. The peak achieved at the end point in the decade of eighties leads to a conclusion that nineties was a dismal decade. One point however is quite clear that the performance during eighties of the sector was quite supportive, but that in early nineties was not bad. Similarly, there is a decline in area, production and productivity of all crops. While area under all crops has shown a marginal increase in growth rate during 1990s, production and yield have shown decreasing/stagnating trends. A comparison of the growth rates in the decades of eighties and nineties can be quite deceptive and therefore, we have resorted to view the trends over the entire period. Figure 2 present this picture.

Figure 1: Growth in GDP Originating From Agriculture

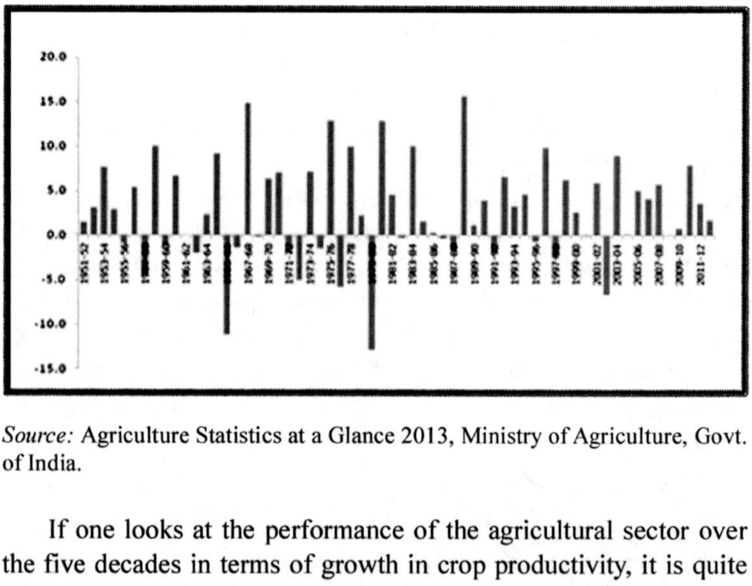

Source: Agriculture Statistics at a Glance 2013, Ministry of Agriculture, Govt. of India.

If one looks at the performance of the agricultural sector over the five decades in terms of growth in crop productivity, it is quite clear that the sector has witnessed alternative cycles of growth and stagnation. The performance between 1980 and 1995 was quite ideal but after that a phase of stagnation seems to have emerged again strongly. This is more visible in the non-foodgrain sector than in the foodgrains.

As among the crops the picture is not very encouraging. The productivity of most of the crops seems to have stagnated at about 1999 onwards with little growth beyond that. The growth is recorded only in the case of wheat, rice and a fluctuating performance of groundnut. Further among these rice and groundnut seem to have rarely caught a plateau. This seems to be a matter of serious concern, especially when we are leading a growth strategy from globalisation and trade angles. The worst sufferers are the farmers growing the crops, other than wheat, paddy and groundnut. The performance of the agricultural sector on the production and productivity front is not very satisfactory. It is well documented that the stagnation is rather due to failure or plateauing of the technology but a lot of it is due to market support for the crops. All these processes have a significant negative impact on the poverty situation in the sector.

Agriculture and Poverty

Sir M. Viswesvaraya in his outline of the scheme for Rural Reconstruction in India expressed that agriculture sector has become the mainstay of the poor due to structural problems. Professor V. M. Dandekar reiterated this statement after five decades without any change. It is now a known fact that across the sectors, agricultural sector has a very high density of poor. This is one historical truth but rarely any attempt is made to look into its genesis, emergence and highlight the differences with other sectors. When Professor Theodore Schultz analysed the transformation of traditional agriculture, he argued about the low level equilibrium (Guatemala and Senapur) and necessity of augmenting the human capital improvement. Schultz also highlighted the 'near zero' marginal productivity in agriculture. Over years situations in agricultural sector have not changed substantially. One can now also affirm that the seed of poverty in agricultural can be located with the capital starvation and the near stagnated marginal value productivity. Rural poverty ratio has always stayed higher than urban poverty ratio and constitutes larger number of the total poor. This result is not simply due to the distribution of population or lack of employment opportunities only. There are some inbuilt cultural peculiarities of agricultural sector that force the inhabitants of the sector to stay poor. Poverty estimates for rural areas could be the best and nearest proxy. The genre of the technology has also contributed significantly towards this situation. We do not contest the fact that poverty has declined in rural areas but would rather search for the residual persistence of poverty.

Poverty: Rural and Urban Scenario

Agriculture emerged with the civilisation as the only livelihood vocation besides hunting. Therefore, the emergence of the term agriculture deals with 'culture'. Its basic function in the early years was that of the only livelihood support system and thus self-sufficiency. Markets did not emerge very strongly till about a hundred years before. During initial development experience livelihood concerns came as the first decision making criteria in the farmers' decision calculus. The remarks of Professor Dandekar came from his logical view of the nature of the work and production organisation associated with agriculture as a typical livelihood system. The argument begins with the seasonal production cycle in crop husbandry. Farmer begins the initial operation more on a clean slate as the summer months would have no direct earnings and the marriage as also the festive seasons of the summer will bring the household economy at a critical threshold with cash crunch. The cultivation begins with the borrowing of 'Taccavi Loans (crop Loans)' and farmer continues the farm operations in the company of the usual risk factors including monsoon. Cultivation operations continue and supported either through the savings of the last year or from fresh borrowings. After harvesting the meek market participation of the agriculturists decides the income flow. Over generations for Indian agriculturists, farming becomes a way of life. Initially, farmer borrows to meet the shortage of funds for the crop cultivation and takes that obvious risk of the crop failure which is associated with more than 20 per cent probability anywhere in the country. A farmer has no alternative but to confront the factor and the product markets with least information and in both arenas farmer is the price taker and not a price leader. That makes a critical difference. Market risks compound the other risks associated with cultivation. It is really a wonder that despite the fact that about 40 per cent of the farmers expressed their preference to quit farming, they continue in the profession till a break point. Finally, it is poverty and association of land based hope that keeps them company in the profession. This has been accepted as a cultural reality by the farmers by now. The logical arguments indicate significant stress on the farmers' income flows and hence poverty will be an unavoidable outcome. But then the question comes as how rural poverty is declining?

Figure 2: Decline in Poverty Ratios: 1973-74 to 2011-12

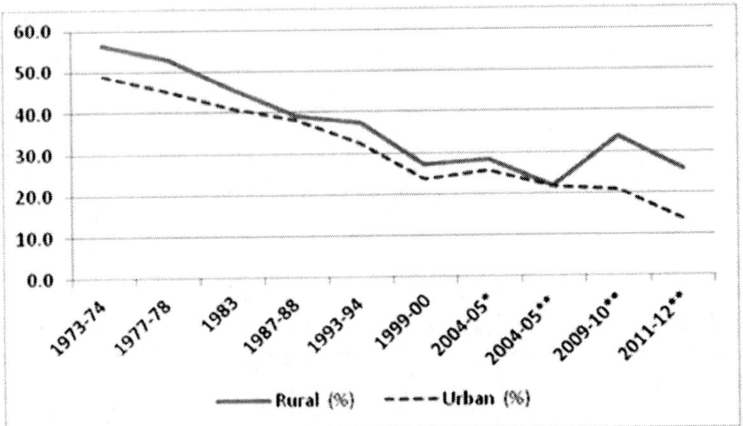

It is well known fact that the quality of absolute poverty in India is not homogenous across sectors or regions. The regional differences are always brought forth in terms of urban and rural poverty both in calorie terms or income accrued. Rural India always stayed at higher level of poverty head count as compared to urban India, not so much due to the availability of food but largely due to access to food. Almost entire food production of India comes from rural areas but when it comes to distribution of consumption, the urban total consumption dominates. The trends in poverty by now indicate that poverty ratios are declining both in rural and urban areas. Figure 2 based on official data of Planning Commission shows declining trend in rural as also in the urban areas. But some subtle differences are interesting. First, the rural poverty ratio stays above the urban areas all the years, even though the growth of urban areas through rural-urban migration is significant. Second, the trend in poverty ratio is declining more smoothly in urban areas as against the fluctuations in the rural areas. This gives a hint that the dependence on monsoon (year to year fluctuations in income flows) plays a critical role in rural poverty decline. The decline of poverty staggers even with a little shock to the agricultural sector but probably urban areas have a cushion effect against this. That is not a big deal of an observation, but during the same stress period the urban poverty still keeps with a declining trend, indicating the availability of the same amount of food in urban India when rural India (producer of total food) confronts food stress.

Table 3: Changes in Workforce: 1991-2011

(Numbers in Lakhs)

	1991	2011	Change
Tot Workers	3141.3	4817.4	1676.1
Cultivators	1246.8	1186.9	-59.9
Agri Workers	859.9	1443.3	583.4

Source: Census of India 1991 and 2011.

The official poverty line of Rs 26 for rural and Rs 32 for urban areas (at 2010-11 prices) has been debated and commented by many. The comments came not only from political circles but equally attracted attention of the academics too. As a field worker and one who travels through rural areas more often I can vouch that 'bare' medical survival is possible with this amount in both rural and urban areas but that cannot be called as survival by any stretch of the meaning of the word. Even the destitute needs slightly higher amount to survive and given the poor safety nets in rural areas, it is quite insufficient even to survive. Let me not get into that debate now but I need to focus on the issue of the quality of rural poverty. In rural India where agriculture is the major occupation the cultivators and agricultural labourers are the two groups that are pre-dominant among the poor. Over the decades as per census of India definition share of 'cultivators' among the workers is declining and the share of 'agricultural labourer' is increasing.

This process indicates economic marginalisation of workers in rural areas and their degeneration in the status from cultivators to agricultural labourers. The decline of the poverty ratio therefore should be credited to the availability of that proverbial Rs 26 to remain afloat the line but probably just above it so that one sinks down at the slightest shock. The disappearing cultivator is a matter of concern. Table 1 shows that as per 1991 census India had 1246.8 lakh workers recorded as cultivators and this number has come down by 59.9 lakhs by 2011. This change in two decades means almost 3 lakh cultivators disappearing from the fold every year. They may get into the fold of 'Other workers' or become 'Agricultural labourer'. The increase in the number of agricultural workers is also substantial and there are enough reasons to believe that the cultivators would have changed to

Figure 4: Total Number of Operational holdings (in 000): 1970-71 to 2010-11

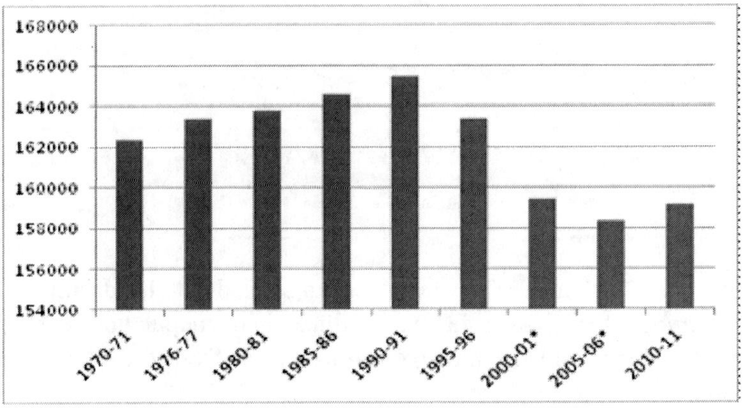

agricultural labourers. The process of marginalisation and swelling of the poverty at the bottom is severe among weaker social groups (Thorat Sukhadeo & Motilal Mahamallik (2005)].

This fact can also be corroborated with the agricultural census data. The figure 3 shows the changes in number of operational holdings as given in the agricultural census over years. There was some increase in the number of operational holding till Agricultural Census of 1990-91 but there is a sharp decline after that till the recent Agricultural Census. Across the agricultural censuses the area operated has also changed substantially. According to 1970-71 Agricultural census the number of marginal and small holdings were 49.6 million this has increased to 117.1 million. The area operated by the marginal and small holdings increased by 36.7 million hectares and the area under the medium and large holdings has reduced by 39.6 million hectares. As a result 29.97 lakh hectares seem to have

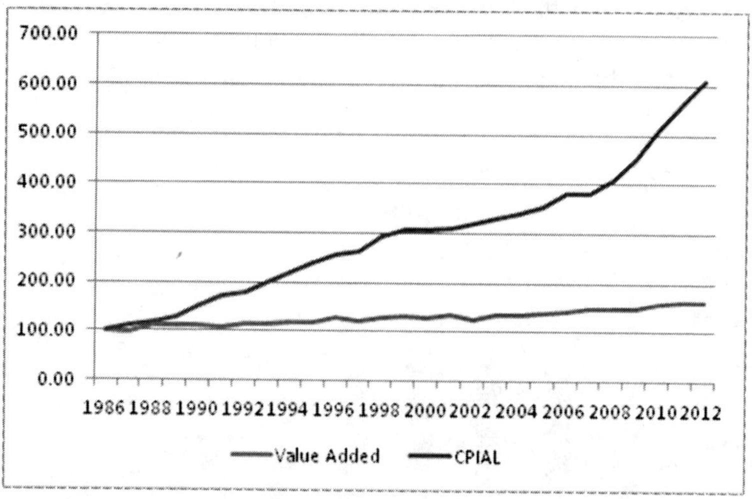

gone out of agriculture. This fact needs to be read with the decline in the number of cultivators that have reduced in the population census and the decline in the poverty ratio as seen from the Planning Commission data. There are only three possibilities. First, the agricultural income per hectare has increased as a result a large number of farmers, despite marginalisation of the size of holding, could cross the poverty barrier. That means farming has become remunerative! Second, if the farming is not remunerative; as indicated by the NSSO 59th round and other sources of data (*Deshpande, R.S.* and *Nagesh Prabhu* 2005), then only the increase in agricultural wages or the availability of other employment opportunities could have helped the farmers/agricultural workers to stay above poverty line. Real wages need to increase for that purpose. Third, there is a possibility of rural poor crossing the official poverty line but staying in the close neighborhood of that income threshold with the help of many ongoing schemes. This is the most probable reason explaining the clustering of persons just "Above Poverty Line" but just near the poverty threshold. The result is therefore deceptive and the dependence culture in the farm sector continues to haunt the sector.

Poverty and Regional Distribution

The hypothesis that poverty declines with agricultural growth was attempted by Montek Singh Ahluwalia (1978 and 1985). Ahluwalia concluds that: "The (second issue considered in this chapter) is the relationship between rural poverty and agricultural income levels per head. Three conclusions have emerged: (1) there is fairly strong evidence of an inverse relationship between agricultural income per head and the incidence of rural poverty, especially, if account is taken of lagged effects." Ahluwalia also cautions that reliance on growth alone may not reduce poverty. A simple piece of evidence is however interesting to note here. We took the data on value added to agriculture per agricultural worker at constant prices compiled by The World Bank and the index numbers of this data along with the index of CPIAL for the period 1986–2012 were plotted together (See Figure 4). It is quite revealing that the CPIAL is growing at quite a fast rate as compared to the value added. That possibly explains that agriculture alone cannot help in alleviating poverty and whatever reduction of poverty ratio visible in rural areas is from the sources other than agriculture. Across the states in India poverty has been varying. Keeping in view the hypotheses tested by Dharm Narain and later by Ahluwalia in the Essays in Honour of

Professor DharmNarain, we worked out simple correlations of important variables with per cent of rural poverty across states in India. Density of cultivators does not show high correlation but that of agricultural workers and labourers indicate that poverty goes closely with the density of this groups. Income generated from agriculture has not recorded the relationship but the growth rates during a short period 2007–12, clearly shows the correlation. The lower magnitude

Table 6: Rural Poverty Correlates

Variables	Corr Coeff.
Cultivators Per cent to total Workforce	0.03
Agri Labours Per cent to total Workforce	0.67
Agri Workers Per cent to total Workforce	0.64
Growth Rate in Per Capita Income-2007–12	-0.17
Growth Rate of Agriculture 2005–13	0.68
Per cent Share of Agricultural GSDP	0.23

Note: Data from Various Economic Surveys for Various Years, and Census of India. Only correlations above 0.6 are statistically significant at 5 per cent level.

Figure 7: Rural Poverty Ratio 2011 and Growth rates in Agriculture: 2005–13

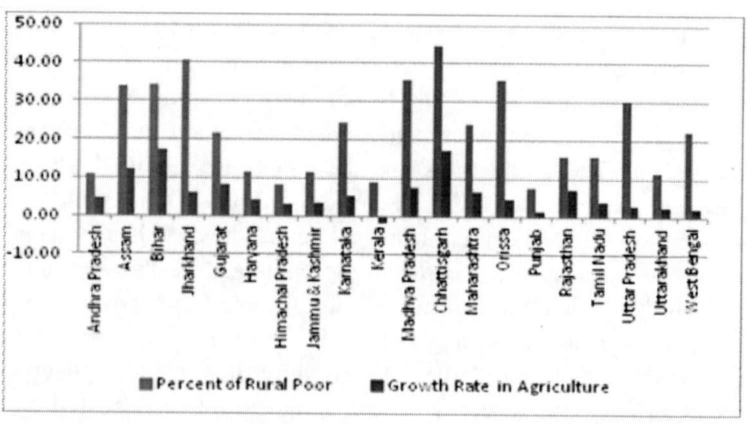

and negative sign of the correlation with *per capita* income in a strict statistical sense means a little. However, the data indicates that it could be the major deciding factor in aiding the cross-over above the poverty threshold. The experience needs to be carefully documented and analysed with larger data set and more rigorously.

The ratio of poverty and the growth rates in agriculture across states do not depict any clear picture of the relationship. It is visible that there are states with high growth and high poverty but as well as there are states depicting high growth with lower poverty ratio. Among the states Chattisgarh, Jharkhand, Bihar, Madhya Pradesh, West Bengal and Maharashtra show a pattern of coexistence of High Poverty with high growth rates in agriculture. Most of the states in this group depict poverty as an institutional existence and these regions will take sufficient time to lower the poverty ratio, besides the agro-climatic conditions also stand as an explanation to these coexistences. There is another interesting group of states that depicts low levels of poverty ratio and lower rates of growth. This group includes Tamil Nadu, Haryana, Uttarakhand, Jammu and Kashmir, Andhra Pradesh and Kerala. There is a significant presence of non-agricultural and allied agricultural sectors in these states. Does that mean growth in agriculture does not matter? Not at all and one cannot reach such a hasty inference basically due to the nature of income flows and processes in agriculture. Even today, with proliferation of market forces, agriculture continues to be an activity plagued with shortage of cash resources and thereby the dependence on other activities. Poverty or near poverty is therefore an obvious outcome.

The Dumping Ground or the Residual Collection Bin

Agricultural sector still continues to be the critical determinant of the performance of the Indian economy. The contribution of the sector to the GDP has slide down from 45 per cent in 1971 through 35 per cent in 2000 and finally to reach 17 per cent in 2012. But that by any means does not reduce the sensitivity of the GDP growth to the performance of the sector. Even with less than 20 per cent contribution to the GDP the failure of monsoon and presence of drought in some parts of the country pulls down the growth rate of

GDP. VKRV Rao in his second book on national income warned about the trends in the rates decline in the contribution of agriculture to GDP at steeper rate than the workforce dependent on agriculture. He cautioned about the density of the poor in the sector. This certainly means that the carrying capacity of the sector has been a critical issue coupled with the near stagnation in value added. Further, the agricultural activities are culturally bounded to the typical organisation of the sector that requires a continuous cash flow as demanded by various activities. As a result the farmers are forced to depend on the supply of cash and as a result become indebted. The evidence shows that rural poverty is declining and it has two specificities. First, the decline is not smooth as that of poverty in urban areas. That gets explained through the typical nature of agriculture. Second, all the other pieces of evidence point out that the process of marginalisation of size of holding coupled with the difference between the trends in agricultural value addition clearly points out the deteriorating economic situation of the farmers. However, the implementation of various schemes and flow of other labour intensive works succeeded in keeping a large share of poor from rural areas afloat. But the distress of agriculturists due to the intense poverty inflicted by the unfriendly markets on one side and the dominant culture of agriculture on the other pushes vulnerable farmers our of the profession. What remains in the rural areas is a cluster of non-poor precariously placed just above the poverty line.

Contrary to the expectations employment in agricultural sector registered a declining trend with increasing workforce density. Employment on 'usual status' basis registered a growth rate of 1.54 per cent per annum during 1983 to 1993-94, and showed a meager growth rate of 0.18 per cent during 1993-94 and 1999-00. Similar is the case with 'current daily status' (2.23 per cent and 0.21 per cent) respectively. Real agricultural wages also increased at a lower growth rate in 1990s (2.5 per cent per annum) compared to 80s (5 per cent). Wage rates of female casual labour in agriculture increased by 3.09 percent in 80s and 2.93 percent in 90s. There are differences across states in the growth of real wages. While Kerala and Tamil Nadu registered highest growth (7.9 per cent and

6.7 per cent) between 1990 and 2000, Assam and Rajasthan registered negative growth rate of -0.7 and -0.8 per cent respectively.

Table 3: Growth of Employment in Agriculture (Usual Status) in India

Period		Growth of Employment in Agriculture
1983-1993-94	Rural	1.38
	Urban	1.54
1993-94 to 1999-00	Rural	0.18
	Urban	-3.4

Source: Brajesh Jha (2004).

Figure 6: Rural Employment by Principal Status under Usually Employed Category in India from 1983-2004-05

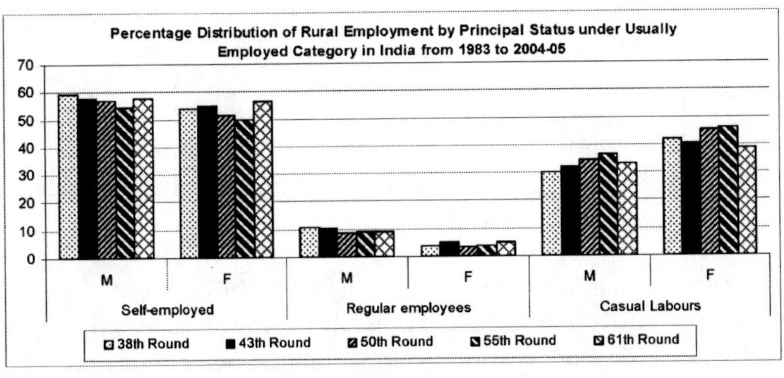

Source: Government of India (2006): "Employment and Unemployment Situation in India 2004-05", NSSO Report No. 515 (Part-I).

It is clearly borne out in tables 4 and 5 that employment has not been increasing in agricultural sector despite expectations. That provokes investigation into the search for a connection between the process of globalisation and typologies of employment. The experience of the last decade brings out that the growth in the agricultural sector has been generating more actualisation of employment and the trends in actualisation are quite bold across the country (see figure 9).

Table 4: Growth rates of Real Agricultural Wages across the States betwen1990 and 2000.

State	Growth rate (%)
Andhra Pradesh	1.3
Assam	-0.7
Bihar	0.3
Gujarat	5.1
Haryana	2.7
Karnataka	3.2
Kerala	7.9
Madhya Pradesh	1.8
Maharashtra	1.6
Orissa	0.7
Punjab	-0.8
Rajasthan	2.8
Tamil Nadu	6.7
Uttar Pradesh	2.5
West Bengal	1.6
All India	2.5

Source: Dreze and Sen (2002).

These trends are sharper in the agriculturally lagging regions. That leads us to the question of the quality of growth in the agricultural sector in the wake of globalisation in addition to the location of growth across regions. At the same time one cannot deny the influence of the quality of growth in the non-agricultural sector also.

Pointers of Distress

The pointers of distress have always focussed on the group of farmers, largely overlooking agricultural labour as an unimportant component. Given the trends in productivity of the crops, except the elite group consisting of rice and wheat, there is enough evidence to believe that the farmers' gross income is not increasing at the rate at which it grew in the years following Green Revolution. This also holds true about the real wages of agricultural labourers. But at the same time prices of the other commodities have increased sharply.

Figure 7: Casualisation of Rural Workforce across the States in India

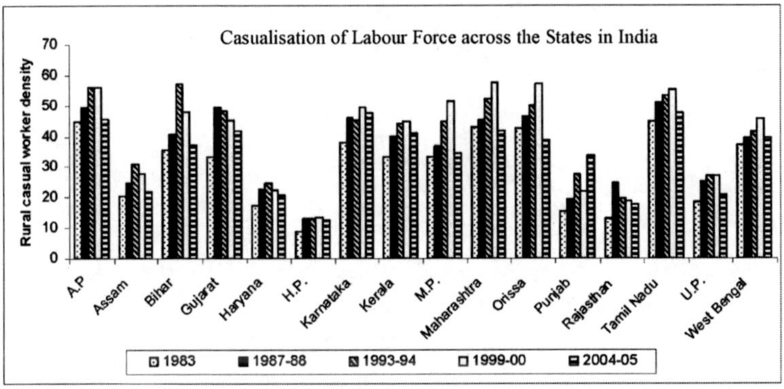

Source: Based on the data from Bhalla et al (2006) and "Employment and Unemployment Situation in India 2004-05", NSSO Report No. 515 (Part-I).

The comparison is attempted in two ways. First, we have looked into the price indices of a few commodities as against the cost of cultivation and the farm business income of farmer. We looked into relative price indices of some of the important commodities and it is quite clear that the prices of farm products have not been growing at the rate at which the prices of other commodities are increasing. We can see the relative income with respect to the gold and silver prices in the country during nineties. The fertiliser prices grew at a very fast rate and the Net business income of the farmer could not keep pace with it. Even though the A2 cost computations of CACP show some relationship with Farm Business Income, the major components of cost are increasing faster than the income.

More than that it is also clear that the Farm Business Income did not grow in tune with the prices of Gold or Silver (representing the historical gold standard). We usually go by the computations of terms of trade, which reveal a little and mask very important observations.

It is necessary to look at the relative prices rather than the terms of trade as revealed from the National Accounts Data (Sen and Bhatia 2004). Second, we also plotted the prices of a few crops along with the Consumer Price Indices of Agricultural Labours. It is clear that

Figure 8: Relative indices

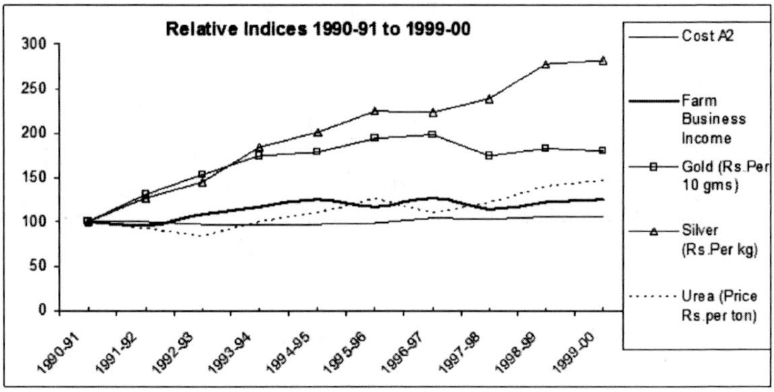

except raw cotton, which showed the price trends above the CPIAL in 1990s, all other commodities have price changes lower than the CPIAL. The farmers produce these commodities and therefore, the farmers feel let down by the market forces and that sets in frustration. Added to this the process of commercialisation in the economy and increased consumerism sets their ambitions at a higher mark. The severe frustration gets manifested into suicides (See table 8), even though there is no one to one correspondence between the two, the distress is quite genuine. We can see that the prices of agricultural commodities except wheat and rice have not kept pace with the Consumer Price Index for Agricultural Labourers. The prices of oilseeds, sugar, gur & Khandsari have shown similar growth trends. That indicates net welfare loss for the farmers growing these commodities. We have also looked into the Farm Business Income series computed from the CACP data and when compared this with the Consumer Price Indices for Agricultural Labourers, it clearly shows that the Farm Business Income did not keep pace with CPIAL, and the gap between the two is increasing fast.

Distress among the farmers in the country is a fact and such situation is quite depressing in a few States including Karnataka, Maharashtra, Rajasthan, Orissa, and Assam. Though one cannot draw any one to one correspondence between distress in the farm sector

Table 5: State wise suicide victims by Farming profession in India

States	1996	1997	1998	1999	2000	2001
Andhra Pradesh	1706	1097	1813	1974	1525	1525
Karnataka	2011	1832	1883	2379	2630	2630
Kerala	1025	1204	1514	1431	1295	1295
Madhya Pradesh	1809	2390	2278	2654	2660	2660
Maharashtra	1981	1917	2409	2423	3022	3022
Punjab	136	111	108	87	73	73
Rajasthan	453	659	705	724	736	736
Tamil Nadu	799	932	1089	804	882	882
Uttar Pradesh	646	568	727	845	735	735
West Bengal	1738	1539	1457	1240	1377	1377
Total (India)	**13771**	**13622**	**16015**	**16082**	**16603**	**16603**

Source: Accidental Suicides in India, Nation Crime Records Bureau, Ministry of Home Affairs, Govt. of India.

and the present spate of suicides in some of the States, the farm and farm related activities have a large stake in explaining the unfortunate occurrences. The loss of welfare to the farmer as a group is consistent and continued and that may affect the economy soon, if not arrested. In a broader economic perspective the farmers who are entrepreneurs and tried to adopt new ventures are likely to be discouraged. The absence of safety nets should not crush this entrepreneurial spirit. This phenomenon of inherent discrimination will have more difficult outcome for the sector in future if not dealt with squarely. Therefore, the State must come out with a strong safety net programme, market reforms and protecting the farm income. The recommendations go a long way in this direction.

In this context it is the small, marginal farmers and agricultural labourers who are caught in a vicious circle of low investment, low productivity, and low income. That requires a Schultzian break to effect a break away from the low level equilibrium The challenge is to empower them with appropriate changes in policy front, technology front and institutional front to enable them to get these constraints released unless some of these addressed through group action by small and marginal farmers with the support of appropriate policy-technology-institution matrix, their survival in the wake of liberalisation will be in danger. Land legislation to enable them to lease in and lease out land and legislation to prevent further subdivision beyond the threshold limit could form a part of policy change. Organisation of group action in rebuilding depleted and degraded natural resource base, in input and output marketing, in putting pressure on agricultural research institutions to develop low cost and risk-free technologies, in approaching the credit institutions for loans, in dealing with agri-business firms, and in availing the benefits public extension system could provide a stage for developing a strong development constituency of small and marginal farmers.

References

1. Ahluwalia Montek S (1978). "Rural Poverty and Agricultural Performance in India," *Journal of Development Studies,* April.
2. Ahluwalia Montek S (1985). Rural Poverty, Agricultural Production, and Prices: A Re-examination in Agriculture Change of Rural Poverty (Eds), Johan Hopkins Press.
3. Bhalla, G. S.(2006). Condition of Indian Peasantry, National Book Trust- India, New Delhi.
4. Chand, Ramesh and Dayanath Jha (2001). "Trade Liberalisation, Agricultural Prices and Net Social Welfare", in S S Acharya and D P Chaudhry (Eds.). *Indian Agricultural Policy at the Crossroads,* Rawat, Jaipur.
5. Dantwala, M. L. (1996). *Dilemmas of Growth – Indian Experience,* Sage, New Delhi.
6. Deshpande R. S. (2002). "Agriculture, Natural Resource Management and Rural Development", Proceeding of a Seminar on, Developmental Reforms for Resurgent India: A Nodal Strategy, Ministry of Culture and Tourism, Government of India (Eds), New Delhi.
7. Deshpande, R S and *Nagesh Prabhu* (2005) 'Farmers' Distress: Proof

beyond Doubt', Economic and Political Weekly, 40(44–45): 4663–4665.

8. Deshpande, R. S. (2003). "Current Land Policy Issues in India", *Land Reforms*, Food and Agricultural Organisation and The World Bank, Rome.
9. Dreze, Jean and Amarthy Sen (2002). *Development and Participation*, Oxford University Press, New Delhi
10. Ghosh, Jayati (1997). "India's Structural Adjustment: An Assessment in Comparative Asian Context", *Economic and Political Weekly*, Vol. 32 No. 20 & 21, May 17-30th.
11. Government of India (2006): "Employment and Unemployment Situation in India 2004-05", NSSO Report No. 515 (Part-I).
12. Jha, Brajesh (2004). " Economic Policies for Augmenting Rural Employment in India", Institute of Economic Growth, Delhi.
13. Nanvati, Manilal B and J J Anjaria (1965). *The Indian Rural Problem*, Indian Society of Agricultural Economics, Bombay.
14. Nayyar, Deepak and Abhijit Sen (1994). "International Trade and the Agricultural Sector in India", *Economic and Political Weekly*, Vol. 29, No. 19, 14th May.
15. Sen., Abhijit and M. S. Bhatia (2004). Cost of Cultivation and Farm Income: State of the Indian Farmer-A Millennium Study, Academic Foundation, New Delhi.
16. Sharma, Devinder (2000). "WTO and Agriculture: The End Result is Zero", Hindu Business Line, New Delhi. September 30th.
17. Thorat Sukhadeo & Motilal Mahamallik (2005), 'Persistent Poverty-Why do Scheduled Castes and Scheduled Tribes stay chronically poor', paper presented at CPRC-IIPA Seminar on 'Chronic Poverty: Emerging Policy Options and Issues' on 29th September 2005, Indian Institute of Public Administration, New Delhi.
18. Visvesvaraya, M (1931). *Rural Reconstruction in India*, Bangalore Press.

Cultural Praxis for Social Transformation: Encountering Modern Tyrannies

N. Manu Chakravarthy

It was a little more than a century ago that two great visionaries of India who were preoccupied with issues of Justice and Equality, involved as they were with the freedom struggle that India had launched against British colonialism, declared in their seminal texts that any civilisation built on narrow ideas of Nationalism and dehumanizing principles of Capitalism would eventually destroy itself. These two outstanding thinkers of India are invoked over and over again by all those who are concerned with the future of humankind whose very survival is threatened by several kinds of violent forces. The reason why those who genuinely believe in a civilisation that cherishes values of Justice and Equality turn to these two thinkers, M.K. Gandhi and Rabindranath Tagore, is that the two men severely critiqued the Imperialism of the West and the imperialist tendencies of the East that was imitating the former in every possible way. Gandhi's "Hind Swaraj" and Tagore's "Nationalism" are two texts that confront the major crises of the modern world without ever endorsing reductionist ideological positions or valorising myopic counter positions that looked like alternatives to hegemony and dominance, but were themselves equally annihilatory in spirit. In other words both Tagore and Gandhi looked for eternal values and lasting visions of peace and harmony without ignoring the complex processes of history. They tried to shape visions of Transcendence locating themselves in the thick of quotidian realities. The kind of transcendental spirit Tagore and Gandhi believed in did not, for a moment, ignore the basic fact that Spiritual Transcendence – of individuals and communities – had to be shaped only by wrestling with complex divisive socio-political and economic forces. It only meant, then, that notions of the Eternal and the Infinite could not exclude temporal realities. The Infinite and the Eternal had to emerge from the thick of everyday struggles and confrontations. Crucial to the ideas of Justice and Equality were very fundamental notions of Culture. Social Transformation was vitally linked to cultural traditions and practices and could not be actualised merely by adopting political methods and strategies. Tagore and Gandhi argued that the evolution of the human self, and thereby human civilisation itself, was organically related to cultural values out of which political action had to emerge. In very violent times such as these there is an absolute need to understand this with great clarity. It is a moral imperative for those committed to the cause of Justice and Equality to fully comprehend the implications of this position, especially when culture has been employed by powerful and cruel elements in the name of National Sovereignty and Ethnic Purity. The reification of cultures – a phenomenon being strengthened by the ugly nexus of the champions of Nationalism and multinational companies who constitute the corporate empire – by vested interests has reduced live cultures to being instruments of oppression and tyranny, apart from converting them into dead archival material to be excavated and dissected by academics with no sense of, or feeling for, the communities that produced them. Thus, there is a massive and deadly concentration of political authority, cultural strength and economic power in a few who determine the course of history and regulate the lives of millions of people. This was what Tagore and Gandhi were up against when they were scathing in their criticism of the dominant paradigms of the West and the methods the East was adopting by copying those paradigms. A century later true democrats are still trying to come to terms with these hegemonic structures. Culture and social transformation have to be understood in relation to the dominant models unleashed by the rich and powerful masters of society.

There are two major territories that people who value a culture of democracy have to enter if they are to entertain visions of social transformation. Both Gandhi and Tagore had marked out these territories in unequivocal terms. The first was the territory called the Nation-state. No genuine transformation is possible without an open encounter with the modern nation-state, an illegitimate construct that arrogates to itself the responsibility of regulating socio-cultural life besides determining the economic models that eventually mar the lives of millions, protecting the interests of only the privileged few. The 'Nation-State', the creation of the modern West, has become ubiquitous and omnipotent and symbolises the accumulated power of all those forces that have absolutely no regard for values of Justice and Equality. It is for this reason that the reality of the community was placed in opposition to the monstrous presence of the Nation-State. The great cultural narratives of our times are essentially political discourses foregrounding the various struggles of communities and individuals against the hegemony of the monolithic Nation-State and bring us face to face with the existentialist realities of oppressed and marginalised sections of society. What needs to be borne in mind is that the power of the modern Nation-State is enhanced by the authority of the corporate world invoking political and economic categories of national security, national integrity, progress, growth, development. Buttressing these are ideas of the technocratic world harping on technical competence and efficiency upholding applied science and technology as supreme values. The loss of the value of the human self is the greatest marker of the nature of the civilisation of modern times, and most certainly of the phase of Globalisation and its attendant principles of liberalisation and privatisation. All great cultural texts of the so-called third world (or post-colonial societies, as often referred to in general terms) reflect the dreams and aspirations of individuals and native communities whose very existence has been threatened by a world order that cannot tolerate any idea of plurality and heterogeneity. To build a homogeneous world where everything is standardised according to the specifications of the technocratic-corporate system justified by a Nation-State that depends on the former for its survival is the prime agenda of the ruling class in the Globalised world. Interrogations of, and confrontations with, this hegemonic order are converted into destructive anti-national sentiments that have no place in a civilized world. The multiple narratives, the plural discourses of communities that believe in a de-centered society where there are no hierarchies between different systems of living, and knowledge, have to deal with the crushing centralized massive singular structure carefully nurtured by the dominant order. Reflections on culture and social transformation necessarily have to engage themselves with this agonising reality of our times.

The strictly academic nature of cultural studies and the merely objective temper of studying social transformation really have to make way for a vibrant and radical analysis of the subversive power of the cultural narratives of diverse communities. There is a need to understand and acknowledge the fact that there is a lot of political energy in cultural texts capable of revising and restructuring our knowledge of social transformation, which might alter the quality of our activism itself. Turning to cultures and societies like India, Africa and Latin America might throw up refreshingly new images of liberation and freedom far different from those given by the dominant West and its carefully manufactured epistemology.

Eurocentric notions are indeed to be replaced by all kinds of alternative narratives that non-Western cultures have always had. Our ideas of human rights, civil liberties, social justice, economic equality, civil society do need to go beyond Western categories and definitions. The vision of oral cultures and traditions and the sweep and range of other non-Western societies point to different experiential realities that, if properly contextualized, have a certain element of "difference" that can add to our dimensions of Equality and Justice. What it actually suggests is the possibility of making political struggles for Equality and Justice holistic in cultural terms. In a world of increasing homogenisation new modes of articulation open up larger spaces of protest and resistance. The great conflicts of modern times do have a need to go beyond readymade frames of reference. Many stereotypes are waiting to be broken by alternative modes of thinking and feeling about the individual self, cultural resistance and political action.

Culture has quite a role to play in the battle against oppression and tyranny.

We also need to move into another territory that Tagore and Gandhi were intensely preoccupied with, for that is a terrain that contains very fundamentally contradictory notions of Justice and Equality. This territory has also been the site of very bitter and violent clashes causing great bloodshed and infinite suffering and misery to humankind. This territory relates to Religion, Religious Cosmology and Imagination and political power and ideology. Culture and social transformation are quite heavily dependent on this specific area of human consciousness. For centuries there has been a debate over the kind of relationship that ought to exist between the political state and the religious institutions leading to the birth of Secularism, especially in the Western context, that believes in a clean separation of Religion and politics. But we have been direct and immediate witnesses not to a distancing between the two, but, like the corporate empire forming a nexus with the ruling State, a conflation of Religion and politics. In fact Religious Institutions and Nation-States reinforce/recreate each other only to increase their power and authority. The manipulative schemes of the two institutions have, both in the name of Religious order and political stability, unleashed enormous suffering on the poor and the deprived. The range and sweep of the brutal power of Religious Institutions and Nation-States will have to be measured in direct relation to the hunger, starvation and the utter poverty of millions of people all over the world even as they have endured the "governance" of religious institutions and Nation-States. The point is that Religious Nationalism – a terrible blend of religion and politics – has not brought either "spiritual salvation" or "secular welfare" for "ordinary" human beings, the "common" people – wherever they exist, much as they see increasing opulence and luxury and limitless power of those who rule over them invoking God and Nationalism. The secularists have always placed themselves in opposition to this disastrous fellowship of religion and politics, and quite rightly so– but only to an extent.

One of the most difficult things for thinkers who (in spite of being fully aware of the catastrophes unleashed on human beings by

Religious Nationalism for several centuries now) believe that there is something invaluable in deep religiosity (which they certainly do not credit capitalism with) that goes beyond the punitive puritanical elements embedded in all religions which can offer "solace" and "salvation" to human life is to extricate religion from the clutches of a tyrannical system of governance. Such thinkers, interestingly enough, identify elements of oppression within the religious institution itself and do not see it as any different from political orders. In other words they foreground the undemocratic political nature of religious organisations and do not see it as an essential part of religiosity. Similarly, they draw attention to the strategies of political orders to use religious sentiments–without really any deep faith in religious experiences – only to mask their own fascist tendencies and practices. Such strategies dissolve profound religious visions and deep political principles into nothing. Further, they engender a wholly negative understanding of serious religious and political concepts that actually uphold the basic dignity of all forms of life wherever they exist. The systematic erasure of genuine religious and political visions that sanctify the very idea of life constitutes the greatest crisis of human civilisation. But it would not do to negate the value of religious and political cosmologies only because they have been rendered foul and ugly by various power structures. Great cultural texts, all over the world, have been attempts at restoring and reviving the monumental dimensions of religious and political values, even running the great risk of being dismissed as "revivalist, reactionary, status quoist etc."

Tagore and Gandhi, while moving away from nihilistic religious and political formations, did turn to the holy aspects of religion and politics (that Tagore differed from Gandhi as regards mixing religion and politics is a different matter altogether) in their struggles to redeem humankind from all kinds of atrocities perpetrated on it by the ruling masters. Tagore and Gandhi did invoke God over and over again, but only by ensuring that such an invocation was free of all religious bigotry and fanaticism and political cruelties and bestialities. This is perhaps the great reason why Tagore and Gandhi never saw any fundamental difference between Islam and Christianity and Hinduism, or the other religious traditions, as far as their conception of a common humanity that bound all races in peace and harmony was concerned. Tagore talked of "Eka needam, Vishwaneedam" (One family, the world as a family) and Gandhi spoke of "Sarvodaya" (the emergence/rise of all) whenever they articulated their views on human destiny. The great works of Tagore (his fiction and his critical essays) and Gandhi's ("Hind Swaraj" in particular) fully reflect this dimension in very unambiguous terms. Both Tagore and Gandhi erased binaries of East and West, too, when they turned to the moral traditions of all religious cosmologies. With a strong sense of history – being fully conscious of Mughal invasion, Portuguese rule and British Colonialism – the two visionaries did not overlook the savagery of history, but looked for alternatives beyond the political realm. Tagore and Gandhi juxtaposed the wisdom that emanated from religious and cultural texts with the cruel lessons that emerged from political theories defending the necessity of a political order. Gandhi drew his lessons from "The Sermon on the Mount", "The Parable of the Owner of the Vineyard" even as he turned to Indian texts that formed his theory of non-violence – Ahimsa – as the only Truth that would save the world from total annihilation. Tagore, too, obtained his vision of the world as one family by embracing diverse religious traditions. During our own times, in Latin America to be precise, Religion has played a crucial role in the struggle for human emancipation. The most important dimension herein is that the religious element shaping cultural and political struggles also attacks the hierarchy that is built into the religious structure. Therefore, the struggle is for decentralised religious practices that recognise human dignity without endorsing the dogmatism of the Institution. Liberation Theology of Latin America is a political and religious struggle at the same time – fighting the hegemony of the Nation-State and the Church simultaneously. (Fidel Castro in his long interview with a Catholic priest talks of how vital a decentralised religious sensibility was to his fight against Capitalist Imperialism. Castro pays tributes to his mother, a devout Catholic, who shaped his vision of Socialism). One can see such an integration of a decentralised religious and political thought in Ivan Illich, a pastor and one of the greatest thinkers of our times, who wanted Mexico, in particular, to evolve into a society of Justice and

Equality. Our notions of culture and social transformation cannot, going by myopic secularist arguments, ignore the democratic struggle within the religious framework. It would not do to believe that political reordering, economic restructuring by themselves would usher in a future of Justice and Equality. There has to be a holistic understanding of the physical and metaphysical needs of human beings in our approaches to socio-cultural and political action. A better future cannot be created by depending entirely on political and economic programmes. Moreover, the humane vision of religion will surely be distorted by barbarians who would convert it into a tool of oppression and exploitation only to further their murderous power. To abandon religion to political wolves and "religious vultures" would be suicidal – Latin America is a great paradigm that we need to accept.

Quite often theories of culture are alienated from cultural practices of living communities that have held on to them to derive comfort and solace in the face of crushing poverty and unbearable suffering. In a world that is making life increasingly painful for the marginalised and the oppressed, activists fighting for the basic values of life, that any sane society would readily accept, ought to use diverse cultural and religious traditions in their movements.

Electoral Reforms in India

M. Vijaya Kumar

Introduction

In India Parliamentary democracy is the structure choosen to ensure the representation of people's aspirations in the process of governance. The electoral system lies at the very heart of democracy. Political parties are indispensable to any democratic system and play a crucial role in the electoral process – in setting up candidates and conducting election campaigns. There are 1,200 political parties in India and of these about 150 are active and functioning. In the post-independent India, big money and influence has played a major role in political representation. As a result only a miniscule minority has grabbed power. The outcome of elections to a large extent has been due to money, gross corruption and criminalisation of politics. This has led to distortions where the democratic credentials of the electoral system are being questioned seriously. There is therefore a widespread and increasing disenchantment with politics and politicians in India. There is a growing public awareness of the rampant entry of criminal elements into the political arena. For example, in the current Lok Sabha, 23.2 per cent of the MPs have reported criminal cases against them. Over 50 per cent have cases that could attract penalties of imprisonment of five or more years. While token attempts at reforming the electoral system have been made from time to time over the last many years to take care of some these distortions, particularly whenever it has suited the party in power, there has hardly been any attempt at making any significant and substantial changes in the electoral system. Electoral reforms are meant to bring about change in the electoral system so that genuine public desires find expression in election results. There have been a number of reports and recommendations on what needs to be done. Some of the significant examples are the Indrajit Gupta Report, the Dinesh Goswami Report, the 170th Report of the Law Commission of India on Review of the working of political parties and Electoral Reforms and the Recommendations of the National Commission to Review the Working of the Constitution (NCRWC). The unfortunate fact however is that almost none of the recommendations of these learned and painstakingly prepared reports have been implemented. The National Commission to Review the Working of the Constitution has come out with a consultation paper especially in relation to elections and electoral reforms.

The Present Electoral System in India

Indian democracy has the 'First Past The Post' (FPTP) as its electoral system to provide representation to voters in State Assemblies and in the Parliament of India. This representation system may allow political parties to come to power, both in the States and at the Centre, with a minority of votes. There are many instances where parties with less than 30 per cent of votes have won a large percentage of seats and had claimed the right to form governments. A vast majority of voters, in this system, are left unrepresented in governance. The present electoral system in India encourages corruption and use of muscle power and communal pull to gain the slight margin of winning votes. Parties that have the power to manipulate voters using their economic power, are more often than not successful in gaining a dominant position in the governance structure.

Political Parties in India

The present political scenario depicts a complex multi-party configuration, reflecting trends of fragmentation, factionalism, casteism, communal politics and regionalism. Endemic within this system is a tendency to form opportunistic alliances for seeking a share in the pie of power, irrespective of any strong ideological or programmatic commitments. The structure and functioning of the political parties in India distort the electoral system. Many political parties in India suffer from a range of structural and functional problems such as absence of inner party democracy, abysmal representation of women in the party leadership, lack of ideology and values in party politics, accommodation of criminals within the parties and acceptance of violence as a legitimate functional mode, to name a few.

A New Electoral System

Proportionate Electoral System is being widely practiced in many democracies of the world. More and more countries are shifting to Proportional Representation. In PR electoral system any party can gain seats only in proportion to the percentage of votes that it gains. There will not be any difference between the percentage of votes and the percentage of seats. This allows parties with a majority voter support to come to power. In PR system majority means more than 50 per cent of votes. The other votes are not wasted. They are given to other candidates in order to provide representation to all voters in the Assemblies and in the Parliament. If parties are unable to gain more than 50 per cent of votes they have to resort to coalitions of parties with similar ideologies before elections in order to influence voters. PR system has multi-member constituencies. This enables two or more members getting elected from the same constituency in order to provide representation to different parties.

In PR electoral system inner party democracy is a must. Political parties prepare a list of candidates before the elections selected through inner party elections and submit the same to the Election Commission. Candidates of parties are declared elected from this list in the same proportion as the percentage of votes that party or a coalition obtains. In the party list the constituency that a candidate will represent is indicated. This enables voters from that constituency to vote for the party to which their popular candidate belongs. If a party fields many popular candidates their percentage of votes increases in many constituencies. Thus, the popularity of party ideology and the popularity of candidates are both reflected in the PR system. In some countries with PR system election expenses are met by the state. This prevents corruption, money and muscle power, malpractices, play of emotions on communal and caste basis etc. Proportionate Electoral System provides ample space for formation of coalitions representing smaller communities that do not have the chance of being represented in FPTP. Smaller parties representing unrepresented communities can make a coalition and gain required percentage of votes in order to come to a winning position of power. This is very important for the survival of democratic governance in India if it is to be pro-poor; corruption and electoral violence are minimised and inner party democracy is enhanced.

AIPF Recommendations for a Reformed Electoral System in India:

1. There will be 2 x 542 = 1084 members of parliament and all state legislatures will have double their present membership. (Presently the strength of Lok Sabha is 542)
2. 50 per cent of the members will be women.
3. 542 members will be elected through nomination by political parties, based on proportional representation (PR), for Parliament.
4. The other MP/MLA in each constituency will be elected by FPTP, but with the condition that he/she should secure 50 per cent + 1 vote to get elected.
5. If in one election, one male MP is elected by PR, the other MP in the same constituency will be a woman elected by FPTP. For the next election, the gender representation is reserved.
6. The current norms for reservation of seats for SC/ST candidates will continue.
7. If an elected representative resigns his/ her seat, he/ she will be disqualified for the term of the house and cannot contest his or any other constituency during this period. A new candidate has to contest in his/ her place.

8. No individual can contest more than one seat.
9. Wherever state legislative councils are in place, graduate constituencies should be abolished and in their place, workers' constituencies should be constituted. Any worker/ employee of any enterprise with ESI card or a valid company ID can register as a voter.

Who are eligible to contest election?

1. Parties choose their candidates by primaries following democratic selection process from within the party. The names of two alternative candidates are publicly declared by publishing them on the Internet. If any objections are raised to the candidatures, the objections are automatically recorded in a webpage put up by the Election Commission.
2. Parties have to nominate their candidates at least 6 months before the election and give sufficient time for the Election Commission to verify the credentials of the candidate, his/ her criminal record, property details etc. If the candidate's nomination is invalid, there will be an alternative and a second alternative candidate. If all three are rejected, the Party can not contest the seat.
3. While educational qualification is not a necessary criterion, the candidate should be able to read and write in his/her native language when he/she contests the state legislature elections and should be conversant in Hindi/ English for Parliament elections.
4. Similarly, advanced age cannot be a bar to nomination, but the candidate should be mentally and physically sound to contest an election and discharge his/ her duties as a law maker.

How does the electorate vote?

All voting is electronic and a voter can cast his/her vote from anywhere in the country for Parliamentary elections and from anywhere outside the state for Assembly elections. Voter identification is by bio-metric ID and a voter ID card is not compulsory. If a voter wants to cast his/her vote from outside an election area (for example: outside the state where elections are being held) or outside the country or for a valid reason while being within the country, he/she should register his/her name through Internet and will be given a unique ID number, which he/she can use to cast his/her vote through Internet.

Voting is compulsory and Election Commission has to ensure that voters will be able to cast their votes with ease. All voting machines are connected to Internet and will be tamper proof. Any public building/workplace can be used for polling and each polling booth will be securely guarded. Voter ID will be through an Intelligent Card, which may also be used for obtaining government permissions, drawing money from banks, making payments, buying air/train tickets etc. The Voter Intelligent ID Card is activated for 5 years, only after a vote is cast. If someone does not cast his/her vote, he/she will cease to be a citizen. His/her passport will also be automatically nullified.

Election Expenses

1. The amount of money deposited by a candidate will be a minimum of 10 per cent of the allowed election expense and shall be included in the total expenditure. If a candidate loses deposit in 2 consecutive elections, his/her deposit amount for the third election will be 50 per cent of the allowed election expenditure. If he/she chooses to contest a fourth time, after losing deposit three times, the deposit amount will be 100 per cent of the allowed election expense. After that he/she will be debarred from contesting any seat. This is for discouraging non-serious candidates.
2. Travel expenses of central party leaders will be included in the candidate's election expenditure. The total allowed expenses of the central party leaders per seat contested by the Party, will be fixed by the EC. This expenditure includes money spent on media advertising, sponsored programs, promotion of parties and candidates by discussion forums

etc., free travel/boarding arranged by private persons/ corporate sector.

3. There should be State funding of elections. This is justified-constitutionally and legally. Such funding should be confined to parties recognised as national or state parties by the Election Commission. To begin with only a part of the financial burden of political parties may be charged to the state. A greater burden could be progressively shifted to the states in future so that ultimately all the legitimate electoral expenses of the Party become a charge on the state. The state funding should be in kind and not in cash. A separate election fund should be created for meeting the expenses on state funding of elections.

Election Ethics

1. Political parties should adhere to strict norms laid out by the Election Commission. Parties and the candidates should be barred from making provocative speeches, inciting violence of a communal/casteist/regional hatred nature, and/or distribute liquor, money, freebies etc. to the electorate. If a candidate or a leader of a political party violates this, not only the candidate, but all the candidates put up by the Party will be disqualified from contesting the election for two consecutive elections. The Party will also be disqualified from participating in two consecutive elections. Video evidence or reports in the media are adequate grounds to initiate action against a candidate or a Party.
2. Criminal and anti-social elements will be identified and any Political Party or its candidate employing these elements for campaigning will also be barred from the election for two consecutive elections.

Political Parties

1. There should be a law requiring all recognised political parties to keep audited accounts and sources of all income

and details of expenditure, with false accounts being a punishable offence.

2. All political parties have to submit a list of its members to the State/Regional Election Commission every year. No political party can nominate a candidate who is not registered as a party member for the last two years, before his/her nomination.
3. Political Parties have to enter into alliances and announce their intention to contest together six months ahead of the election. Anti-defection law should be applicable to alliances also. If parties decide to break their alliance, then all the candidates belonging to the alliance will have to forfeit their seats also.
4. Support to be rendered to any government from "outside", i.e. without joining the coalition government, should be legally barred. Only a party having at least 25 per cent of seats in the Lower House of parliament or Assembly should be entitled to form the government.

What Kind of Governance

1. Yardsticks used for prosecuting government servants facing criminal proceedings and placed under suspension until cleared by the courts, should be applied to politicians as well.
2. There should be strict norms for the functioning of the legislative bodies. Any member who indulges in the use of the office for personal business promotion during the term of his office should forego his/her seat.
3. Members who are not present for 80 per cent of the time of house business in a year will automatically cease to be members. This should also include those who suffer from chronic sickness.
4. Any member of a legislative body will face charges of sedition and will be tried for treason and anti-national activities, if he/she makes provocative speeches or makes

such statements that incite violence as well as regional, communal and casteist sentiments. Video evidence or reports in the media are adequate grounds to initiate action and to frame charges against such a member.

5. AIPF suggest that every elected representative should seek the confidence of the voters in his/her constituency once in a year. The confidence vote will be recorded electronically. Though this may cause a heavy burden on the state, this will ensure that the elected representatives enjoy the confidence of the voters throughout their term of office. In case, an elected member loses the confidence (gets less than 50 per cent+1 of the valid votes) there will be re-election in that constituency. There will be no campaigning for the confidence vote.
6. For the large parliamentary membership we recommend that there will be only two weekly sessions of the house for each sitting. For the rest of the period, the members have to be nominated by their respective political parties to various panels that will transact business. For example, there can be a panel on internal security, one on finance, another on commerce, one on foreign affairs etc. This will enable the house to devote more time to all issues and ensure that all members participate in the debates and make their voices heard. The joint session will review the proceedings of each panel.

Political Parties and the Current Reform Agenda

Sindhujaa Iyengar

One of the more interesting quirks of Indian polity is the parity in the influence that Constitutional and extra-Constitutional institutions exercise over the country's governance systems and processes. It may be considered reasonable to expect that Constitutional bodies would command a greater role in shaping public affairs than extra-Constitutional ones do. Instead, the average political observer finds several instances where the latter trumps over the former. In one camp are reformist institutions such as the Election Commission (ECI) and the Supreme Court – to whom the Constitution entrusts the task of protecting the interests of the largest stakeholder in governance, the citizens. In the other camp are some extra-Constitutional bodies from whose ambitions the citizen must be protected – Political Parties being the foremost amongst these.

Ongoing political skirmishes indicate that the two camps are equally matched in their struggle to shape political processes into a form that suits their respective values, or lack thereof. For the purpose of this discussion, it will suffice that we take into account the ongoing tussle between political parties on one hand, and the ECI and/or the Supreme Court on the other. And, the disturbing fact is that the extra-Constitutional institution of Political Parties is able to thwart repeated attempts by the Constitution-mandated ECI and Supreme Court to make the former act in accordance with the spirit of the Constitution. Cases in point are the Political Parties' assertion that they shall continue to announce freebies in their respective election manifestos[1], and their opposition to the call to bar those who are charge-sheeted[2] or jailed[3] from contesting polls.

The issue becomes all the more complex when a Constitutional body conscientiously refrains from overstepping its jurisdiction. Political parties use the Parliament as an instrument to modify electoral laws to enhance their convenience to themselves. The ECI has refused to push its stand on the debate over banning Opinion Polls: "We are not a competent authority. The decision has to be taken by the government."[4] The latter is reflected in the 61st Report of the Parliamentary Standing Committee on Personnel, Public Grievances, Law and Justice which seeks to derogate the ECI's power to issue a Model Code of Conduct[5], as well as the political parties' coming together in Parliament to attempt to insulate from the Right To Information (RTI) Act[6]. These inherent attitudes in the two institutions give political parties the advantage of *realpolitik* over the idealism of the ECI and Supreme Court. Under the circumstances, perhaps the way to bolster reformist undertakings by the ECI and Supreme Court in the face of resistance by political parties is the public call for party reforms aimed at strengthening Indian democracy through equity, transparency and accountability. Needless to say, the party's opposition to reforms initiated by the former is likely to be diluted when the same are demanded by the electorate on the impending strength and lurking threat of the vote. Hence, the need for Civil Society organizations to consolidate and give form to such public calls for party reforms cannot be overemphasized.

A recent attempt at this is 'The Political Parties (Registration and Regulation of Affairs, etc) Draft Bill 2011', prepared by a committee Chaired by Justice M.N. Venkatachalaiah and advocated by the Association for Democratic Reforms, the National Election Watch[7] and the Centre for Standards in Public Life[8]. This has apparently been prepared in the backdrop of suggestions on party reforms by committees and commissions initiated by the state. These include the Tarkunde Committee Report on Election Expenses (1978) which even three decades ago recommended against company donations to political parties and the audit of party accounts.[9] The

Dinesh Goswami Committee on Electoral Reforms (1990) had recommended the restriction of candidates from contesting in multiple constituencies[10], lowering the age limit of contesting for elections[11], and providing statutory backing for certain provisions under the Model Code of Conduct[12]. The Vohra Committee Report (1993) appears to support this argument when it says, "the cost of contesting elections has thrown the politician into the lap of (criminal) elements"[13]. The Indrajit Gupta Committee Report on State Funding of Elections (1998) had insisted that "state funding of elections is fully justified – constitutionally, legally and also in the larger public interest."[14] The Law Commission of India's 170th Report (1999) had emphasized the necessity for providing laws to ensure intra-party democracy.[15] The National Commission to Review the Working of the Constitution (2002) had amongst other concerns emphasized laying down adequate criteria for the registration and deregistration of political parties.[16] And, the Second Administrative Reforms Commission in its Fourth Report (2007) had recommended the "tightening" of the anti-defection law[17] and a ban on post-poll alliances[18], amongst other reforms.

The Political Parties Draft Bill 2011 declares itself to be "an Act to regulate the constitution, functioning, funding, accounts, audit, and other affairs of and concerning political parties participating in elections." To this end, it proposes party reforms that may be broadly categorized into Structural and Functional ones.

At the Structural level, the Bill proposes (a) that the Chief Election Commissioner be recognized as the Registrar of Political Parties[19]; (b) that every political party shall have a constitution that is consistent with the provisions of the Constitution of India[20]; (c) unambiguous party organization and structure through clearly defined office bearers[21]; (d) the maintenance of an updated membership registry with the party's state unit[22], including details of the numerical strength of each category of members[23]; and (e) that political parties are included under the RTI Act[24]

At the Functional level it proposes (a) that only registered parties can contest polls[25]; (b) that no party shall promote itself through any activity or property associated with a religion[26]; (c) that parties can own movable and immovable property within the territory of India[27], and can sue or be sued[28]; (d) the provision that "the Registrar may call for such other particulars as he may deem fit" from parties[29]; (e) that the Registrar shall decide whether to register a body as a political party or not, and that the "decision of the Registrar shall be final[30]"; (f) that the Executive committee will determine which party members are to be given poll tickets[31]; (g) the regulation of party finances[32] and donations[33]; (h) that the Registrar can inquire, either suo moto or otherwise, into political parties' non-compliance with the provisions of the Act[34], and can levy penalties for the same[35]; and (i) that the Central Government can make rules to give effect to the Act after consulting the Registrar[36].

The Bill attempts to make a powerful consolidated presentation of citizens' concerns over the quality of work produced by political parties and its impact on quality of governance. It is unfortunate that the Bill is compelled to reiterate several suggestions that earlier commissions and committees on party reforms have already raised. This clearly indicates that repeated requests over the years for a clean party system have been falling on unwilling ears. Certainly, all the suggestions that the Bill proposes merit deep consideration and discussion in public forums. Some of them, however, catch the author's eye due to their potential for not only party reform, but also *progressive* reform:

1. The *first* amongst these is the Bill's suggestion that the Chief Election Commissioner functions as the Registrar of Political Parties and be allowed to exercise full discretion in the registration and deregistration of parties, entrusted with the authority to penalize parties that fail to comply with the Act. To penalize implies the placement of judicial authority in the hands of an Executive-appointed body. Moreover, the Bill, in certain provisions, is more general than specific. Also, the term "*provisions* of the Constitution" appears to suggest that parties must necessarily subscribe to the *letter* of the law. It would be unwise for the Bill to assume an

originalist position on the Constitution and assume that a party's stand against its letter is necessarily equivalent to a stand against its spirit. This is not to suggest that the Bill should not grant the ECI the power of penalty, or that it should permit political parties to violate the Constitution. Instead, the Bill could consider the creation of checks and balances on the ECI's discretionary powers, perhaps by requesting the apex Court to extend its power of judicial review over the Commission's pronouncements. In the absence of such a check on its decisions, there exists the danger that every order of the ECI is dismissed by political parties as the ill-conceded hegemony of minimally accountable office-bearers. On the other hand, when the ECI's decisions do not meet with the disapproval of the judiciary, they will enjoy greater insulation from the attacks of political parties seeking to wriggle out of their obligation to comply.

2. *Secondly,* the Bill suggests that each political party shall be headed by an Executive Committee which shall gain office through intra-party elections. The "practice of nominating members of the Executive Committee is prohibited."[37] This is a laudable provision as it will go a long way towards minimizing dynastic, hereditary and non-merit leadership within the parties. However, the Bill's provision that "the Executive Committee and local committees shall take decisions and elect their office bearers on the basis of simple majority vote" is disappointing. It is now common public knowledge that our *First-Past-the-Post* (FPP) model of electoral winner-determination leaves much to be desired towards the provision of a truly representative elected body. Recognizing this, the Law Commission of India, in its 170th Report on the Reform of Electoral Laws[38] makes a case in favour of supplementing the FPP system with the List System to make our legislatures more representative. In fact, even members of the Rajya Sabha are elected by Single Transferable Vote and Proportional Representation rather

than by FPP. Clearly the singular advantage that FPP presents in Lok Sabha and Vidhan Sabha elections is the simplicity of the system which makes it comprehensible to every member of our teeming masses. Perhaps, the practice of healthier electoral alternatives in intra-party elections will help spread awareness about them amongst the masses; this in turn may hasten voter-comprehension of the alternate system, enabling its adoption in General and Assembly Elections at an early date. Further, if the Bill requires political parties to function in accordance with Constitutional provisions, it appears reasonable to expect them to follow the Constitution's provisions for affirmative action as well. Can it be considered that party Executive Committees reserve a percentage of seats for backward communities and women? Perhaps the concept of representation of the marginalized sex can be expanded to include even the trans-sexual community? Here, the Bill's provision that each party maintain a record of the numerical strength of its members under "each category"[39] may be considered to include gender and sex-based categories. Intra-party representation could perhaps pave the way for an easy transition towards equal access of all sexes to policy-formulation, through Parliamentary representation.

3. *Third,* the Bill seeks to introduce accountability and transparency in party finances by providing for the office of party Treasurer and Assistant Treasurer who will have the sole responsibility for the custody and control of party funds.[40] The party shall regularly submit these accounts for external audit. Moreover, "the Registrar may direct a special audit of the accounts of any year of a party or of any local unit."[41] Also, party funds shall be kept in a scheduled bank, and the account number/s be intimated to the Registrar. These provisions of account and audit are supplemented by regulations pertaining to the acceptance of donations made to the party. Here, the average citizen would perhaps be happy to note that the Bill seeks to break the politics-

business nexus by regulating donations from corporate bodies. However, it may be argued that the business-political nexus and consequent tradeoffs will continue until such time that parties have access to non-private funds to finance their election campaigns. The latter can be realized only through state-funding of elections, which the Bill prohibits through its above-stated provision that parties cannot accept funds from Union and State governments. This is worrisome, as it may be argued that state-funding will address the systemic flaw that permits candidates with monetary resources to have an unfair advantage over those who do not. The Electoral System should provide that a candidate's poll prospects are determined by the quality of her/his manifesto, and policy capability and intent, and not by extraneous factors such as money-power. To this end, every candidate should enjoy ascertained access to campaign funds at par with every other candidate. This will encourage 'good' candidates to join the electoral fray unworried by the tenuous nature of private funding that makes candidates enter into unhealthy Business-Politics nexus.[42] Here, it is interesting to note that state-funding of elections would require political party reforms to be undertaken at a systemic level, which is a level higher than the structural and functional reforms laid down in the Bill as it stands.

4. *Fourth,* is the glaring omission by the Bill to deal with the phenomenon of party defection through post-poll alliances. It is now commonly accepted that Post-Poll Alliances are undemocratic, as they prevent the voter from making an informed choice. Hence, any document on party reforms may be expected to provide for the maximisation of the voter's Right to Information by calling for a ban on post-poll alliances. Moreover, political parties that contest as members of coalition alliances should be required to lay their joint coalition manifesto before the electorate, and not just individual party manifestos. Today, commonly, the voter is able to access only individual party manifestos

before the polls. The coalition manifesto tends to be framed and adopted only after the polls. Consequently, the joint Coalition Manifesto may be very different from the individual Party Manifesto on the basis of which the voter had cast her/his vote. Hence, the voter finds oneself cheated of one's right to know the nature of the government that s/he is voting to power. [43]

5. *Fifth,* on a related note, the Bill requires every political party to possess a written constitution, "defining its aims and objects"[44] and certain functional details[45]. When political parties enter into a (pre-poll) coalition alliance, each member-party should be required to state the Coalition Constitution alongside the Party Constitution. Like the party constitutions, coalition constitutions also must state the aims and objectives of the alliance, enlist its member parties, and state its functional details. The Executive Committee of the alliance should be elected in a manner similar to the election of party committees. This will ensure that intra-party democracy is supplemented and enhanced through intra-coalition democracy.
6. *Sixth,* the Bill provides that "*The Central Government may, after consulting the Registrar, by notification in the Official Gazette, make rules for carrying out the purposes of this Act*"[46], *and that "every rule made by the Central Government under this Act shall be laid, as soon as may be after it is made, before each House of Parliament...*"[47] This is a welcome provision that ensures two essentials: (a) that certain essential provisions of the Bill and recommendations of the ECI to give effect to them can be granted Executive and Statutory backing; and (b) that neither the Executive nor the Parliament can take a decision related to the Act in the face of opposition from the ECI. The merit of this provision lies not only in the fact that it provides for a holistic inter-relationship between the Executive, Legislature and ECI (as also the Judiciary by way of Judicial Review) in legislation related to political party reforms. Rather, it also

minimizes the friction between these bodies post-decision making, by ensuring that all decisions are thrashed out at the policy formulation stage. This helps minimize the consequences that a clash of will between the bodies may have on the quality of policy implementation.

7. *Seventh,* the Bill does not provide for the introduction of the much-debated '*None of the Above*' (NOTA) option for voters. Although certain sections of civil society may be disappointed at the non-inclusion of NOTA, this author finds no reason to complain. Although one may agree with NOTA in principle on the ground that the Right to Vote *For* includes the Right to Vote *Against*, NOTA's feasibility appears unlikely from a *realpolitik* perspective. Any provision of NOTA must necessarily include a threshold percentage of negative votes polled by the electorate which, if crossed, the election must be declared *null and void* and a fresh election with fresh candidates be declared. An unacademic prediction of voter behavior under the circumstances would arguably suggest that the average voter is so disillusioned with the existing political system, party conduct and candidate quality that s/he may well register a NOTA vote repeatedly at each successive election, until such time that the greater consequences of NOTA to the nation sinks into the electorate's comprehension. (The disillusionment is likely to be enhanced by the unfortunate fact that the electorate in most constituencies is forced to elect the least evil instead of the greatest good.) The greater consequences of NOTA and the repeated elections that it causes include the immense financial, man-power and temporal cost that the nation must bear to conduct each election. Also worrisome is the arguable likelihood that successive elections within a short span of time would lead to not only voter apathy, but also increasing lassitude amongst the administrative staff (polling officers, police et al.). This could result in a decline in the quality of voter mandate as well as poll conduct.

8. *Finally,* on a related note, a case could be made for the Bill to incorporate compulsory voting, at the cost of disincentives for failure to comply. The precise nature, content and degree of such disincentives can be placed on the agenda for contemporary public debate.

Concluding Observations

India has spent most of her Independent years debating the nature and content of political party reforms. The only consensus on the issue seems to be over the urgent need for reform, with only political parties standing opposed to this view. It is little wonder that the functioning of political parties worries the nation *en masse*, as despite their extra-constitutional origin, they remain the cornerstone of India's parliamentary democracy. Each evil and good in the functioning of our polity, economy and society is directly or indirectly influenced by our party culture. For this very reason, we are compelled to engineer party reforms in a gradual and incremental manner rather than in a revolutionary and absolute manner; each party reform must be allowed the time required to live out its tremor in the society and economy, before a new upheaval is introduced in the nation's polity. Perhaps this is the reason why reform suggestions are borne out after decades of their introduction, and the recommendations put forth by each reform committee perforce overlap with those of the committees that immediately precede and succeed it.

Notes

1. Balaji, J. (2013). *Parties Assert Right to Announce Freebies in Election Manifestoes.* The Hindu. Retrieved 30th October, 2013 from http://www.thehindu.com/news/national/parties-assert-right-to-announce-freebies-in-election-manifestos/article5015517.ece.
2. Press Trust of India. (2013). *Bar Chargesheeted People from Contesting Polls, EC tells Supreme Court.* India TV. Retrieved 30th October, 2013 from http://www.indiatvnews.com/politics/national/bar-chargesheeted-people-from-contesting-polls-ec-tells-supreme-11945.html
3. Vaidyanathan, A. and Phukan, S. (2013). *Jailed Politicians Can't Contest: Supreme Court Ruling Faces Legal Challenge?* NDTV. Retrieved 30th October, 2013 from http://www.ndtv.com/article/india/

jailed-politicians-can-t-contest-supreme-court-ruling-faces-legal-challenge-391306.

4. Shakil, M. (2013). *Political Parties Divided over Banning of Opinion Polls.* IBN Live. Retrieved 10th November, 2013 from http://ibnlive.in.com/news/political-parties-divided-over-banning-of-opinion-polls/433019-37-64.html
5. Press Trust of India. (2013). *Panel Recommends Taking Away Certain Powers Vested with EC*. The Hindu. Retrieved 30th October, 2013 from http://www.thehindu.com/news/national/panel-recommends-taking-away-certain-powers-vested-with-ec/article5061463.ece?ref=relatedNews
6. Balaji, J. (2013).*Reprieve for RTI as Bill to Insulate Parties is Deferred.* The Hindu. Retrieved 30th October, 2013 from http://www.thehindu.com/news/national/reprieve-for-rti-as-bill-to-insulate-parties-is-deferred/article5096990.ece
7. Venkatachaliah, M.N. (Chair). (2011). *The Political Parties (Registration and Regulation of Affairs, etc.) Draft Bill, 2011.* (P: 3). Retrieved 30th October, 2013 from http://adrindia.org/sites/default/files/Political%20Parties%20Bill%202011%20Draft%20Booklet_0.pdf
8. Staff Reporter. (2011). *Draft Bill on Reforming Parties Out.* The Hindu. Retrieved 30th October, 2013 from http://www.thehindu.com/todays-paper/tp-national/tp-karnataka/draft-bill-on-reforming-parties-out/article2002575.ece
9. Tarkunde, V.M. (Chair). (1978). *Report of the Committee on Election Expenses.* 8(c) and 8(d). Retrieved 30th October, 2013 from http://lawmin.nic.in/ld/erreports/TarkundeCommitteeReport.pdf
10. Goswami, D. (Chair). (1990). *Report of the Committee on Electoral Reforms.* Chapter V.1, V.2 and V.6. Retrieved 30th October, 2013 from http://lawmin.nic.in/ld/erreports/Dinesh%20Goswami%20Report%20on%20Electoral% 20Reforms.pdf
11. *Ibid.* Chapter V.2.
12. *Ibid.* Chapter V.6.
13. Vohra, N.N. (Chair). (1993). *Vohra Committee Report.* 6.2(iii). Retrieved 30th October, 2013 from http://networkedblogs.com/cfegj
14. Gupta, I. (Chair). (1998). *Committee on State Funding of Elections Report.* Retrieved 30th October, 2013 from http://lawmin.nic.in/ld/erreports/Indrajit%20Gupta%20Committee%20Report.pdf
15. Jeevan Reddy, B.P. (Chair). (1999). *Law Commission of India's 170th Report on Reform of the Electoral Laws.* 3.1.1. Retrieved 30th October,

2013 from http://www.lawcommissionofindia.nic.in/lc170.htm# Necessity for providing law relating to internal

16. Trivedi, R.K. (Chair). (2002). *NCRWC's Consultation Paper on Review of the Working of Political Parties Specially in Relation to Elections and Reform Options.* 8.2 and 8.3. Retrieved 30th October, 2013 from http://lawmin.nic.in/ncrwc/finalreport/v2b1-8.htm
17. Moily, V. (Chair). ((2007). *Fourth Report of the Second Administrative Reforms Commission on Ethics in Governance.* 2.1.3.2. Retrieved 30th October, 2013 from http://arc.gov.in/4threport.pdf
18. *Ibid.* 2.1.4.3.
19. Venkatachaliah, M.N. (Chair). (2011). *The Political Parties (Registration and Regulation of Affairs, etc.) Draft Bill, 2011.* Chapter II.3. Retrieved 30th October, 2013 from http://adrindia.org/sites/default/files/Political%20Parties%20Bill%202011%20Draft%20Booklet_0.pdf
20. *Ibid.* Chapter II.4.3.
21. *Ibid.* Chapter II.5.3.
22. *Ibid.* Chapter II.5.2.
23. *Ibid.* Chapter II.6.1.d.v.
24. *Ibid.* Chapter V.13.
25. *Ibid.* Chapter II.6.2.
26. *Ibid.* Chapter II.6.1.d.v.
27. *Ibid.* Chapter II.5.5.
28. *Ibid.* Chapter II.5.6.
29. *Ibid.* Chapter II.6.1.f.
30. *Ibid.* Chapter II.6.1.g.
31. *Ibid.* Chapter II.8.
32. *Ibid.* Chapter III.10.
33. *Ibid.* Chapter III.11.
34. *Ibid.* Chapter IV.12.1.
35. *Ibid.* Chapter IV.12.2.
36. *Ibid.* Chapter V.14.1.
37. *Ibid.* Chapter II.7.1.
38. Jeevan Reddy, B.P. (Chair). (1999). *Law Commission of India's 170th Report on Reform of the Electoral Laws.* Retrieved 30th October, 2013 from http://www.lawcommissionofindia.nic.in/lc170.htm#Necessity for providing law relating to internal

39. Venkatachaliah, M.N. (Chair). (2011). *The Political Parties (Registration and Regulation of Affairs, etc.) Draft Bill, 2011.* Chapter II.6.1.d.v. Retrieved 30th October, 2013 from http://adrindia.org/sites/default/files/Political%20Parties%20Bill%202011%20Draft%20Booklet_0.pdf
40. *Ibid.* Chapter III.10.1.
41. *Ibid.* Chapter III.10.2.
42. Author's suggestions towards the Law Commission of India's Consultation Paper on Electoral Reforms. (2013).
43. Author's suggestions towards the Law Commission of India's Consultation Paper on Electoral Reforms. (2013).
44. Venkatachaliah, M.N. (Chair). (2011). *The Political Parties (Registration and Regulation of Affairs, etc.) Draft Bill, 2011.* Chapter II.4.3. Retrieved 30th October, 2013 from http://adrindia.org/sites/default/files/Political%20Parties%20Bill%202011%20Draft%20Booklet_0.pdf
45. *Ibid.* Chapter II.5.1.
46. *Ibid.* Chapter V.14.1.
47. *Ibid.* Chapter V.14.2.

References

Venkatachaliah, M.N. (Chair). (2011). *The Political Parties (Registration and Regulation of Affairs, etc.) Draft Bill, 2011.* (e-Source).

Tarkunde, V.M. (Chair). (1978). *Report of the Committee on Election Expenses.* (e-Source).

Goswami, D. (Chair). (1990). *Report of the Committee on Electoral Reforms.* (e-Source).

Vohra, N.N. (Chair). (1993). *Vohra Committee Report.* (e-Source).

Gupta, I. (Chair). (1998). *Committee on State Funding of Elections Report.* (e-Source).

Jeevan Reddy, B.P. (Chair). (1999). *Law Commission of India's 170th Report on Reform of the Electoral Laws.* (e-Source).

Trivedi, R.K. (Chair). (2002). *NCRWC's Consultation Paper on Review of the Working of Political Parties Specially in Relation to Elections and Reform Options.* (e-Source).

Moily, V. (Chair). ((2007). *Fourth Report of the Second Administrative Reforms Commission on Ethics in Governance.* (e-Source).

Technology and Social Processes in India

Dr. Narendar Pani

Sanjay Biswas belonged to that rare breed of distinguished Scientists who were acutely aware of the interaction between science and society. His many achievements as a Professor in the Indian Institute of Science, Bangalore, only added to his commitment to work towards what science could do to create an equitable society that was free of prejudice. Over the decades that I knew Sanjay I cannot claim to have met him very frequently, but each meeting had a lasting impact. The last time I met him was when the Indian Institute of Science had decided to launch its undergraduate degree. Sanjay was keen that the programme had a meaningful social science component and asked me to offer a course. After teaching the quick-thinking teenagers I realized the many dimensions of the task of getting emerging young scientists to adequately recognize that they did not live in a social vacuum. It would then be most appropriate to remember Sanjay through an essay on the role of technology in post-Independence Indian society targeted at those just entering the heady world of learning science.

Technology and Society

To assert that science and society are closely linked is, in a sense, to state the obvious. Scientists are also social beings and what they do, or do not do, will be reflected in society. But once we go beyond such obvious generalities the relationship between science and society can be a much more complex one, influenced by a variety of factors.

The social ethos could determine what the scientists believe they would like to do. Even the idea that scientists should be left free to do whatever they want is not free of social influences. After all scientists have to survive as they pursue their interests. And it is society which determines just how they will do so. Take the case of Sanjay's own Indian Institute of Science. When it was set up early in the twentieth century there was a view that it should focus on students of independent means so that they had the capital to make use of the knowledge gained in the institute. It was left to then Maharaja of Mysore, Krishnaraja Wadiyar IV, to point out in 1911 "that if a hard and fast rule is made against the grant of scholarships, the result may be to shut out an occasional student who has brilliant abilities without the means of supporting himself during his course of study at the Institute".[1] The extent and manner in which scientists are allowed to pursue their own interests are thus themselves socially determined.

The interaction between science and society is reflected in, among other spheres, the way technology unfolds. This is evident once we explore the distinction between science and technology. As JD Bernal wrote in *Science in History,* "A technique is an individually acquired and socially secured way of doing something; a science is a way of understanding how to do it in order to do it better".[2] Implicit in this conceptualization are at least three points where society interacts with the creation and choice of technology. First, there is the relationship between the individual and technology that determines how a technology is individually acquired. Second, there is the process through which society secures a particular way of doing something. And third, there is the social influence on the relationship between science and technology.

The social relationship between the individual and technology is most evident when individuals have the ability to choose a particularly technology. Individuals who can afford to buy the most expensive cell phone have a wide range of options to choose from. Their choice is invariably influenced by advertising which in turn reflects the social mores that are marketed at a point of time. At the same time there is a more significant, if less spoken about, determinant of the relationship between the individual and technology: the access to a particular technology. The access to a technology can be constrained by a number of factors, the most obvious one being the cost of the technology being greater than the individual can afford. But it is also possible for that access to be constrained through other means, such as a government ban on the import of a foreign technology.

The social process through which society secures a particular way of doing something has several dimensions. There is the social pressure to do something that increases one's status in society. In a completely commercialized environment this could be reduced to merely owning products that are the most expensive. But there are also influences that go beyond crass commercialism. It may be more fashionable to own gadgets that can do more things, even if we do not find the time or inclination to use all the applications a gadget can provide. And it is not even always necessary that the movement is from low technologies to higher technologies. There are times when fashion can push the change in technology in the other direction. One striking example of this reversal is the case of the global garment industry. In the 1950s the middle and high fashion garment industry was largely concentrated in the relatively high technology, high fashion centres of the advanced world, like Paris. With the youth rebellion in the 1960s through musical events like Woodstock, it became fashionable to wear the clothes of the working class. As denim and jeans – including torn ones – took over fashion, production moved a few notches down the technology ladder. Indeed, it went down far enough to allow production itself to be relocated in the less developed parts of the world.

The social influences on the relationship between science and technology can be seen at different points in the development of a particular science and its conversion into technology. The access to science is itself socially determined. In a country where even literacy is not universal it is evident that not everyone has access to the basic education that is required to take the first step in the ladder of science learning. Social processes play a predominant role in determining which groups in society gain this access and which groups do not. And this is not a matter of economic affordability alone. Some social groups may value a science education more than others. The next step of tapping scientific knowledge for technological innovations is also not independent of social processes. In an extreme case scientists can be so completely insulated from society that their knowledge is not easily available to those who can use it to create socially relevant technologies.

The nature of the three social influences on science and technology – on the individual, on social support for a technology, and on the scientist – is itself not unchanging. As society is transformed so are these influences. An attempt to capture the working of these influences in post-independent India must then be made in the context of the social, economic and political trends of the period. And in this exercise it is useful to break up the history of post-Independence India into three broad phases: the Nehruvian Era, from Independence till the mid-sixties; the Garibi Hatao Era, from the mid-sixties till the mid-eighties; and the Liberalization Era, from the mid-eighties onwards.

The Nehruvian Era

In dealing with issues of technology in the years soon after Independence India faced a challenge created by its ideals. It had committed itself to being a democracy despite a vast majority of its population being illiterate. The democratic process could then generate elected representatives whose constituents were not particularly concerned about issues related to technology. The government of Jawaharlal Nehru addressed this dilemma by creating policy making bodies that reported directly to the prime minister, particularly the Planning Commission and the Atomic Energy Commission. These bodies were headed by intellectuals who had the trust of the prime minister. A common feature in the leadership of these commissions was that they shared, among other things, a belief in a prominent place for large high technology projects. This was most evident in the Homi Bhaba led Atomic Energy Commission. The Planning Commission did allow for a wider range of projects to be taken up. But the Second Plan put in place a strategy that provided a prominent place for large high technology projects.

The Second Plan strategy was based on the belief that growth over long periods of time would only be possible if an economic base was first created. The first task was then to develop a base of heavy industry. Given the levels of knowledge available in the country at the time the entire process would necessarily be a long drawn out one. The high capital costs involved and the long gestation periods meant that this investment was largely beyond the reach of India's largely infant industry. The state thus had to take on the role of being the major investor. Industry was protected from competing with imports through strict restrictions on what could be imported. It was assumed that once the base was created, the private sector would be able to build on it and grow.

Built into the creation of a successful heavy industry base was the recognition of the need for high technology. This would initially involve the import of substantial amounts of technology, but it was expected that this technology would be transferred to India. A patent regime was created where it would be easy for imported technologies to be absorbed and replicated. The focus was on process patents rather than product patents. Thus a product could be replicated in India without breaching its patents as long as the process through which it was produced was even slightly different. As Indian industry was given time to grow, imports of goods embodying higher technologies were restricted.

As a result of this strategy the technology an individual could access in this era was necessarily limited. This is perhaps best reflected in the Ambassador car. The Morris Oxford II model car was produced in Britain between 1956 and 1959. In 1958 the first Ambassador car was made using this technology. The continued protection against imports however ensured that there was no great pressure to keep upgrading the product. The limited competition ensured that this transfer of technology did not result in a longer-term transformation of the car industry. The consumer then had a limited range of products embodying modern technology available to her.

The acceptance of this limited availability of products was the result of two facets of the social ethos of the time. The first was an idealist view that the sacrifices being made at that time would result in much more rapid growth in the future. The commitment to the building of a new nation made the acceptance of relatively low technology products seem a minor price to pay. The second aspect of the ethos that enabled the acceptance of relatively low technology products was a sense of equitable independence. The pride in a country building its own technology led to the celebration of achievements that were important steps toward the top of the technological mountain, even as there was awareness that these steps were still some distance from the peak. And the emphasis on equity meant that it was important to focus on products that anyone could access even if that meant the few who could afford products embodying the most sophisticated technologies would not be able to access them.

Built into this approach was also a particular notion of the relationship between science and technology. The focus on the end products meant a subtle shift in emphasis from science education to technology education. If the pre-Independence era saw the setting up of the Indian Institute of Science, the post-Independence years saw the emergence of several Indian Institutes of Technology. More than the nomenclature of these institutes there was a shift in emphasis away from pure science. In an ethos which celebrated the ability to transfer technologies, there was understandably little incentive to spend a lifetime in the uncertain world of pure science. It was much more rewarding to do a competent job of adapting technologies developed elsewhere.

The Garibi Hatao Era

By the mid-sixties the patience involved in waiting for the Second Plan strategy to bear fruit was beginning to wear thin. Weakened by two wars the country was finding it more difficult to keep its idealistic spirit going. To make matters worse the Second Plan did not have a prominent place for agriculture. This contributed in no small measure to India slipping to near famine conditions for two consecutive years in 1964-65 and 1965-66. India became dependent on food granted to it under the US Public Law 480. The dependence on PL 480 made a mockery of the emphasis on technological self-sufficiency in industry.

Mrs. Indira Gandhi as Prime Minister decided there was little room for continuing to wait for the Second Plan strategy to live up to its promises. She began to focus on a strategy of more immediate and visible gains. She sought to boost food grain production through the Green Revolution and later stepped up welfare schemes for the poor to realize her 'Garibi Hatao' slogan.

The average Indian's access to products embodying technology arguably grew the most rapidly during this period. This may seem an odd claim to make in the context of popular notions of products embodying technology. Indians still had to wait years for a telephone connection or even a two-wheeler. But in a country that was still far from being free of starvation and had high levels of food insecurity the products that mattered the most were various food grains. The Green Revolution technologies fundamentally transformed yields in rice and wheat. With the Public Distribution System distributing the rice and wheat at heavily subsidized prices, the benefits of technologically enhanced yields in rice and wheat were widespread. A technological transformation that drew millions of Indians away from starvation must be treated as India's most successful technological breakthrough.

The social process that secured this technological transformation was built around an acceptance of a welfare state. The political class began to see welfare as the major, if not sole, instrument of democratic politics. The welfare system was further consolidated through an increasingly entrenched mechanism of patronage politics. The influence of a welfare oriented ethos on technology extended beyond agriculture and the rural population. Large high technology public sector plants too began to be located in areas where they were expected to provide the greatest political dividend. Locating these units in areas where they were economically unviable dramatically reduced their chances of survival. Thus while the welfare ethos may have provided political dividends in the short run, it soon destroyed the faith the ordinary Indian had in large public sector projects.

The policy towards converting science into technology gained a sense of urgency in this era. There was a much greater emphasis on immediate results. In agriculture, an entire extension network was created to take the benefits of achievements in the laboratory to the land. Even in more high technology areas the focus was on visible achievements. The Indian Space Research Organization was created during this period. By 1975 India had put its first satellite, Aryabhata, into space. And the emphasis on achievement was so intense that an Indian was sent to space, even if that had to be done in a Soviet mission. If in the beginning of this era the focus was still on creating Indian science and technology, by the end there was a subtle but significant shift towards seeking success even if it was on the shoulders of others.

The Liberalization Era

The Second Plan strategy of state investment to create a base for industrialization may have been more long drawn out than originally intended, and its course distorted during the Garibi Hatao era, but it was not without its long term consequences. The growth of the public sector had created an economic base, even if it fell short of achieving its full potential. It had also created a large organized working class that had access to state investment in education at various levels. The growing confidence of the working class saw a shift in the savings habits of Indians. From relying entirely on the safety of post office deposits they began to move to nationalized banks. The more confident among then began to venture into capital markets. At the same time the next generation that had benefited from higher education became a significant manpower base. Some Indian industrialists tapped both the savings through the capital markets and the manpower to create rapidly growing industrial houses. At the same time the communication revolution enabled local technological manpower to be utilized in meeting global demand. By the mid-eighties the owners of several Indian business houses had begun their journey towards joining the club of the richest individuals in the world.

The consolidation of this process demanded greater access to the most advanced technologies available. The software industry could not be expected to compete with the rest of the world unless they were given access to the best computer hardware. This meant lowering the tariff and other barriers that were in place from the early era of protecting infant Indian industry. It was also argued that if the manufacturers were not to simply take the benefit of imports of inputs without transferring at least a part of that gain to consumers, they would have to be forced to compete with imports of the finished products. To this end the domestic market was also opened to foreign consumer goods.

One of the consequences of this regime was that the individual's access to products embodying the most sophisticated technologies increased visibly. The major beneficiaries of this access were undoubtedly those who could afford the hi-tech products that were now being imported. There were vast sections of Indian society that had no access to these products. Even as the advertising world celebrated the arrival of cars with the latest technological features, it was clear that these products were well out of the reach of the vast majority of the people of the country. There were no doubt important exceptions where the less well off could break into the fringes of these markets. Arguably the most notable of these innovations was that of a missed call, a system that enabled users of a mobile telephone to convey messages without a charge. But most Indians could not access the benefits of imported technology in consumer goods that had now become the norm.

Social processes played an important role in ensuring this unequal distribution of the benefits of technological change were accepted. Among the many social instruments that served this purpose there was a prominent role for aspirations. The celebration of inequality, including the use of hi-tech products to flaunt wealth, gained acceptance largely by the poorer classes being encouraged to aspire to be a part of the rich. The earlier social norms developed in the Garibi Hatao era actively played on the class divide, often advocating violence against the rich. But the aspiration based social norms of the liberalization era promoted the idea that the class divide was best addressed by those on the losing end of the divide today aspiring to be on the other side in the future. And when this aspiration was clearly unrealistic, it was replaced by the aspiration that even if the current generation of the poor could not cross the class divide, their children would be able to.

This import dominated strategy had its effects on the process of transforming science into technology. With Indian technology institutions losing out to imports, the best of local scientific talent had less professional incentive to remain within the country. They found it much more professionally, and financially, rewarding to work abroad themselves. This in turn increased the demand for foreign education that would make it easier for them to gain employment in the advanced world. It could be argued that this was not an entirely negative process. There was the possibility that at least some of those who had moved abroad would later in their professional careers return to India. It was also expected that the success of those of Indian origin abroad would translate into benefits for the country including the transfer of funds. But it did have a negative impact on the technological institutions – especially the state led ones – within the country.

The Indian experience with the interaction between social processes and S&T is too varied to be captured in the brief overview this essay has sought to provide. But it is quite clear that every major turn Indian society has taken since Independence has not left its science and technology untouched. Individual access to the benefits of science and technology has moved from an era of waiting in hope to one of merely seeking imports. This access has also not been uniform across different section of Indian society. While the Green Revolution did have a major impact on the worst off Indians, the impact of the other social transformations on these sections of society was far less equitable. And the Science and Technology establishment has itself moved a fair distance down the road from being temples of progress to becoming what are predominantly spectator galleries.

Notes

1. *Speeches of His Highness Sri Krishnaraja Wadiyar Bahadur, 1902-1920*, Bangalore: Govt. Press, 1921, pp 123-128.
2. JD Bernal *Science in History*, Vol 1, Penguin, Hammondsworth, 1969, p. 47.

Hunger Pangs: India is World's Hunger Capital!

Justin John

India is going through a paradoxical phase of nutritional challenge. Modern India is a place in which majority of the population is still starving whilst an ever increasing number of people are becoming morbidly obese. Both of these phenomena can be attributed to structural adjustment demands. On one had there is a demand for cut in food subsides along with a demand to incentivise private corporations. Food security and the right to food have become political issues in India today. The passage of National Food Security Bill in Parliament: a promise made in the UPA's "first 100 days" agenda after its return to power in 2009 was dubbed as 'Vote Security' by the opposition. This political banter by the opposition is a stark evidence of food insecurity in India. However, eradicating hunger requires concrete action, rather than hollow promises. India has been ranked in the 'alarming' category of the Hunger Index prepared by the International Food Policy Research Institute. What is shocking to discover is countries like Burkinao Faso, Sudan, Rawanda, and Zimbabwe were feeding their people better than India. Even war ravaged countries like Afghanistan and Iraq perform better than India on Hunger. Pakistan, Nepal and Sri Lanka outperform India. Out of 79 countries, India ranked 65th on the 2012 Global Hunger Index. According to World Food Program, India is home to about 25 per cent of the world's hungry people. The State of Food Insecurity in the World 2008 released by the Food and Agricultural Organisation estimates that India is home to more than 230 million undernourished people, which is 21 per cent of the national population.

Catastrophic situation of nutrition in India based on NFHS II provides evidence of mass deprivation among children and women. According to the survey, 46 per cent of all Indian children are undernourished, 52 per cent of all adult women are anemic, and 33 per cent of women and 28 per cent of men have a body mass index (BMI) below normal. One of the WHO criteria to determine famine defines a community with more than 40 per cent of its population having a body mass index (BMI) of less than 18.5 as famine stricken. By this yardstick, Indian children as a whole and many other communities are in the grip of perpetual state of famine.

Hunger map of India (IFPRI)

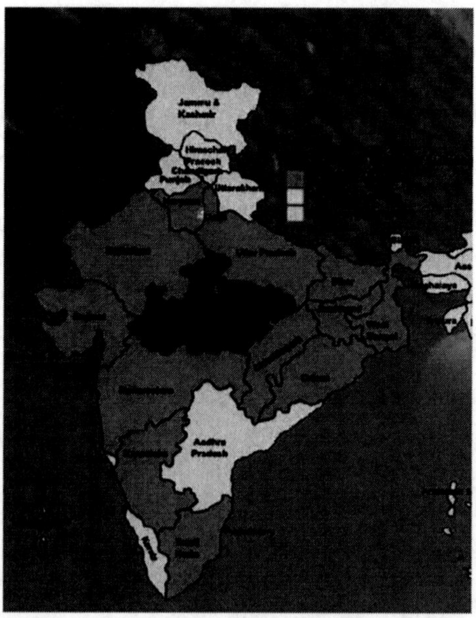

According to the National Sample Survey Organisation's (NSSO) large survey of 2004-05, the average daily intake of calories of rural population has dropped by 106 kcal (4.9 per cent) from 2,153 kcal

Table 2: The India State Hunger Index and its Underlying Components

State	*Prevalence of calorie under-nourishment (per cent)*	*Proportion of under-weight among children <5 years (per cent)*	*Under-five mortality rate (deaths per hundred)*	*India State Hunger Index score*	*India State Hunger Index rank*
Punjab	11.1	24.6	5.2	13.63	1
Kerala	28.6	22.7	1.6	17.33	2
Andhra Pradesh	19.6	32.7	6.3	19.53	3
Assam	14.6	36.4	8.5	19.83	4
Haryan	15.1	39.7	5.2	20.00	5
Tamil Nadu	29.1	30.0	3.5	20.87	6
Rajasthan	14.0	40.4	8.5	20.97	7
West Bengal	18.5	38.5	5.9	20.97	8
Uttar Pradesh	14.5	42.3	9.6	22.13	9
Maharashtra	27.0	36.7	4.7	22.80	10
Karnataka	28.1	37.6	5.5	23.73	11
Orissa	21.4	40.9	9.1	23.80	12
Gujarat	23.3	44.7	6.1	24.70	13
Chhattisgarh	23.3	47.6	9.0	26.63	14
Bihar	17.3	56.1	8.5	27.30	15
Jharkhand	19.6	57.1	9.3	28.67	16
Madhya Pradesh	23.4	59.8	9.4	30.87	17
India	20.0	42.5	7.4	23.30	18

Note: The India State Hunger Index represents the index calculated using a cal19orie undernourishment cutoff of 1,632 kcals per person per day to allow for comparin of the India State hunger Index with the Global Hunger Index 2008. The ISHI score for India using this cutoff is 23.3 and corresponds more closely with the GHI 2008 score for India of 23.7 than any other calorie cutoff.

Sources: Calorie undernourishment: IIPS 2007; child underweight: IIPS 2007 and authors calculationl

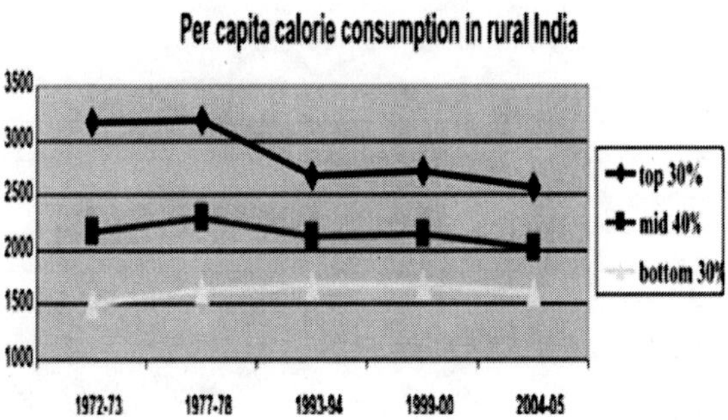

from 1993-94 to 2004-05 and by 51kacl (2.5%) from 2,071to 2,020 kcal in urban areas. NSSO data indicates that the calorie intake of the economically poor continues to be 30 to 50 per cent less than the calorie intake of the economically better off of the population, despite poor needing more calories because of hard manual work. Whereas the economically better off of in India consumed 2564 kcal per day 2004-05, the economically poor consumed only 1607 kcal per day, which is to be seen as a sign of distress and hunger. India which is trying to secure a permanent seat in the UN Security Council, and aiming to become a 'superpower' by 2020 has to acknowledge hunger and call malnutrition as a national disaster and come out with a holistic approach to combat nutrition problem gripping it, if the country desires to take its place among the developing countries of the world.

Agrarian Crisis and Hunger

The Green Revolution brought about fundamental changes in the Indian agriculture. Pure technical solutions were offered to remedy food crisis looming large. Usage of hybrid seeds were introduced and farmers were pushed to use chemical fertilisers and pesticides. Mechanised agriculture was encouraged to increase food production. Green revolution did increase production of certain food grains, and led to prosperity of farmers in certain pockets of India. But in the long run Green Revolution has greatly damaged Indian agriculture.

Farmers' Suicides in India

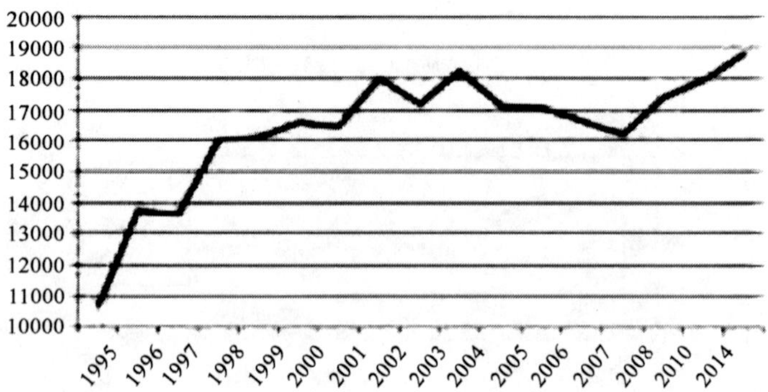

Small and marginal farmers have been decimated. Farmers have lost control over the seeds they were sowing, and have become dependent on traders and large multinational corporations. Cost of cultivation has shot up beyond the control of the farming communities. Opening up Indian economy ensured farmers had to face volatile market situations and unfair competition from highly subsidized corporate farmers. All these factors together led to an agrarian crisis that saw more than 2,50,000 farmers mostly growing cash crops committing suicide between 1995 and 2011 across India. Most of the victims belong to small and marginal farmers, and many belonging to backward classes and scheduled castes. According to the data available from National Bureau of Crime Record the number of farmers suicides have been on increase year after year.

Land Grab and Food Insecurity

Large tracts of agricultural land being diverted to non-agricultural purposes will have cataclysmic implications on food security. With a over a one billion population to be fed, and agricultural returns diminishing, it is important to protect cultivable lands and take measures to make arid land into cultivation to safeguard food security of India. Only 46 per cent of India's land area is under agriculture. Rapid urbanisation and demand for land from non-agricultural sectors have led to cultivated area going down by 1.5 per cent. In terms of percentages it might be a miniscule drop. But in absolute terms it amounts to 21 lakh hectares. Considering the feudal landscape of India, farmers from marginalised communities are going belly up. Access to land holding in India is still dismally low in spite of land reforms. Land reform measures have failed. 41 per cent of the rural households are still landless and depended on agricultural labour for livelihood. All across the country, agriculture land is shrinking. In Kerala, the area under paddy is around 3.5 lakh hectares as against 10 lakh hectares in 1980. As a result the demand for rice is about five times higher than what is produced by the state. Mineral-rich Orissa is losing agricultural land to mining and power projects. Even in the case of a small state like Himachal Pradesh the net sown area has declined by 33,000 hectares between 1991 and 2001. SEZ (Special

Economic Zones) are at the heart of the problem. The establishment of an SEZ generally requires the forced acquisition of land and the eviction of its previous users mostly farmers. This has had consequences in terms of food sovereignty of India.

National Food Security Act

National Food Security Act with all its limitations has the potential to wipe out hunger and starvation deaths in India. It promises a minimum entitlement of 5kg of cereal per person, per month, to 75 per cent of India's rural population and 50 per cent of the urban poor at a price ranging from Rs 3 – Rs 1 a kg. Along with ensuring 800 million people get at least a minimum level of food required for sustenance, it also provides for Rs1,000 per month to pregnant and lactating mothers for a period of six months and a nutritious meal to all children from 0 to 3; and then, through the mid-day meal scheme, upto the age of 14 the scheme has promised to provide food to the hungry. National Food Security Act is being hailed as the largest welfare scheme in the world. Most important aspect of enactment of National Food Security Act is articulation of the right, which makes right to food a justiciable right. Right to food to its people is welfare state's obligation towards its citizens.

Market Reactions

Markets have registered pointed disapproval of the food security bill when passed in the parliament. Media also played a role in giving undue air time to crisis mongers preaching free market fundamentalism and dishing out statements in relation to damaging consequences to India's fiscal deficit but being forgetful of capabilities of millions of Indians lost due to damaging consequences of hunger and malnutrition.

National Food Security Bill would entail an expenditure of Rs1.25 lakh crores. Food subsidy has been rising year after year on its own, mainly due to rising support and procurement prices. Expenditure on National Food Security Bill, which has large positive impacts on lives of the marginalised, should be juxtaposed with exorbitant tax write-offs and exemptions for the rich, industry and exports.The budget 2013 had let go off revenues of Rs 5.74 lakh crore. The diamond and gold industry alone got Rs 60,000 as tax exemptions. Financial consequence to ensure right to food should be viewed as retributive justice by the Indian state to its majority of impoverished citizenry. The fight to ensure right to food for all has to be an ongoing effort to ensure hunger free India. This struggle has to transcend cultural, class barriers and involve all quarters of the society. Hunger is a blot on the Indian democracy, with a potential to disturb our democratic structures.

WTO and its hurdles on National Food Security Act

India's food security Act was on the top of the negotiating agenda at the WTO ministerial conference held at Bali in Indonesia. WTO was worried about India's food bill on the global markets. Sovereign India has to bargain with the developed countries trying to push the developing countries to subsidise trade interests of its corporations and agribusiness giants. Speaking at an event organised by CII and FICCI, WTO Director General, Roberto Azevedo had asserted that "India will soon be breaching aggregate measurement of support committed to WTO due to its new food security program". The real worry of WTO is increased procurement of wheat and rice from poor Indian farmers would lead to market loss for international market and leading to a distortion of trade. US/EU continues to oppose the proposal floated by India through G-33 countries. G-33 countries include China, India, Indonesia, Pakistan and others which has come together to protect food security, livelihoods and rural development by seeking amendments in trade policy. India wants its enhanced subsidy outgo for food procurement from small farmers is not to be seen as trade distorting. These subsidies, required to meet the food security needs of hungry population, and thus needs to be kept outside the limit of 'Aggregate Measurement of Support'.

Bonded Labour and Modern Day Slavery in India

Kirankamal Prasad

Does slavery exist in India? Answer could be a strong 'no'. Does bonded labour find a place in the modern globalised India? Going by the government records, the answer seems to be, 'probably not'or at the most, it could only be found in some remote villages. What about modern slavery? No one seems to have a clue about it. On 17th October 2013, "Walk Free Foundation", Australia came out with its first edition of a Global Slavery Index, providing, country by country, for 162 countries, of the number of people living in modern slavery. The report revealed that modern day slavery in its various forms is a global phenomenon affecting even the developed countries and not just those in the global south. The key finding from this Index is that there are an estimated 29.8 million people in modern slavery all over the world. Of these, India alone accounts for nearly half the number, i.e., 13,956,010, which is the highest number of people in modern slavery in a country. The other nine countries that come after India with the highest number of enslaved people are: China (2,949,243), Pakistan (2,127,132), Nigeria (701,032), Ethiopia (651,110), Russia (516,217), Thailand (472,811), Democratic Republic of Congo (462,327), Myanmar (384,037) and Bangladesh (343,192). Taken together these ten countries account for 76 per cent of the total estimated enslaved people. The ten countries with the lowest number of enslaved persons are: Norway (652), Panama (548), Mauritius (535), New Zealand (495), Trinidad and Tobago (486), Brunei (417), Ireland (321), Luxembourg (69), Barbados (46) and Iceland (22).

India Fourth in Modern Slavery

In terms of the prevalence of modern slavery to the total population of a country, India ranks the fourth (13,956,010 among 1,236,686,732), coming after Mauritania (151,353 among 3,796,141), Haiti (209,165 among 10,173,775), Pakistan (2,127,132 among 179,160,111), Nepal (258,806 among 27,474,377), Moldova (33,325 among 3,559,541), Benin (80,371 among 10,050,702), Cote d'Ivoire (156,827 among 19,839,750), The Gambia (14,046 among 1,791,225) and Gabon (14,046 among 1,632,572). The ten countries with the lowest prevalence of modern slavery are: Denmark (727 among 5,590,478), Finland (704 among 5,414,293), Luxembourg (69 among 531,441), Norway (652 among 5,018,869), Sweden (1,237 among 9,516,617), Switzerland (1,040 among 7,997,152), New Zealand (495 among 4,433,100), United Kingdom (4,426 among 63,227,526), Ireland (321 among 4,588,798) and Iceland (22 among 320,137). These figures point out to the widespread prevalence of modern slavery all over the world. India not only tops the list, it accounts for almost half the number of enslaved persons in the world. The second country with the highest number of enslaved people is China but it accounts for only 21 per cent of those in India. And the third country with the highest number is Pakistan, which accounts for 15 per cent of the enslaved persons in India. The next country is Nigeria, which has only 5 per cent of the people in modern slavery. All this should remove any doubt in us about the existence and high prevalence of modern slavery in India which includes bonded labour.

What is Modern Slavery?

GSI includes slavery, slavery-like practices like bonded labour, debt bondage, forced marriage, sale or exploitation of children, human trafficking and forced labour in all forms of modern slavery. To understand these realities clearly and to grasp their inter-linkages, we require to take note of the definitions in the relevant international covenants and our national legislation. Slavery means the status or condition of a person over whom any or all of the powers attaching to the right of ownership are exercised - slavery, servitude, forced labour and similar institutions and practices according to the

Convention of 1926. Slavery-like practices are debt bondage, forced or servile marriage, sale or exploitation of children (including in armed conflict) and descent-based slavery. Forced Labour means all work or service which is exacted from any person under the menace of any penalty and for which the said person has not offered himself voluntarily [Convention Concerning Forced or Compulsory Labour, 1930 (ILO No. 29].

Trafficking in Persons has the following elements:

Recruitment, transportation, transfer, harboring or receipt of persons by means of threat or use of force or other forms of coercion, abduction, fraud, deception, the abuse of power or a position of vulnerability or the giving or receiving of payments or benefits to achieve the consent of a person having control over another person (these means are not required in the case of children) with the intent of exploiting that person through prostitution of others, sexual exploitation, forced labour, slavery (or similar practices), servitude, and removal of organs (UN Protocol to prevent, suppress and punish trafficking in Persons, especially Women and Children, 2000).

Bonded Labour

According to the Bonded Labour System (Abolition) Act, 1976 bonded labour system is a type of forced labour in which a debtor either for a loan or advance or any other economic consideration or hereditary or customary or social or caste obligation is made to render service for no wages or only a nominal wage or is prevented from selling labour or the product of labour or to anyone else or is prevented from moving about freely. The Supreme Court has clarified that forced labour need not only involve physical or legal compulsion; it is also found in situations of economic hardships because of which a person agrees to work for nominal wages. Thus, Supreme Court has given even broader definition for force than the ILO definition. The Indian Constitution prohibits, as a fundamental right, *begar* or free labour, forced labour and trafficking in persons. Slavery like practices including bonded labour and debt bondage, forced labour and trafficking in persons are intimately related. If slavery denotes absolute right of ownership over the person of a slave, slavery like practices also denote some, though not an absolute, control over a person. If forced labour and bonded labour both denote extracting labour from a person, in bonded labour, the person has to be totally at the disposal of the master or owner. Slavery like practices include also forced labour, human trafficking for both labour and sexual exploitation, forced marriage, sale and exploitation of children and removal of organs. If slavery, slavery like practices, forced labour and bonded labour denote the end result, human trafficking reveals the process. In a way all these realities are inter-related and, in some sense, overlapping. In the Indian context, what we have to bear in mind is that all these forms are to be found in varying degrees, with bonded labour and debt bondage accounting for the highest proportion among all the forms of modern slavery, may be 75 to 80 per cent. No one can deny there is forced or bonded labour in India. The lofty provisions in the Constitution and the Statute on Bonded Labour, and the numerous stipulations and directions from the Supreme Court, now and again, only give witness to this stark reality in India. But the administration, the police, the judiciary, the politicians and even the public and the civil society organisations, by and large, seem to ignore this grim reality and may even deny its existence.

There is a denial

Bonded labour in India is linked to the deep rooted caste system. In the typical caste system, the untouchables performed all forms of menial labour to families and to the village community without any wages. It was their caste duty to render those services. They were looked after by the families to whom they were attached traditionally. Remnants of these forms of caste based services are still to be witnessed in villages throughout India. The 'caste slave labour' was replaced to a great extent by the present day bonded labour during the times of British Rule in India through a process of indentured labour. The community owned land was privatised. Wage labour and cash payments became more and more the norm. Dalits (untouchables) and moolnivasis (indigenous people) were forced to sell their labour for wages which were not sufficient to look after their individual needs, leave alone those of their family members. They resorted to taking advances or loans, and, in lieu of that, they started mortgaging their and their family members' labour to the creditor. These practices went by various names in different regions and states of India as captured in the Bonded Labour Act, e.g., *adiyamar, baramasia, basahya, bethu, bhagela, cherumar, garru-galu, hali, hari, harwari, holya, jana, jeetha, kamiya, khundit-mundit, kuthia, lakhari, munjhi, mat, munish, nit-majoor, paleru, padiyal, pannayilal, sagri, sanji, sanjawat, sewak, sewakia, seri*and*vetti*... Apart from these terms, many other local nomenclatures for bonded labour are still to be found in many rural areas of the country. Thus we have in Karnataka various terms for bonded labour even today like *sambaladalu, alumaga, manemaga, maneholeya, manemadiga, bittichakri* and so on.

Individuals as Bonded

Nowadays, it is very rare to find in agriculture whole families being held in bondage. It is the norm now for individuals to enter into bonded service. Migrant labour is the emerging trend especially after the process of globalisation set in motion since the 1990s. Many of the moolnivasi and dalit families from among the migrants are likely to get into bonded labour. It is very common now for poor labourers to migrate from the northern districts in Karnataka to the south or to the neighbouring states and from the neighbouring and northern and eastern states to Karnataka and quite a few of them, sometimes with their entire families get trapped in bondage. Similarly, moolnivasi and dalit families from central and eastern states migrating to north and western states in search of labour opportunities are most likely to enter into bonded service. Children from moolnivasi and dalit families as domestic servants to the well off in the metropolitan cities and towns are also most likely to work as bonded labourers and it is an escalating phenomenon. Apart from agriculture, sericulture and horticulture, migrant bonded labour, whether inter-state or intra-state, is found predominantly in rural and urban unorganised sector industries like brick kilns, stone quarries, crushing mines, rice mills, popped rice mills, beedi manufacturing, carpet weaving, construct, power looms, cotton handlooms and various processes under the textile industry, gem cutting, lock making, fireworks, match box, fish processing, leather processing, sugar factories, garages, hotels and tourism spots, massage parlours and so on. Quite a few of these migrant labourers are likely to be ensnared into bondage conditions.

SCs/STs are Bonded

According to a report of the World Bank, in 2012, 32.7 per cent of Indians lived below the international poverty line of less than US$1.25 per day. It is dalits and moolnivasis who still constitute an overwhelming majority among the bonded labourers even today. It some instances, they constitute 90 to 95 per cent among the bonded labourers in a locality or a region. This fact throws light on a very important aspect of the problem of bonded labour. Bonded labour in India is not just an issue of poverty. It is mainly a social issue and a continuing element of the all pervading caste system. Therefore not only while grasping the reality but mainly in trying to find suitable solutions to bonded labour, we require to link economic aspects of poverty with social aspects of the caste system. Incidentally, we can also note that all the major social evils facing the country have caste dimensions to them. Every manual scavenger is from a dalit community. Nearly half the people involved in daily underpaid wage labour in the unorganised sector are from dalit and moolnivasi communities. A great percentage of illiterates come from those communities. An overwhelming majority of child labour and out of school children are from these communities. A significant number of families in the slums belong to these communities.

Treatment to Bonded Labourers

Physical violence, verbal abuse and sexual exploitation rounds off the picture of indignity and oppression inherent in the system of bonded labour. Any delay or slowness in work, even caused by a valid reason, say physical injury while on work or indisposition due to sickness, invites abuse and even violence. Threat of severe physical violence keeps bonded labourers from attempting to escape or run away. Being a bonded labourer itself is demeaning and lowers one in the esteem of the family members and other villagers. Sexual violence of the wives of bonded labourers by the landlords is quite frequent; even seeking sexual favours by the wives of landlords from well built and handsome young boys and men is not uncommon.

The inherent injustices and indignities of the bonded labour system are accentuated by other difficulties. Migrant bonded labourers face enormous difficulties in accessing protections and government entitlements, such as ration card for food, which is based on a worker's residence. Likewise for those who are bonded in their own area, corruption or non-performance of safety nets (such as the Mahatma Gandhi National Rural Employment Guarantee, food rations, primary health care and pensions) and practices of land grabbing by high caste groups or for commercial development leaves people without protections. Many of those who succumb to bonded labour do not officially exist: they have no birth registration or any other identity card so it can be hard for them to access protective entitlements. Most of the poverty alleviation schemes of the government do not reach bonded labourers at all. Even non-governmental efforts at ameliorating poverty do not seem to have an impact on the lives of bonded labourers. The structures and the minimum requirements envisaged under these schemes, be they of the government or of NGOs, keep the bonded labourers miles away.

Modern Slavery

Apart from the traditional and emergent forms of bonded labour within India, there are different types of modern slavery also found in India. Cross-border migration affects India on quite a large scale. Low skilled migrant workers – both internal and foreign (regular and irregular) – are vulnerable to bondage like situations. Many Nepali and Bhutanese migrants, who are exempt from Indian migration visa regulations, fall prey to the machinations of unscrupulous recruiters who exploit their vulnerability as new arrivals. The undocumented and unskilled Bangladeshis, who are not able to qualify for employment visas, take the help of illegal brokers to facilitate employment. The 2012 Global Report on Trafficking in Persons by the United Nations Office on Drugs and Crime has noted that Indian nationals who have migrated for work have found themselves in conditions of modern slavery–often involving recruitment intermediaries and debt bondage–around the world. They have been exploited in various industries including construction, mining, agriculture and hospitality, in manual labour and commercial sexual exploitation, as well as in private domestic work and as domestic staff at Indian diplomatic missions abroad.

Sexual Exploitation

Sexual exploitation of women, men and transgender people, both adults and children, is widespread in India. In north Karnataka, it is linked to dedicating young dalit girls to temples and goddesses through a system called *devadasi* and *muttukattuvudu*. Commercial sexual exploitation takes place in specific established areas in towns and cities. It is also now much more dispersed in disguised forms into rural areas, transport hubs, roadside restaurants and houses in suburban areas, extensively using cell phones, which makes it hard to locate and tackle. Women from Nepal and Bangladesh have been mostly identified in situations of commercial sexual exploitation in India. Other 'non-labour' forms of modern slavery, like forced and servile marriage, fraudulent adoption and organ trafficking have also been identified in India. Poor moolnivasi and dalit as also some minority communities fall prey to the forced marriage of their young girls and sale of young children. They also fall prey to organ trafficking. Forced marriage is to some extent fuelled by sex-ratio disparity. Those states, with worst disparity, and, which happen to be rich, import girls into servile marriages from poorer states.

Government Apathy

The Government of India has stated in a 2008 Report that since the enactment of the Bonded Labour Act in 1976, 287,555 bonded labourers have been identified, of whom 267,593 had been rehabilitated. In contrast to the vast number of persons in modern slavery in India, estimated at 14 million, these figures do not even touch the tip of the ice-burg. Since 1980, the government has consistently donned a denial mode regarding bonded labour. It was the Supreme Court from the early 1980s that has consistently upheld the relevance of the Bonded Labour Act and goaded the administration to take up the challenge of facing bonded labour in the country and in different states and union territories. Even then the governments have not been moved to action at all. While hearing a Writ Petition (Civil) No. 39722 of 1985 in 1997, almost all the states filed affidavits before the Supreme Court that there was no bonded labour in the states or, conceded that if at all it existed, there could be some stray cases. It was to the credit of the then Chief Justice who was hearing the case that he did not accept any of the affidavits and summarily disposed them off by appointing two commissioners each to twelve states mandating them to investigate on bonded labour and report to the Supreme Court. Only the commissioners of Tamil Nadu brought to light the existence of ten lakh bonded labourers in that state just in one year of 1998 or so.

Ray of Hope

The Supreme Court while hearing the same Writ Petition directed the National Human Rights Commission in 1996 to monitor the implementation of the Act on Bonded Labour. Ever since that year, the NHRC has been impressing on the state governments to do the needful. Even then the denial mindset of the government does not seem to have changed much. The Supreme Court has again come to the rescue of bonded labourers in 2012. While finally disposing of the same Writ Petition (Civil) No. 39722 of 1985, it has given a number of strong directions to each of the states and union territories for necessary implementation. If these directions are implemented in letter and spirit by all those concerned, bonded labourers are sure to get justice and we can hope to fully eradicate bonded labour as also all other forms of modern slavery. The most important direction was that every state and union territory was to carry out a survey on bonded labour every three years. These surveys were to be carried out by the District and Sub Divisional Vigilance Committees, which have to be reconstituted every three years. The reports on the results of the surveys should be computerised and sent to the NHRC and the findings are to be displayed in the websites of all the concerned, i.e., the states, the union territories, the NHRC and the union government. Other directions were Gram Panchayats and local bodies must report on bonded labour to the district magistrates; all states and union territories must constitute Vigilance Committees within six months; the district magistrates must carry out their tasks regarding bonded labour with diligence, empathy and sensitivity and effectively implement Sections 10, 11 and 12 of the Act; the investigating officers must follow SR Sankaran's Guidelines on identification of bonded labour, which stipulate, among other things, that the investigation to be done in the settlements of dalits and moolnivasis and, on no account, in the presence of the master of a bonded labourer; the states and union territories must calculate the firm requirements for integral rehabilitation and enhance the present limit of Rs. 20,000; the district magistrates and the state and union territory governments must ensure effective implementation of the Minimum Wags Act, the Employees' Compensation Act, the Inter-State Migrant Labour Act and the Child Labour (Prohibition and Regulation) Act; and all states and union territories must continue to submit the six monthly reports to the NHRC. We have to see now if these latest directions by the Supreme Court will have any impact on the administration, the police, the judiciary and the politicians, both at the centre and in the states and union territories.

Civil Society Organisations

At this juncture, it will be worthwhile to reflect on the experience of the few civil society organisations so far that have worked on bonded labour in India. We can consider every non-governmental formation as civil society organisation, be it a movement, a trade union, a community based organisation, a charitable or rights based organisation, society or trust. Compared to any other social evil, groups working on bonded labour are very few and can be counted on fingers. The mainstream trade unions have not taken up the issue of bonded labour at all. The dalit or moolnivasi or other progressive movements have also not taken up the issue systematically; if at all, they have addressed it only sporadically. Among the few organisations that have spearheaded the cause of bonded labour, Bandhua Mukti

Morcha under the leadership of Swami Agnivesh, stands out the most. It was because of BMM, we have been able to get some of the extraordinary judgments from the Supreme Court. There have also been other organisations based in different states that have addressed the issue. Some of these organisations have also promoted collectives of bonded labourers, be they trade unions, cooperatives, self help groups or other village based groups. But almost all those organisations have adopted one main strategy to get justice to bonded labourers, i.e. to file writ petitions in the High Courts or Supreme Court or file cases in the district courts. Most of these efforts have not brought speedy justice to bonded labourers.

Jeevika Vimukti Karnataka

Jeeta Vimukti Karnataka–Bonded Labour Liberation Front in Karnataka; Bandhana Mukta Jeevana–Bondage Free Life was formed at the state level in 1993 but having its roots in the experiences in one Taluk from 1987 to 1990. The last two dates are given because they have different significances for the movement of JEEVIKA. In 1987, the Founder of the movement Kiran Kamal Prasad had to face social boycott in a village while living and working with dalits in that village; and during the period of that social boycott, he was forced out of the village, with one person kicking him from behind just once; the police officer of the rank of SP while investigating the cause of the riot, asked for the number of bonded labourers in that village; and when a list of the names of 40 bonded labourers was given to her a week later, she had remarked, "Now I know why they are against you."

The concern of Kiran while starting to stay in the village in 1986 was to learn from the life of dalits and promote conscientisation among them and through that process build up a strong organisation under their own leadership which would address all the issues of their life. When the SP had asked for the number and names of bonded labourers in the village after the riot and had given her remark, Kiran started thinking of addressing the issue head on and systematically. He was aware that the Government of Karnataka was denying the existence of bonded labour in the entire state since 1980. Till then, the government had identified nearly 65,000 bonded labourers, the highest in the country till 1997. Kiran did not think in terms of what could be done to get justice to the 40 bonded labourers identified recently. Even if that were to be done, it would have been very difficult to take it up given the hostile situation in the village. The intuitive understanding was that the denial mode of the government must be broken proactively through valid data pertaining to an entire region and gathered scientifically through questionnaires and interviews; and that region was identified as one Taluk of Anekal in Bangalore Urban district comprising of around 275 villages. Hence action oriented research aiming to tackle the issue systemically and not bogged down by addressing individual cases, which was also necessary, was to be one of the basic pillars of JEEVIKA.

The data gathered painstakingly for two years visiting 275 villages was tabulated and analysed through the help of a research and training institute in Bangalore. Just as the data was put together, a prominent founder and leader of the powerful dalit movement in Karnataka, Dalita Sangarsha Samiti (DSS), and also a powerful and witty orator, a great poet, writer, researcher, crusader and professor in a university, Dr. Siddalingaiah, was nominated to the Karnataka Legislature in 1990. Kiran had developed friendship with him just a few months prior to that through his work on adult education in Kannada on the lines of Paulo Freire. Dr. Siddalingaiah had also done some pioneering work on adult education on the lines of Freire in the slums of Bangalore. He readily accepted the proposal to table a few questions on bonded labour in the legislature based on the data from Anekal. It was 20 June 1990. The very first question drew a very positive response from the Minister concerned, which said that the government was aware that the evil of bonded labour was still alive and that it was determined to undertake appropriate action under the law. This was a great achievement and the credit mainly goes to Dr. Siddalingaiah. On the same day of tabling a question on bonded labour in the legislature, the bonded labourers began to be gathered into informal unions in the villages and given awareness and trainings. The nascent union took up a number of struggles in the taluk and the district headquarters to address various issues of bonded labourers. Hence the twofold strategy of JEEVIKA broadly is to lobby and advocacy, at one level, aiming at bringing about change in policies at the highest level possible and, at another level, more basic and even more important, to conscientise and organise/unionise bonded labourers themselves or the people concerned with. Further, the thrust was to promote the former strategy through the latter.

Bringing about change in policy was not restricted to one taluk. While dealing with the issue of bonded labour in that one taluk, policy interventions were sought for the entire state. The ministry monitoring bonded labour in the state, the Rural Development and Panchayat Raj (RDPR) Department was also moved from the beginning to address the issue of bonded labour in the entire state. The state government started ordering surveys in all the districts since 1993, though not much came out of those exercises till 2000. To address the issue of bonded labour systemically, efforts were made to create a movement on bonded labour reaching out to the entire state of Karnataka. The immediate desire was to collaborate with DSS, which had just witnessed its first split in 1987. A proposal was given to both the factions to take up the issue and all support under their banner was assured. But the promised collaboration did not materialise. The Federation of Voluntary Organisations for Rural Development – Karnataka (FEVORD-K), a network then of nearly 150 organisations, was then approached to take up the issue; a sub-committee on bonded labour was formed; but only two or three member organisations took part in that. Karnataka then was very week in voluntary action compared to other southern states; and hardly any of those organisations was involved in agricultural labour, leave alone bonded labour, or were managed by dalits or moolnivasis. Thus, bonded labour was not an issue that concerned the dalit movements nor the voluntary organisations in Karnataka. The next course was to launch an independent movement, under the banner of JEEVIKA and aim at networking with all like-minded and progressive movements and groups. JEEVIKA became a reality at the state level in the middle of 1993.

While launching JEEVIKA, an important advice given was that JEEVIKA should not resort to going to courts as a first step; that it should exhaust all the possibilities with the administration; and after exploring all the avenues with the administration, it should go to courts, if needed. This advice was adhered to fully and it has shaped the praxis of JEEVIKA. An important aspect of this praxis is that by concentrating on impacting on the administration, it has been able build up considerably the agency of the union leaders as well as the movement leaders who are all from villages and Kannada medium schools. In the process, the state apparatus has been demystified considerably in the eyes of the union and the movement.

The informal union of bonded labourers begun in one taluk was formalised and registered as a state level trade union in 1997. To have a greater impact, the union membership consisted of bonded labourers and landless agricultural workers. The name of the union was Karnataka Jeetadalu mattu Krashi Karmikara Okkuta (Union of Bonded Labourers and Landless Agricultural Workers in Karnataka). Since bonded labourers in agriculture were mostly men and boys, women were brought into the movement by promoting self help groups (SHGs) among women in the families of bonded labourers and agricultural workers. To effectively tackle bonded labour in the long run, JEEVIKA started advocating universal quality elementary education (UNIQUE) and common school system. It also started to run one year residential bridge courses in a few taluks to bonded and other working children and after the year to mainstream them into government schools and hostels.

The activists of JEEVIKA were promoted from the villages and in their own native taluks, who would then function as capable and committed leaders of their community. Since most of the bonded labourers were from dalit and moolnivasi communities, it was decided to promote activists only from those communities. It has been a common experience that, given the deep seated caste prejudices, the issues affecting dalits and moolnivasis are not addressed, by and large, by non-dalits and non-moolnivasi people, whether in the government or outside the government. Therefore, to promote the interests of bonded labourers or enable them to secure justice, it was recognised that activists and leaders must be promoted from dalit and moolnivasi communities. Since a vast majority from those communities would still be very poor, a programme for bonded labourers supporting the activists from those communities would also mean empowering those communities and in a way building up resilience of those communities against bonded labour. Work on bonded labour to succeed must promote youth from dalit and moolnivasi communities in a large way. It is also a fact that most of the dalit and moolnivasi students passing through government schools and colleges in villages and towns fail to acquire the required skills making them employable in a competitive market. The large number of youth from dalit and moolnivasi communities acquire school and college degrees; they are talented; they are eager to serve their community; but they cannot find jobs; neither do their families are in a position to provide them any alternative source for their livelihood, since they are assetless and have to maintain their life as daily wage labourers.

Though policy level changes were effected at the state level in 1990 and later through the efforts of JEEVIKA, bonded labourers were not identified, released and rehablitated in the field till 2000 except for the initial efforts in Anekal in 1990 and 1992. The activists and the union leaders were forced to exploit other means to secure livelihoods for the former bonded labourers. This was done by accessing various poverty alleviation schemes of the government. Through the activism of dalit and moolnivasi youth, a large number of benefits are being regularly proocured for the union members. To develop the leadership of the union members as also of the activists and strengthen decentralisation of democratic power, they are encouraged to contest Gram Panchayat elections and function as responsible members or leaders in the Gram Panchayats.

Though the concern was to reach out to the entire state, JEEVIKA could mobilise resources to promote activism in ten among the thirty districts in the state. When the state government took a strong resolve to implement the Act on Bonded Labour in 2000, JEEVIKA activists toured the length and breadth of the state conducting sensitisation programmes to the officials in the districts and taluks. But ultimately most of the nearly 3000 bonded labourers identified were from the seventeen taluks of JEEVIKA's involvement. For action on bonded labour to be effective, not only strong political will and administrative resolve is required; it has to be accompanied by people's pressure from below. To promote this, efforts were made since 2006, to strengthen Vigilance Committees on Bonded Labour in the districts and the sub divisions by motivating dalit and moolnivasi youth and leaders to get into them and raise their voice there on behalf of bonded labourers. Another round of motivating dalit and moolnivasi youth to take up the cause of bonded labour was made in 2009 and 2010 in the context of the publishing of the Karnataka Action Plan on Bonded Labour 2008 by the government. But purely appealing to altruistic action alone does not help if not accompanied by suitable financial support.

Though resources and energy were devoted to building up the agency of bonded labourers and dalit and moolnivasi youth, JEEVIKA was also able to make impact in formulating policies and carrying out sensitisation programmes to top level administrators precisely because of its strong base at the grass roots. In 2004, the RDPR Department invited Kiran to draw up an Action Plan on Bonded Labour for Karnataka. This was approved in 2007 and a large number of copies were printed in 2009 and distributed all over Karnataka. In 2006, Kiran was nominated to the NGO Core Group in the NHRC, and in 2011 to the NHRC Core Group on Bonded Labour. In the same year, JEEVIKA was nominated to the Karnataka State Level High Powered Committee on Bonded Labour. JEEVIKA has also been taking a lead in collaboration with National Law University Delhi (NLUD) since November 2012 to propose a new set of effective Rules to the Bonded Labour Act to be notified by the Central Government. These experiences from JEEVIKA throw a lot of light on how best to tackle bonded labour in India. In that regard, it would be worthwhile to consider the suggestions for India in the Global Slavery Index 2013. The present article is concluded by reproducing them fully below:

"India should:

- Report annually on implementation and progress of efforts to combat all forms of modern slavery, including through provision of criminal justice statistics. This will require the establishment of protocols on the collection and compilation of data.
- Undertake national prevalence estimates on modern slavery.
- Ratify and implement the Convention on the Worst Forms of Child Labour, and the Domestic

Work Convention.

- Require States to report on how they have followed up on the Supreme Court Judgement of October 15,2012, requiring all states to carry out surveys to identify and release those in bonded labour. The efforts currently being made in the State of Karnataka should be promoted and followed by other States.
- Update rules for use in implementing the Bonded Labour Act.
- Update the 2008 integrated Plan of Action to combat human trafficking so that it reflects current conditions, the new law and targets the full spectrum of modern slavery.
- At the State level, develop and implement action plans on bonded labour in every state and union territory, following the example of the Karnataka State Action Plan on Bonded Labour 2008. Appoint a high level responsible officer at the State and District level, who focuses only on tasks related to bonded labour and other forms of modern slavery. Official District Bonded Labour Vigilance Committees should be made active, involving committed NGO representatives and slavery survivors.
- Undertake an assessment to understand whether the AHTUs established are consistently applying relevant laws and guidance, and understand whether all forms of modern slavery are in fact being investigated and prosecuted.
- Strengthen protections for victims of modern slavery and ensure that they are not criminalised. Victimsmust be protected (including protecting their identities) throughout the duration of their cases and methods of speeding up trials should be implemented. Ensure follow-up with reintegrated survivors.
- Invest in well-supported outreach to typical sites of slave labour to raise awareness about rights.
- Upgrade shelter homes and take steps to ensure that the human rights of shelter home residents are observed and

penalties imposed on those who violate their rights. Sheltering of victims (by both NGOs and government) should not in reality be a system of false imprisonment and punishment.The qualification of leadership of these institutions, as well as the training and re-training of staff should be given close attention. A programme of investment in upgrading and of independent participation in unannounced inspections should be initiated.

- Clarify legal, policy and law enforcement responses to commercial sexual exploitation, and respect the human rights of those affected by any response, including those who depend on working in the sex industry for survival, who are not in slavery.
- Ensure 'raids' follow victim-centred procedures to ensure they help more than harm.
- Strengthen efforts directed at stamping out corruption and complicity of government officials in modern slavery, including through encouraging innovative, no-cost mechanisms to report suspected official complicity.
- Continue efforts directed at addressing the underlying causes of modern slavery–such as poverty, illiteracy, under employment, violence against women, discrimination, lack of access to entitlements such as functioning schools and health services, and social exclusion.
- Seek to address the 'grass is greener over there' stories with information dissemination about the realities of migration, and mobility – and also build specific institutional capacity to inform people and communities about mobility."

Contributors

1. Dr Ambrose Pinto SJ, the Editor of the Volume taught Political Science in St. Joseph's College, Bangalore for more than 25 years. He was the Principal of St. Joseph's Evening College, Bangalore (1994–1998, 2001–2003, St. Joseph's College, Bangalore, (2003-2011), Director of the Indian Social Institute, New Delhi (1998-2001), Fellow at the Indian Institute of Advanced Study, Shimla (2011- 2012) and presently Principal of St. Aloysius Degree College, Bangalore. He has several articles and books to his credit. His recent books are – "Five Years of Saffron Rule in Karnataka" (Ed.) (2014), "Dalits in Karnataka: In search of Identity and Equality" (2014) both brought out by Manak Publications, New Delhi and "From Democratic Socialism to Neo-liberalism: The Story of India's Democracy" from the Indian Institute of Advanced Study, Shimla.
2. Dr Arun Mitra is an Ear Nose Throat Surgeon by profession working as consultant in the city of Ludhiana in Punjab. He is National General Secretary of Indian Doctors for Peace and Development (IDPD). Besides this he is an elected member of the Punjab State Medical Council (PMC). He is also member of the Central Working Committee of Indian Medical Association (IMA). He has been Senior Vice President IMA Punjab in 2009 and President IMA Ludhiana in 2007 and 2008. As a medical student he was National President of All India Medicos Federation. Has been actively involved in the peace movement since his student days in the All India Peace and Solidarity Organisation (AIPSO).
3. A founder member of Alternative Law Forum, Arvind Narrain has done a bachelor's in law from National Law School of India

University, Bangalore followed by a Masters in the University of Warwick on a Chevening scholarship. He has spent two years at the NLSIU Centre for the Child and the Law where he was actively involved in working on child rights and juvenile justice. He also taught courses at the NLSIU on human rights law and ideology, ethnic conflict, law; poverty and development. Arvind now works full time at ALF dividing his time between litigation on the criminal side and research and advocacy on sexuality and minority related issues.

4. Dr Anil Rajimwale is the leader of Communist Party of India and one of the party's leading theoretician. He writes extensively to journals and magazines.
5. Professor Sen Gupta is a Visiting Professor, National Institute of Science, Bangalore.
6. Sri C. Balakrishna President, Karnataka Progressive Forum has been active in several issues in the city. He has worked closely with Medha Patkar in the National Alliances of People's Movement, taken up the cause of the scavengers, minimum wage and other concerns.
7. Dr R. S. Deshpande is currently National Fellow, Indian Council of Social Science Research (ICSSR) and former Director of Institute for Social and Economic Change (ISEC), Bangalore. His specialisations include, Agricultural Development Policy, Watershed Development, WTO - Agriculture & Trade, Rural Policy and Poverty, Economics of drought-prone Areas and rain fed regions, Economics of Irrigation, Policy Analysis and Applied Econometrics. Professor Deshpande has authored 17 books and more that 110 research papers published in national and international journals. Among his books Agrarian Crisis and Farmer Suicides, where water seeps, NGOs and Farmers' Movements in India, Moon in the Mirror: Farmers and MSP in Karnataka are a few. Professor Deshpande has contributed significantly as a member of the many policy bodies which include Advisory Body of the Ministry of Commerce, Government of India, WTO Cell of Government of Karnataka, Committee on Farmers' Suicides appointed by the Government of Karnataka, etc. He is currently editor of the Journal of Social and Economic

Development, and on the Editorial Board of Agricultural Economics Research Review, and a reviewer of some of the reputed journals. Apart from all these he is a poet and an artist.

8. Sri Justin John is a youngster working with the Hunger Project, an NGO for the last four years. An MSW, he has been deeply concerned with issues of hunger, famine, drought and poverty alleviation progrmmes.

9. Kiran Kamal Prasad is the Founder and present Coordinator of Jeevika, an organisation for the eradication of bonded labour's EEVIKA is the recipient of the 2010 Harriet Tubman Freedom Award, presented annually by Free the Slaves to one community-based organisation that demonstrates how slavery can be dismantled and destroyed. Kiran has done tremendous work on the issue of bonded labour.

10. Dr Narendra Pani is Professor in the School of Social Sciences in the National Institute of Advanced Studies, Bangalore. His most significant research contribution is reformulation of the Gandhian method to make it an effective tool to understand contemporary policy making. An economist by training, he has, over the last thirty years, written extensively on a variety of subjects. He is the author of Inclusive Economics: Gandhian Method and Contemporary Policy, Redefining Conservatism: An Essay on the Bias of India's Economic Reform, and Reforms to Pre-empt Change: Land Legislation in Karnataka. He has published a number of academic articles in India and abroad. He is also the author of an explainer on the WTO, two novels, a booklet on theatre and several hundred articles on the editorial pages of newspapers.

11. Dr Gampalahalli Ramakrishna popularly known as Dr GR has been a guiding spirit to many pro-people movements in Karnataka. Hailed as a pro-people scholar, he has been espousing many causes in the overall interests of society. He was a long time associate of Dr Debiprasad Chattopadhyaya, a Marxist Philosopher of repute, who made seminal contributions to the alternate discourse on Indian Philosophy among others. From 1967 to 1993 he was Professor of English at National College, Basavangudi, Bangalore. He was a Visiting Professor at Kannada

University, Hampi from 1994 to 1996, during which period he wrote the book '*The Path of Indian Science*'. As an independent publisher, Dr GR established Ma–Le Prakashana in 1980 to bring out progressive literature in Kannada and English. For 25 years, he was the publisher of '*Achala*', a women's monthly magazine in Kannada of Jagruthi Mahila Adhyayana Kendra. He has several publications to his credit. Dr GR has been the Chief Editor of *Hosathu*, a progressive monthly magazine published in Kannada since 1999. He was also in the Editorial Board of the newsletter of Samudaaya, a reputed cultural troupe of Karnataka, known for its espousal of people's causes through theatre. Presently, Dr GR is the Chief Editor of the Kannada Version of the series *Global Philosophy for Everyman*, comprising eight volumes, published first in English by Navakarnataka Publications Pvt. Ltd, Bangalore in December 1993.

12. Dr Mary Mathew is a Professor at the Department of Management Studies, Indian Institute of Science (IISc). Her Ph.D is in the area of Organisation Change and Technology Management. She looks at process changes (organisation design) required in R&D management practice to make innovative patents happen in R&D companies. She has evolved measurement approaches to assess innovation at the national and organisational levels. She has led research projects with grants from European Commission, The Flanders Ministry in Belgium, The Ministry of Science and Technology, the Ministry of Communications and IT, WIPRO, CSB, CPRI, KPMG and the Kelley Business School. She is the co-author of two books on Organisational Theory and Design, co-authored together with Prof Gareth Jones from Texas A&M and Professor Stephen Robbins of San Diego State University. She is working on her third book on management of intellectual property. Her recent publications are in the Journal of Innovation, Journal of Intellectual Property Rights, Vikalpa, CURIE Journal, and the South East Asian Journal of Management. She is an active member of the Academy of Management and the country head for the PICMET the technology management conference run by Portland State University.

13. N. Manu Chakravarthy has been teaching English for the last three decades at the under-graduate and post-graduate levels. He has written books in English and Kannada on cinema, music, politics and cultural theory. Awarded with the Swarna Kamal by the President of India at the 58th National Film Awards for contribution to film criticism, his book on culture and politics, *Madhyama Marga* won the prestigious VM Inamdar Award in 2010. His interest in reviewing films makes him a film theorist. He is a distinguished critic who has made valuable contribution to literary and cultural criticism in English and Kannada. He has written extensively on literature, music, feminism, politics and cinema. He has written perceptively about major figures of Kannada Cinema like Vijay Bhaskar, K. S. Ashwath, Raj Kumar and Ananth Nag. "Re/Viewing Iranian Cinema", "Imaging the Oppressed", "Of Icons and the Spirit of the Times", "The Marginalised as the Invisible", "Lensing the Middle Class Spirit" are some of his conceptual writings on cinema. His writings seek to project the deep humanism and concern that guide the creativity underlying films as works of art. His book "Culturing Realism: Reflections on Girish Kasaravalli's Films" is a collection of articles on the outstanding Kannada film maker, Girish Kasaravalli. These are not commissioned pieces. They are critical reviews and interviews previously published, mainly in film journals. He was on the editorial board of the film journal "Deep Focus". He is one of the key resource persons for the annual cultural course conducted by Ninasam, Heggodu.
14. Vijaya Kumar is the Vice-President of All India Progressive Forum. Active in the campaign for electoral reforms he is involved in offering workshops to students and the public on entreprenurship.
15. Dr Yugal Rayalu is from Nagpur winner of the coveted Karamveer Chakra 2012. An Electrical Engineer, he remains committed to empower deprived sections of society. Vocational education professor from Nagpur, he was given the best Teacher Award in 2010 and an award in the 'Education to Society' category jointly by United Nations Volunteers (under United Nations Development Programme) India and ICONGO (Indian

Confederation of NGOs) in 2012. He is the Head of the Vocational Department of Dharampet M. P. Deo Memorial Science College and one of the Secretaries of the All India Progressive Forum.

16. Dr Thelma Narayan is an epidemiologist, health policy analyst and activist who coordinates CPHE (Centre for Public Health and Equity) and is Director of the CPHE Madhya Pradesh Initiative. She is one of the original co-initiators of Community Health Cell (CHC) and currently works with various national health initiatives. A member of the Task Force on Health and Family Welfare, Karnataka, she has evolved public health and primary health care oriented state health policies in Karnataka and Orissa. She was a member of the measurement and evidence knowledge Network of the WHO Commission on social determinants of Health. She is an active member of the People's Health Movement network and was the joint convenor of the Jan Swasthya Abhiyan (PHM India) till recently. She is also a contributor to the Global Health Watch and a faculty member of the International People's Health University. Dr Ravi Narayan is an active member of the People's Health Movement network. He was the joint convener of the Jan Swasthya Abhiyan till December 2002 and later coordinator of the Global Secretariat of People's Health Movement from January 2003 to July 2006. Currently he is a member of WHO Advocacy Circle of PHM and also part of the PHM Steering Council and Coordinating Council. He is associated with the Global Health Watch and a faculty of the International People's Health University. He is a council member of the Global Forum for Health Research and founding governing body member of the Public Health Foundation of India. He is a member of the Task Force on Primary Health Care of the Planning Commission of India and is closely associated with two major initiatives of the Central Ministry of Health, the National Rural Health Mission and the AYUSH and Public Health Initiative. He is also a member of the International Advisory Committee and the speciality advisor on public health of the British Medical Journal.